CORINTHIACA

CORINTHIACA

Studies in Honor of Darrell A. Amyx

Edited by Mario A. Del Chiaro

Associate Editor, William R. Biers

Ellen Macnamc

University of Missouri Press
Columbia, 1986

Library of Congress Cataloging-in-Publication Data
Corinthiaca: studies in honor of Darrell A. Amyx

   Bibliography: p.
   Includes index.
     1. Corinth (Greece)—Antiquities. 2. Greece—
Antiquities. 3. Corinth (Greece)—Civilization.
4. Pottery, Greek—Greece—Corinth. 5. Amyx,
Darrell A. (Darrell Arlynn), 1911- . I. Amyx,
Darrell A. (Darrell Arlynn), 1911- . II. Del Chiaro,
Mario Aldo, 1925- . III. Biers, William R.,
1938- .
DF261.C65C67 1986 938'.7 86–4375
ISBN 0–8262–0617–4 (alk. paper)

Copyright © 1986 by
The Curators of the University of Missouri
University of Missouri Press,
Columbia, Missouri 65211
Printed and bound in the United States of America

Frontispiece photograph of Darrell Amyx by Lensart
Studio, Berkeley, California.

In memory of Professor H. R. W. Smith,

who has been an inspiration to both Dick Amyx and me.

Preface

A native Californian, Darrell A. Amyx joined the faculty of the University of California, Berkeley, in 1946 as Professor of Ancient Art, a position he held with distinction until his retirement in 1978. Born at Exeter in 1911, Professor Amyx took his Bachelor of Arts degree in Classics at Stanford in 1930. His graduate training was completed at Berkeley, where he obtained the degrees of Master of Arts in Latin (1932) and Doctor of Philosophy in Latin and Classical Archaeology (1937). His early academic career was interrupted for some three years (1942–1945) when he served with the United States Office of Censorship in San Francisco during the Second World War.

During his tenure at the University of California, Berkeley, Professor Amyx served unselfishly and brilliantly as Chairman of the Art Department (1966–1971), Assistant Dean in the College of Letters and Science (1964–1965), and Curator of Classical Art in the University Art Museum (1965–1976) and in the Robert H. Lowie Museum of Anthropology (1958–1978). His grants and honors are many and noteworthy: Fellow of the American School of Classical Studies, Athens (1935–1936); two Guggenheim Fellowships (1957–1959 and 1973–1974); Fulbright Senior Research Grantee to Greece (1957–1958); four grants from the American Council of Learned Societies (1941, 1962, 1970, and 1980); Fellow of the American Council of Learned Societies (1965–1966); two grants from the American Philosophical Society (1956 and 1976); Phi Beta Kappa; and Corresponding Member of the Istituto di Studi Etruschi ed Italici, Florence, and the Deutsches Archäologisches Institut, Berlin. In addition, Professor Amyx is a member of the Archaeological Institute of America and the American Philological Association. During the years 1968–1972, he served as Associate Editor for the California Studies in Classical Antiquity (volumes 1–5).

This volume of essays is presented to Darrell A. Amyx by his many friends and colleagues—some former students—as a token of their admiration and affection. A distinguished scholar and an effective teacher, Professor Amyx fully deserves the intended accolade that places special attention on Corinth, that ancient Greek center for which he has become the leading expert on its archaic vase painting. The impact of his painstakingly researched and perceptive scholarship is readily attested by the endless references to his published works and by the innumerable comments that may be encountered when consulting archival and inventory data in both public and private collections—national and international. As a teacher, Professor Amyx has few peers. In addition to those students enriched and inspired by his graduate courses throughout the years, there are those who comprise the steady stream of Master and Doctoral students in Classical Art, all of whom have unquestionably profited from and will always remember the breadth of his learning, his astute advice, his integrity, and his infectious warmth and keen sense of humor.

His writings—published, in proof, or yet in manuscript—have gathered momentum since retirement for the simple reason that he no longer need to devote so much time—dutifully and unselfishly provided in the past—to students at all levels of studies, but he can now focus on his own special investigations. Subsequently, we can now look forward to the appearance of important and significant publications, not to mention occasional appearances at public lectures and symposia. This volume has been shaped to honor Darrell Amyx's significant contributions to the understanding of ancient Corinth. Would it were within our power to present this eminent scholar the "keys to the city," that is, *ancient* Corinth. However, since such a mayoral function is not in the offing, this *Festschrift* may serve to recognize these past and forthcoming contributions in advancing our knowledge of the role played throughout the entire Mediterranean region by this once prosperous and influential Greek city and its citizens at home and abroad.

Mario A. Del Chiaro
Santa Barbara, California
Spring 1986

Acknowledgments

As his first Ph.D. student, I felt it a duty and a privilege to organize the present publication as a tribute to Professor Darrell A. Amyx. In terms of publication, I am most grateful to two members of the Department of Art History and Archaeology, University of Missouri, Columbia, William R. Biers and Saul S. Weinberg (Emeritus), for their unflagging support in bringing this enterprise to the attention of the University of Missouri Press.

Although a number of essays are concerned with subjects and themes other than the pottery of ancient Corinth, the intention of this *Festschrift*—as *Corinthiaca* in the publication title implies—is to acknowledge the life-long interest of Professor Amyx in this subject. This is readily apparent by the bulk of contributions devoted to various aspects of Corinthian and allied vase painting.

I must once again thank all contributors, not solely for their interesting and significant essays but also for their patience and their understanding of the delays not surprisingly encountered by such projects. Many of the articles in this volume were submitted as early as 1982. It must be pointed out that these authors had yet no knowledge of the recently published *Wealthy Corinth. A History of the City to 338 B.C.* (Oxford, 1984) by J. B. Salmon. I am indeed grateful to them for their time and their effort to honor Darrell A. Amyx, an extraordinary teacher and scholar.

The following list comprises a tabula gratulatoria:

Ekrem Akurgal
Petre Alexandrescu
Pierre Amandry
John K. Anderson
William S. Anderson
Ermanno A. Arslan
Ann H. Ashmead
Paul Åström
Tomris Bakir
Evelyn E. Bell
Ernst Berger
Marie-Louise Bernhard
Jane C. Biers
William R. Biers
Darice Birge

Mary Blomberg
John Boardman
Nancy Bookidis
Maurizio Borda
S. P. Boriskovskaya
Dietrich von Bothmer
Cedric G. Boulter
Jan Bouzek
Frank Brommer
Oscar T. Broneer
Marie-Louise Buhl
Herbert A. Cahn
Denise Callipolitis-Feytmans
Alexander Cambitoglou
Giovannangelo Camporeale

Fulvio Canciani
Herschel B. Chipp
Christoph W. Clairmont
Paul A. Clement
J. N. Coldstream
Giovanni Colonna
Brian F. Cook
J. M. Cook
Robert Manuel Cook
Mauro Cristofani
Georges Daux
Aaron Dechter
Hanita Dechter
Christina Del Chiaro
Mario A. Del Chiaro

Ernesto De Miro
Jean-Paul Descoeudres
Tobias Dohrn
José Dörig
Sterling Dow
H. S. Ettlinger
L. D. Ettlinger
Klaus Fittschen
Joseph Fontenrose
Barbara Ann Forbes
Alison Frantz
Jiří Frel
Arthur E. Gordon
Virginia R. Grace
J. R. Green
Crawford H. Greenewalt, Jr.
A. Greifenhagen
George M. A. Hanfmann
Evelyn B. Harrison
John W. Hayes
D. E. L. Haynes
Madeleine von Heland
Sharon Herbert
Reynold Higgins
Dorothy K. Hill
Nikolaus Himmelmann
Betty Homann-Wedeking
Ernst Homann-Wedeking
Robert John Hopper
Wilhelm Hornbostel
Henry R. Immerwahr
Michael H. Jameson
Flemming Johansen
Hans Jucker
Ines Jucker
Vassos Karageorghis
Semni Karouzou
J. H. C. Kern
Karl Kilinski II

W. Eugene Kleinbauer
Ursula Knigge
Norbert Kunisch
Annie-France Laurens
Patricia Lawrence
Phyllis Williams Lehmann
Kurt T. Luckner
Reinhard Lullies
Anna Marguerite McCann
James R. McCredie
Paul M. McDermott
A. Dean McKenzie
Ian McPhee
Guglielmo Maetzke
Marina Martelli
Margaret Ellen Mayo
Benjamin Dean Meritt
Lucy Shoe Meritt
Henri Metzger
Ann B. Miller
Stella G. Miller
Stephen G. Miller
David G. Mitten
Warren G. Moon
Mario Moretti
Kees Neeft
Joseph Veach Noble
Frank A. Norick
Piero Orlandini
Massimo Pallottino
Enrico Paribeni
Paola Pelagatti
Elizabeth G. Pemberton
Barbara Philippaki
Kyle Meredith Phillips, Jr.
W. Kendrick Pritchett
Antony E. Raubitschek
Isabelle K. Raubitschek
Brunilde Sismondo Ridgway

Martin Robertson
Henry Robinson
Rebecca Robinson
Carl Roebuck
Susan I. Rotroff
Judith Schaeffer
Konrad Schauenburg
Karl Schefold
Margot Schmidt
Axel Seeberg
Brian B. Shefton
Hellmut Sichtermann
Arthur W. Silver
Marjorie Silver
Erika Simon
Hans von Steuben
Andrew F. Stewart
Conrad M. Stibbe
Ronald S. Stroud
Janos G. Szilágyi
Dorothy B. Thompson
Homer A. Thompson
Margaret Thompson
Mario Torelli
A. D. Trendall
Vincenzo Tusa
Georges Vallet
Eugene Vanderpool
Cornelius Vermeule III
Emily Vermeule
Michael Vickers
Klaus Vierneisel
Giuseppe Voza
Gladys D. Weinberg
Saul S. Weinberg
Charles K. Williams, II
Nicholas Yalouris
Fausto Zevi

Introduction

Saul S. Weinberg

DEPARTMENT OF ART HISTORY AND ARCHAEOLOGY
UNIVERSITY OF MISSOURI-COLUMBIA

It is more than fifty years since Humfry Payne, in *Necrocorinthia*, established in broad outline the developmental sequence and the chronology for Corinthian vase painting of the Archaic period in particular, as well as for Corinthian sculpture, fictile revetments, and metal work of the same period. Only two years later, in *Protokorinthische Vasenmalerei*, he began a more detailed analysis of the earlier phase of pottery manufacture at Corinth, and this would have been followed, no doubt, by other detailed studies, had not his life been ended so abruptly and prematurely in 1936. Among the many scholars who carried on with the work that Payne had begun so brilliantly, none has contributed more to Corinthian studies than has Dick Amyx. The bibliography of his publications included here attests both to his broad interests in classical and, particularly, Corinthian studies, as well as to his concentration on Corinthian vase painting and its derivatives.

Thus, it is wholly fitting that a group of Amyx's friends, colleagues, and former students has joined in contributing a number of studies in his honor; it is only natural that these should all center around Corinth. The resulting volume, *Corinthiaca*, is a highly significant contribution, adding much that is new to our knowledge of many, varied aspects of Corinthian arts and crafts, as well as to our knowledge of Corinth's history and literature. That thirteen of the twenty-three studies are on Corinthian and Corinthianizing pottery is commensurate both with the far greater amount of pottery that is preserved, as compared with other artifacts of Corinthian manufacture, and with the major interest of the honoree.

Probably more than any other of the essays, that of Patricia Lawrence, student and long-time collaborator of Amyx, gives the essentials of connoisseurship and the methodology of stylistic study of Corinthian pottery that Amyx has spent a lifetime in formulating and is passing on in his teaching and writing. An excellent example of these principles in practice is the article entitled "Middle Protocorinthian Periodization" by Jack Benson, whose independent researches on early Corinthian pottery have paralleled and complemented those of Amyx for the past three decades.

Of special importance is the coincidental bringing together in this volume of five interesting studies that shed much new light on early Corinthian my-

thology, religion, history, and topography; they range in date from late Mycenaean times to the fourth century B.C. Most important for Corinthian studies in a variety of areas is Charles Williams's study of the cult of Aphrodite at
Corinth through many centuries of the city's history. Certainly this was much
discussed in recent years when Williams, Director of the Corinth Excavations,
played host to Amyx at Corinth, where he was preparing his latest volumes
on Corinthian vase painting, which are eagerly awaited. Thus, as we review a
past of forty-five years of brilliant achievement, we can, at the same time,
look to an equally productive future for Dick Amyx and wish him many more
years of active scholarship.

Works by Darrell A. Amyx

Books and Articles

"The Gorgon-Hydria from Eretria." *AJA* 43 (1939), 305 (summary).

"The Gorgon-Hydria from Eretria." *AJA* 45 (1941), 64–69.

"An Amphora with a Price-Inscription in the Hearst Collection at San Simeon." *University of California Publications in Classical Archaeology* 1:8 (1941), 179–206.

"Note on Juvenal XIV: 227–232." *CP* 36 (1941), 278–79.

"Corinthian Vases in the Hearst Collection at San Simeon." *University of California Publications in Classical Archaeology* 1:9 (1943), 207–40.

"A New Pelike by the Geras Painter." *AJA* 49 (1945), 508–18.

"Geometric Platform Bronzes." *AJA* 53 (1949), 147–48 (summary).

"The Amphoras of Alcibiades." *AJA* 59 (1955), 169 (summary).

"The Geladakis Painter." *Hesperia* 25 (1956), 73–77.

"Inscribed Sherds from the Amyklaion." *AJA* 61 (1957), 168–69.

"The Attic Stelai, Part 3: Vases and Other Containers." Report. *American Philosophical Society: Year Book for 1956* (1958), 335–38.

"The Attic Stelai, Part 3: Vases and Other Containers." *Hesperia* 27 (1958), 163–307.

"A Corinthian Kotyle in Mainz." *Jahrbuch des Römisch-Germanischen Zentralmuseums, Mainz* 6 (1959), 101–9.

"A Forged Corinthian Animal Frieze." *Bulletin of the Brooklyn Museum* 21, 2 (1960), 9–13.

"The Medaillon Painter." *AJA* 65 (1961), 1–15.

"I vasi Corinzi di Reggio Calabria." *Klearchos* 3 (1961), 5–16.

"The Honolulu Painter and the 'Delicate Style.'" *Antike Kunst* 5 (1962), 3–8.

"Xenokles in Seattle." *AJA* 66 (1962), 229–32.

"A 'Pontic' Oinochoe in Seattle." *Collection Latomus* 58 (1962), 121–34.

"The Alabastron of Oinanthe." *AM* 76 (1962), 12–14.

"An Alabastron by the Herzegovina Painter." *BABesch* 38 (1963), 89–91.

"*Adversaria Critica*: In and Around the Sphinx Painter." With P. Lawrence. *AJA* 68 (1964), 387–91.

"Some Etrusco-Corinthian Vase-Painters." *Studi in Onore di Luisa Banti* (Rome, 1965), 1–14.

"The Second Edition of Beazley's *ARV*: Review Article." *CP* 60 (1965), 186–92.

"Vases from the Etruscan Cemetery at Cerveteri." Exhibition Leaflet, University of California at Berkeley Art Gallery, 1965, pp. 1–12.

"Ancient Vases in the Seattle Art Museum." *AJA* 69 (1965), 164 (summary).

"The Mingor Painter and Others: Etrusco-Corinthian Addenda." *Studi Etruschi* 35 (1967), 87–111.

"A 'Corinthian' Forger Unmasked." *AJA* 72 (1968), 161 (summary).

"The Case of the Dunedin Painter." *CSCA* 1 (1968), 13–34.

"Observations on the Warrior Group." *CSCA* 2 (1969), 1–25.

Contributor to Herbert A. Cahn, ed., *Münzen und Medaillen*, and A. G. Basel, *Kunstwerke der Antike, Auktion* 40 (13 December 1969), esp. pp. 16–22.

"Dodwelliana." *CSCA* 4 (1971), 1–48.

"Isthmia Pottery, 1952–1960." *AJA* 75 (1971), 195 (summary).

Cypriote Antiquities in San Francisco Bay Area Collections. Joint author with V. Karageorghis, et al. *Studies in Mediterranean Archaeology 20,* 5 (1974).

Echoes from Olympus: Reflections of Divinity in Small-Scale Classical Art. Editor and author with students. Berkeley, 1974.

Archaic Corinthian Vases and the Anaploga Well. With P. Lawrence. *Corinth* VII, part 2. Princeton, 1975.

"Collection Paul Canellopoulos, VII: A Corinthian Cylindrical Lekythos." *BCH* 99 (1975), 401–7.

"San Simeon Revisited: Corinthian Vases." *CSCA* 8 (1975), 17–31

"The Orpheus Legend in Art." *Archaeological News* 5 (1976), 25–41.

"A Postscript to Orpheus." *Archaeological News* 5 (1976), 71.

"Corinthian Vase-Painting of the Archaic Period." Report. *American Philosophical Society: Year Book for 1978*, p. 303. Philadelphia, 1978.

"Two Etrusco-Corinthian Vases." *Studies in Honour of Arthur Dale Trendall*, pp. 13–19. Sydney, 1979.

"The Many Loves of Zeus (and their Consequences)." *Archaeological News* 8 (1979), 98–115.

Contributor, entries nos. 14 and 15. In Warren G. Moon and Louise Berge, *Greek Vase-Painting in Midwestern Collections.* Chicago, 1979.

"Héraclès et l'Hydre de Lerne dans la céramique corinthienne." With P. Amandry. *Antike Kunst* 25 (1982), 102- 16.

"Archaic Vase-Painting vis-à-vis 'Free' Painting at Corinth." In Warren G. Moon, ed., *Ancient Greek Art and Iconography*, pp. 37–52. Madison, 1983.

"An Inscribed Corinthian Neck-Amphora." *AJA* 88 (1984), 236 (summary).

Contributor to K. Kilinski II, *Classical Myth in Western Art: Ancient through Modern.* Southern Methodist University, Dallas, 1985.

"A Curious 'Padded Dancer' Vase in Milan." *Rassegna di Studi del Civico Museo Archeologico e del Civico Gabinetto Numismatico di Milano* 31–32 (1983), 27–28.

In Press

"Corinthian and Etrusco-Corinthian Vases in Bloomington." *Indiana University Art Museum Bulletin.*

Corinthian Vase-Painting of the Archaic Period (Berkeley).

"Some Problems in Archaic Corinthian Prosopography." *Studies in Honour of Professor George E. Mylonas* (Athens, Greece).

Book Reviews

Trendall, A. D. *Paestan Pottery. CP* 34 (1939), 78–80.

Maxey, M. *Occupations of the Lower Classes in Roman Society. CP* 34 (1939), 248.

Hafner, G. *Viergespanne in Vorderansicht. AJA* 43 (1939), 164–66.

Robinson, D. M., et al. *CVA: Robinson Collection,* fasc. 3. *AJA* 43 (1939), 713–14.

Plaoutine, N. *CVA: Louvre,* fasc. 9. *AJA* 43 (1939), 713–14.

Eilmann, R., and Gebauer, K. *CVA: Berlin Antiquarium,* fasc. 1. *Classical Weekly* 33 (1939–1940), 100–101.

Levy, H. *A Latin Reader for Colleges. CP* 36 (1941), 204–5.

Chase, G., and Pease, M. *CVA: Fogg Museum and Gallatin Collections. AJA* 46 (1942), 596–97.

Richter, G. *Attic Red-Figured Vases, A Survey. AJA* 50 (1946), 500–502.

Cabré Aguiló, J. *Corpus Vasorum Hispanorum:* Cerámica de Azalia. *AJA* 51 (1947), 206–9.

Mylonas, G. *The Hymn to Demeter and Her Sanctuary at Eleusis. CP* 43 (1948), 67–68.

Botsford, G., and Robinson, C. *Hellenic History,* 3d ed., 1948. *AJA* 53 (1949), 336.

Beazley, J. D. *Etruscan Vase-Painting. AJA* 53 (1949), 409–11.

Yavis, C. *Greek Altars. American Historical Review* 55 (1949- 1950), 957–58.

Memoirs of the American Academy in Rome 19 (1949). *Classical Weekly* 43 (1949–1950), 220.

Buschor, E. *Das Hellenistische Bildnis. Classical Weekly* 45 (1951–1952), 104–5.

Richter, G. *The Sculpture and Sculptors of the Greeks,* 3d ed., 1950. *AJA* 57 (1953), 38–39.

———. *Archaic Greek Art. College Art Journal* 12 (1952- 1953), 292–94.

Kübler, K. *Altattische Malerei. AJA* 57 (1953), 294–95.

Beazley, J. D. *The Development of Attic Black-Figure. CP* 49 (1954), 141–43.

Vian, F. *La guerre des géants. CP* 50 (1955), 267–69.

Lullies, R. *CVA: Munich, fasc. 2. Gnomon* 28 (1956), 550–51.

Hafner, G. *CVA: Karlsruhe, fasc. 1. Gnomon* 28 (1956), 550–51.

———. *CVA: Karlsruhe, fasc. 2. Gnomon* 29 (1957), 394–95.

Hampe, R., and Simon, E. *CVA: Mainz, fasc. 1. AJA* 65 (1961), 210.

Ghale-Kahlil, L. *Etudes Thasiennes, VII: La céramique grecque. AJA* 66 (1962), 101–2.

Davison, J. *Attic Geometric Workshops. Archaeology* 15 (1962), 291–92.

Devambez, P. *Greek Painting. AJA* 67 (1963), 426–27.

Bruckner, A. *CVA: Geneva, fasc. 1. AJA* 69 (1965), 76–77.

Villard, F. *CVA: Louvre, fasc. 13. AJA* 70 (1966), 295–97.

Boardman, J., and Hayes J. *Excavations at Tocra, 1963–1965: The Archaic Deposits, I. Gnomon* 41 (1969), 681–84.

Benson, J. *Horse, Bird and Man: The Origins of Greek Painting. The Art Bulletin* 56 (1974), 118–20.

Blomberg, M., et al. *CVA: Stockholm, fasc. 1. AJA* 89 (1985), 699–700.

List of Abbreviations

AA	*Archäologische Anzeiger*	*CSCA*	*California Studies in Classical Antiquity*
ABV	J. D. Beazley, *Attic Black-figure Vase-painters* (Oxford, 1956)	*CVA*	*Corpus Vasorum Antiquorum*
AdI	*Annali dell'Istituto di Corrispondenza Archeologica*	*HSCP*	*Harvard Studies in Classical Philology*
AJA	*American Journal of Archaeology*	*IG*	*Inscriptiones Graecae*
AJP	*American Journal of Philology*	*JdI*	*Jahrbuch des deutschen archäologischen Instituts*
AM	*Mitteilungen des deutschen Archäologischen Instituts, Athenische Abteilung*	*JHS*	*Journal of Hellenic Studies*
ArchEph	*Archailogike Ephemeris*	*JOAI*	*Jahreshefte des Oesterreichischen Archäologischen Institutes*
ARV²	J. D. Beazley, *Attic Red-figure Vase-painters*, Second edition (Oxford, 1963)	*MonPiot*	*Monuments et mémoires publ. par l'Académie des Inscriptions et Belles-Lettres, Fondation Piot*
AZ	*Archäologische Zeitung*	*Necrocorinthia*	H. Payne, *Necrocorinthia. A Study of Corinthian Art in the Archaic Period* (Oxford, 1931)
BABesch	*Bulletin van de Vereeniging tot Bevordering der Kennis van de Antieke Beschaving*	*PAPS*	*Proceedings of the American Philosophical Society*
BASOR	*Bulletin of the American Schools of Oriental Research*	*Perachora*	H. Payne, T. Dunbabin, et al., *Perachora. Excavations of the British School of Archaeology at Athens*, vol. 1 (Oxford, 1940); vol. 2 (Oxford, 1962)
BASP	*Bulletin of the American School of Prehistoric Research*		
BCH	*Bulletin de correspondance hellénique*	*RA*	*Revue Archéologique*
BMMA	*Bulletin of the Metropolitan Museum of Art, New York*	*RE*	Pauly-Wissowa, *Real-Encyclopädie der klassischen Altertumswissenschaft*
BSA	*British School at Athens, Annual*		
CIL	*Corpus Inscriptionum Latinarum*	*RendNap*	*Rendiconti della [R.] Accademia di Archeologia, Lettre ed Arti, Napoli*
Corinth	*Corinth. Result of Excavations Conducted by the American School of Classical Studies in Athens*	*RM*	*Mitteilungen des deutschen archäologischen Instituts, Römische Abteilung*
CP	*Classical Philology*	*TAPA*	*Transactions of the American Philological Association*
CR	*Classical Review*		

Contents

1. Theseus at the Isthmus

Antony E. Raubitschek

CLASSICS DEPARTMENT, STANFORD UNIVERSITY

In the Catalog of Ships (*Iliad* 2.546–559), Athens, Salamis, and Argos are mentioned in this order; the area of Megara and the Isthmus is unaccounted for. Whether this omission is original or whether it is the result of a later (Athenian) interpolation, the fact remains that at least in the sixth century, and perhaps already in the eighth, it may have been thought that the territory of Athens in the heroic period extended as far as the Isthmus.

This impression is confirmed, indirectly, by Sophocles and Herodotus. The former, in his *Aigeus*, says that Aigeus ruled over Attica and Megaris, and the local historians of Attica, Andron and Philochorus, specifically mention that the Isthmus was the border of Attica (Strabo 9.1.6). Herodotus asserts twice (9.26.3 and 27.2) that the Herakleidai (who were supported by the Athenians) met the Peloponnesians at the Isthmus, which implies that the border between the Ionians (Athenians) and the Peloponnesians was there, and this is exactly what Strabo says (9.1.5).

Strabo also reports that Peloponnesians and Ionians often disputed the boundaries between them (9.1.6) and that they finally set up a stele with the inscription τάδ' ἐστὶ Πελοπόννησος οὐκ Ἰωνία (This is Peloponnesos not Ionia) on one side, and τάδ' οὐχὶ πελοπόννησος, ἀλλ' Ἰωνία (This is not Peloponnesos but Ionia) on the other side. Strabo knew, of course, that after the founding of Corinth and Megara, the stele was de-stroyed and the border of Attica pushed back to where it was in historical times, west of Eleusis.

Pausanias also knows that the Athenians controlled, in the time of Pandion, the Megaris as far as the Isthmus (1.39.4), but it is Plutarch who tells in his *Theseus* (25) the full story how Theseus brought Megara firmly under Athenian control and set up the stele with the two inscriptions in trimeters. Theseus is also credited with having renewed the Isthmian Games, which were originally a nocturnal festival for Melikertes (Palaimon); the credit for this information is given to Hellanicus, a younger contemporary of Thucydides.

The inscription on the two sides of the stele at the Isthmus has a close parallel in the inscription on the two sides of the Arch of Hadrian in Athens:[1] Αἵδ' εἴσ' Ἀθῆναι Θησέως ἡ πρὶν πόλις (This is Athens of Theseus, the early city) and Αἵδ' εἴσ' Ἀδριανοῦ καὶ οὐχὶ Θησέως πόλις (This is the city of Hadrian not of Theseus).[2] Meter and diction are the same, and so are the historical and topographical interest and the knowledge of early history that the texts reveal. There is no doubt that the Arch of Hadrian was erected at the edge of what was thought to be the city of Theseus; its location agrees fully with the statement of Thucydides (2.15.4) on the

---

1. *IG*, II², 5185.
2. See J. Travlos, *Pictorial Dictionary of Athens* (London, 1971) 253–57.

oldest city of Athens on the south slope of the Acropolis.

What is amazing is that, after all these years, there should have been kept alive in Athens the memory of conditions which existed during the thirteenth and twelfth centuries B.C., and which were obliterated by the Dorian Invasion.

There is a possibility that the Mycenaean Wall which O. Broneer discovered at the eastern part of the Isthmus may be connected with the conflict between the Ionians and the Peloponnesians and with the stele allegedly erected by Theseus.[3] P. A. L. Greenhalgh has called our attention[4] to another wall at

Thermyopylae that Herodotus mentions (7.176.3–5) as being very old and dilapidated when the Greeks under Leonidas restored it as a defensive wall against the Persians. Originally, it had been built by the Phocians against the Thessalians. In the case of the wall at the Isthmus, something similar may have occurred; the old wall of the Mycenaean period may have served as a model for the Peloponnesians who built the defensive wall against the Persians.

At both Olympia and Nemea, the excavations of the sanctuaries of Pelops and of Opheltes have confirmed the literary tradition that claims a Mycenaean origin of the festivals held at these places. The same should be true for the Isthmia, the earliest history of which may be confirmed by future excavations.

3. See *Hesperia* 35 (1966) 347, 355, 357; 37 (1968) 26 and 31; J. Wiseman, *The Land of the Ancient Corinthians* (Göteborg, 1978) 17–18 and 59.

4. In *Acta Classica* 21 (1978) 6 and 11–12.

2. Labda, Lambda, Labdakos

CLASSICS DEPARTMENT, STANFORD UNIVERSITY

I

Two figures of Greek story owe their names to a letter of the Greek alphabet. One is Labda, the lame daughter of an otherwise unknown Amphion of Corinth, a member of the ruling group of Bakchiads in the seventh century B.C. No Bakchiad would marry her so she became the wife of Aëtion (Eëtion), son of Echekrates, who claimed Lapith ancestry. She gave birth to Kypselos, destined to overthrow the Bakchiads and establish a tyranny.[1] Kypselos's ascension to power dates to the mid-seventh century.[2] His mother is not likely to have been born later than circa 700 B.C. or to have married later than circa 680 B.C.

The other figure is Labdakos, the father of Laios and grandfather of Oidipous of Thebes. Labdakos's lameness is apparently not mentioned in any ancient text and few incidents are attached to him, but the combination of his grandson's name, "Swellfoot," and the close resemblance of his own name to that of the lame Labda have led most scholars to suppose that Labdakos meant "the Lame One."[3]

There has also been agreement that both Labda's and Labdakos's names probably or certainly derive from the Phoenician letter *lamed*, known in Greek as *labda* and *lambda*.[4] Ancient support for the derivation of Labda's name has been found in the *Etymologicum Magnum*, s.v. βλαισός (p. 199 Gaisford), where the condition is that of being splay-footed, knock-kneed, or bandy. The lexicographers knew only the classical and later the Ionic form [∧] and interpreted the woman's condition accordingly. More plausibly, philologists have taken the *lambda* to be the archaic form with one stroke shorter than the other, thus [∧]. Her lameness would have been the result of having one leg shorter than the other.[5]

---

1. Herodotos, 5.92.β-ε, Nikolaos of Damaskos (Jacoby, *Fragmente der griechischen Historiker* 90 F57), cf. Pausanias 5.18.7; Plutarch, *Moralia* 163F–164A.

2. In support of the traditional "high" date, see Russell Meiggs and David Lewis, *A Selection of Greek Historical Inscriptions to the End of the Fifth Century B.C.* (Oxford, 1969) p. 11; Jean Servais, "Hérodote et la chronologie des Cypsélides," *L'Antiquité Classique* 38 (1969) 28–81; Alden A. Mosshammer, *The Chronicle of Eusebius and Greek Chronographic Tradition* (Lewisburg, Pa., and London, 1979) 234–45. The low chronology with Kypselos coming to power circa 620 B.C. was favored by Edouard Will, *Korinthiaka* (Paris, 1955) 363–440.

3. For Labdakos's name, see August Fick and Fritz Bechtel, *Die griechischen Personennamen*² (Göttingen, 1894) 429; Carl Robert, *Oidipus. Geschichte eines poetischen Stoffs im griechischen Altertum* (Berlin, 1915) 59; Otto Gruppe, *Griechische Mythologie und Religionsgeschichte*, vol. 1 (Munich, 1906) 504, note 2; Pierre Chantraine, *Dictionnaire étymologique de la langue grecque* (Paris, 1968) s.v. *labda*. On Oidipous's name, see Fick and Bechtel, *Die griechischen Personennamen*, 403; L. W. Daly, *RE* 17, s.v. Oidipous, 2104–5 and *Suppl.* 7, 786; and Lowell Edmunds, *HSCP* 85 (1981) 233–36 (who argues that it was in origin a plant name). On Laios's name, see below, note 34.

4. On the name of the letter see Eduard Schwyzer, *Griechische Grammatik*, vol. 1 (Munich, 1939) 140; and Chantraine, *Dictionnaire* s.v. *labda*.

5. Robert, *Oidipus*, 59; Fick and Bechtel, *Die griechischen Personennamen*², 429; Ulrich von Wilamowitz-Moellendorf, *Aischylos. Interpretationen* (Berlin, 1914)

The coining of these two names requires that the Greeks had adopted the Phoenician alphabet and had gained sufficient familiarity with it for the allusion to the letter to be understood easily. The names, therefore, originated at a date later than circa 800 B.C. and most likely later than circa 750 B.C.[6] This easily accommodates the seventh century Corinthian woman, Labda, and confirms the impression that Labdakos had no long history, even as he had no distinctive myth or personality. A single source mentions his death while opposing Dionysos, a fate said to have resembled that of Pentheus, and a border war with the Attic king Pandion (Apollodorus 3.40 and 193). But it has been noted that the form of the *lambda* required to produce the Theban king's name is not Boiotian, which in the epichoric alphabet was turned upside down, [$\vee$], as it was also in neighboring Euboia and Attica.[7] The coast of Asia Minor and the Aegean islands had the requisite hooked *lambda*, and Ionic poetry of the early archaic period could have been the source of Labdakos's name. But

Corinth had the same *lambda*, as did her small neighboring states and Aigina and the northwestern part of the Peloponnesos. The name of Labda, the other one of our two alphabetic figures, was certainly at home in a local Corinthian story. A recent study of early Corinthian writing on vases sees the slanting *lambda* with one short leg as standard in the seventh and sixth centuries and argues that in general Corinth was more developed in its letter forms than other areas.[8] Writing was a familiar adornment of pottery and one would suppose that in Corinth, with its active commercial life, writing was commonly used at an early date.[9] In this context the limping letter form was easily used for the lame woman, the mother of Kypselos. The name of the Theban king, Labdakos, may also, I suggest, have originated in Corinth.

The generations of Theban kings between Kadmos and Oidipous were relatively obscure, and they have been taken to be linking figures, conjured up to attach Oidipous and his parents to the founder of the line.[10] The seven generations of kings through which Teiresias had lived are mentioned but not

---

105 and *Kleine Schriften* (Berlin, 1935) 218 = *Hermes* 34 (1899) 64; S. I. Oost, "Cypselus the Bacchiad," *CP* 67 (1972) 17, n. 29. Ernst Curtius, *Grundzüge der griechische Etymologie*[5] (Leipzig, 1879) 655, derived Λάβδαχος as well as Λάϊος from λαϝός (but he has not been followed).

6. On the introduction of the Phoenician alphabet, P. Kyle McCarter, Jr., *The Antiquity of the Greek Alphabet and the Early Phoenician Scripts* (*Harvard Semitic Monographs*, no. 9 [Missoula, Montana, 1979]), especially 123–26 (on *lambda*, 83–84); B. S. J. Isserlin, *Cambridge Ancient History* 3[2], 1 (Cambridge, 1982) 816–18 and L. H. Jeffery, ibid., 830.

7. Robert, *Oidipus*; Francis Vian, *Les Origines de Thèbes. Cadmus et les Spartes* (*Etudes et Commentaires* 48 [Paris, 1963]) 178, n. 6, tries to keep the Theban origin by citing Herodotos's comparison (5.59) of Kadmeian letters with Ionian. But the evidence for the Boiotian epichoric alphabet is unequivocal. The most convenient place to examine the letter forms of the early alphabets is the "Table of Letters" at the end of L. H. Jeffery, *The Local Scripts of Archaic Greece* (Oxford, 1961 [reprinted in *Cambridge Ancient History* 3[2], 1, 823–24]), together with the detailed tables for each local alphabet. The Boiotian, Euboian, and Attic alphabets preserve the stance of the Semitic letter while the Ionic and Corinthian, among others, have turned it upside down.

8. Fritz Lorber, *Inschriften auf korinthischen Vasen* (Deutsches Archäologisches Institut. *Archäologische Forschungen*, Band 6 [Berlin, 1979]) 99 and 16. Cf. Renato Arena, "Le iscrizioni corinzie su vasi" *Memorie della R. Accademia Nazionale dei Lincei*, ser. 8, vol. 13.2 (1967). The information in Lorber is neither complete nor altogether accurate, as is shown by the reviews of Alan Johnston in *JHS* 101 (1981) 223–24 and Alan L. Boegehold, in *AJA* 87 (1983) 281. I am much indebted to Prof. Boegehold for allowing me to read this review in manuscript as well as his discussion of inscriptions from the Corinthian "Potters' Quarter," to be published as an appendix to *Corinth* XV, 2. He would now date the earliest examples of writing from the "Potters' Quarter" (*AJA* 37 [1933] 605–10 = Jeffery, *Local Scripts*, 120–21 and 130, no. 1 and pl. 18) to between 720 and 650 B.C.

9. The notorious scarcity of public inscriptions at Corinth in the Classical and Hellenistic periods is another matter. The nature of Corinthian political life, the lack of local marble, and possibly the use of wooden boards may all have contributed. See S. Dow, *HSCP* 53 (1942) 113–18; and J. H. Kent, *Corinth*, VIII, iii. *The Inscriptions 1926–1950* (Princeton, 1966) pp. 1–2.

10. Robert, *Oidipus*, 59; Vian, *Les Origines de Thèbes*, 178, 198–99.

named in a fragment of the *Melampodia* (Fr. 276 Merkelbach-West), a poem at times attributed to Hesiod in antiquity but now thought to have been a later product. Only Kadmos's son Polydoros is mentioned by Hesiod (*Theogony* 978). The name of Labdakos, the next in line, is not preserved from any author before Pindar, *Isthmian* 3.16, of 461 B.C., where it is implicit in the name of his descendants, the Labdakidai, said to be still living in Thebes. The full sequence, Kadmos, Polydoros, Labdakos, and Laïos, is found in Herodotos 5.59.

The Cyclic Epics, however, offered a number of occasions for the mention of Labdakos. In the *Cypria* Nestor is said to have told of Oidipous in a digression that also covered Epopeus's rape of the daughter of Lykos (elsewhere Lykos is king of Thebes in Laïos's minority),[11] the madness of Herakles, and the story of Theseus and Ariadne.[12] Three of these four incidents touch on Thebes. But in a digression the most that might be expected, despite Nestor's garrulousness, is the naming of Labdakos as the grandfather of Oidipous or the grandnephew of Lykos. The introduction of a figure with such a distinctive name into epic poetry for the first time seems unlikely under these circumstances. Other early poems, the *Thebaïs* and the *Oedipodeia*, told of Laïos, Oidipous, and Oidipous's children.[13] It is improbable, perhaps impossible, that Laïos bore no patronymic, and no alter-

native to Labdakos as his father has come down to us, but there is no indication that stories about Laïos's father were included in these two epics. Thus an allusion to Labdakos with no recounting of tales connected with him or with others of the intermediate generations seems likely in one or more of the Cyclic Epics—*Cypria*, *Thebaïs*, or *Oedipodeia*. We need to look elsewhere for a fuller account of the generations after Kadmos. The source should be no earlier than the late eighth or early seventh century, to judge from the alphabetical reference in Labdakos's name, and not much later if that name was to become available for use by the composers of other archaic poems.

II

A version of Oidipous's genealogy is given in Apollodorus (3.39–48). (See below)

Elements from the chain of stories attached to this genealogy were used by Euripides and other classical and Hellenistic poets. It is reasonable to suppose that they elaborated on or deviated from an Archaic source or sources even though in the state of our knowledge it may not be possible to distinguish the earliest material in late syntheses such as that of Apollodorus.[14] While Labda-

11. Apollodoros 3.40, Hyginus 9.1.
12. Proclus *Chrestomathia* (ed. Allen), p. 103, 20–24.

13. Fragments in G. Kinkel, *Epicorum Graecorum Fragmenta* (Leipzig, 1877) 8–13; cf. Albert Severyns, *Le Cycle épique dans l'école d'Aristarque* (Liége and Paris, 1928) 211–12; G. L. Huxley, *Greek Epic Poetry from Eumelos to Panyassis* (Cambridge, Mass., 1969) 39–50.
14. Besides the versions of the Pentheus story, see Eu-

kos is young, his maternal kin, Nykteus and Lykos, each hold the Theban kingship in turn. Lykos's daughter Antiope, a figure associated with Mt. Kithairon, turns us toward Corinth and Sikyon. Later in the genealogy Oidipous too is associated with Kithairon, Corinth, and Sikyon. When Oidipous's story is stripped down by the rationalizing Palaephatus, he is left as "a Corinthian man" and a successful soldier with a fast horse. Influence of Corinthian poetry on the formation of the familiar story has, understandably, been suggested.[15]

The name of the poet Eumelos, son of Amphilytos, a Bakchiad (Pausanias 2.1.1), is the only one that has come down to us associated with Corinthian poetry, despite Pindar's praise of the Corinthian muse (Olympian Odes 13, 22), and this has caused some surprise. But just as the names of Homer and Hesiod gathered to them anonymous poetry of Ionic and Central Greek origin respectively, it is likely that what was known to be Corinthian came to be attached to Eumelos's name.[16] Of the poems attributed to him, three are relevant to our problem: (1) a prosodion to Delian Apollo, composed for the Messenians around the time of their first struggle with the Lakedaimonians, in the late eighth century B.C.;[17] (2) a Europia; and (3) a Corinthiaca, known to Pausanias only in a prose version.

The Europia told how Amphion (Antiope's son) learned from Hermes the use of the lyre with which he charmed stones to form the walls of Thebes. Kadmos, the first in line of the Theban kings, was a kinsman of Europa and came to Thebes in the course of his search for her (the only surviving reference to either figure in this work is the name of the poem). The poem also dealt with Dionysos, son of Zeus and Kadmos's daughter Semele—his purification at Kybela in Asia Minor by Rhea, his organization of rites and acquisition from her of paraphernalia, his reception with songs and honors among all men until he meets with persecution at the hands of the Thracian king Lykourgos.[18]

The Dionysian stories may have been attractive to the Corinthians, the inventors of the dithyramb,[19] whose rulers in the late eighth century derived themselves from a certain Bakchis.[20] If the Europia told of later generations of Kadmos's descendants, there would have been further Dionysiac elements: Pentheus, son of Kadmos's daughter Agave, engaged in fatal conflict with the god; Labdakos was said to have followed Pentheus's path (Apollodorus 3.40); Dirke, Lykos's wife, was a devotee (Hyginus 7 and 8). One hears anticipations (or are they echoes?) of Euripides's Bacchae in the miraculous falling away of chains from Antiope imprisoned by Dirke and Lykos; and Dirke, having planned

ripides' Antiope, TGF² 410–26; Denys L. Page, Greek Literary Papyri (London, 1942) pp. 60–71.

15. On Antiope, see Wernicke RE 1, s.v., 1. The Hesiodic Catalogue had an Ehoea of Antiope that connected her with Boiotian Hyaria on the Euripos and told of the twin sons building the walls of Thebes with the lyre and of their marriages, Fr. 181–83, Merkelbach-West. On Oidipous as a Corinthian, Palaephatus 4 (7), p. 12 Festa (Mythographi Graeci 3, 2), cf. Pausanias 9.26.2.

16. Cf. C. M. Bowra, "Two Lines of Eumelus," Classical Quarterly 13 (1963) 148.

17. Kinkel, Epicorum Graecorum Fragmenta, pp. 193–94; D. Page Poet. Mel. Graec. N. 696, from Pausanias 4.33.2; in 4.4.1 Pausanias refers to it as the only

genuine work of Eumelos. For discussion, see Bowra, "Two Lines of Eumelus," 145–53; Huxley, Greek Epic Poetry, 62. On the date of the first Messenian War, see Jeffery, Archaic Greece. The City-States c. 700–500 B.C. (London and Tonbridge, 1976) 115, 735–715 B.C. On the ancient dates for Eumelos, see A. Mosshammer, Chronicle, 195–203.

18. Kinkel, Epicorum Graecorum Fragmenta, pp. 186, 192–93, and Pausanias 9.5.8, in an account of the whole Kadmeian line; Huxley, Greek Epic Poetry, 75–78 (60–79 are on Eumelos); T. F. R. G. Braun, Cambridge Ancient History 3³, 3, 30. Corinth, with its early contacts with the Near East, might well have been interested in Europa and Kadmos.

19. Pindar, Olympian Odes 13, 19, cf. Herodotos 1.23, attributing its invention to Arion, who flourished at the court of Periandros in the late-seventh century; but the dithyramb in some form was known earlier, Archilochus 120 West.

20. Pausanias 2.4.4, cf. Heraclides Ponticus, Müller, Fragmenta Historicorum Graecorum 2, 212–13; 5 (ap. Aristot. Fr. 611.20 Rose).

Antiope's death by impalement on a bull, suffers this fate herself (Apollodorus 3.43). With its Theban and Dionysian themes, a Corinthian *Europia* of the Bakchiad period, perhaps by the poet of the hymn to Delian Apollo, would be an attractive candidate for supplying the linkage generations of the Kadmeian line, including Labdakos.

A third work sometimes attributed to Eumelos, the *Corinthiaca*, is very different from the first two we have considered and is less relevant to our problem, but it needs to be examined because of a discrepancy with what I have attributed to the *Europia*. This third work furnished a Corinth painfully barren of heroic traditions with a legendary past by identifying the Homeric Ephyra with Corinth and by appropriating the Argonautic adventures. There is no hint of an interest in Thebes, and two key figures in the genealogy cited above from Apollodorus, Antiope and Epopeus, appear in very different positions. Antiope is now the mother by Helios of Aloeus and Aietes, and Aloeus is the father of Epopeus. Antiope is thus Epopeus's grandmother, not his bride, and there is no reference to her bearing the Theban heroes Amphion and Zethos. Epopeus, to be sure, retains his unpleasant personality. His son Marathon flees from him to Attica, returning only after his father's death, when he divided the land in two, leaving Ephyra to his son, the eponymous Korinthos, and Asopia to the equally eponymous Sikyon.[21]

The *Corinthiaca* shows disagreement with the treatment of Antiope and Epopeus, which I have suggested was derived from the *Europia*. The interests of the two poems were different, and it is by no means necessary that

they were by the same poet. The *Corinthiaca* was just what its name indicated, a poem on Corinthian matters, and its attribution to the most famous Corinthian poet is not surprising while there is no obvious reason why the Messenian commission for a hymn to Delian Apollo or the Theban subjects of the *Europia* should have been attributed falsely to Eumelos. The authorship of the *Europia* is not essential to the argument. Nonetheless, these two works, in contrast to the patriotic focus of the *Corinthiaca*, suit a poet of the late eighth century B.C. with wide contacts and interests (Messenia, Delos, Boiotia); the poet himself was perhaps a member of the Bakchiad ruling elite which, it should be noted, is said to have furnished Thebes with a legislator by the name of Philolaos (Aristotle, *Politica* 1274B 2–5).

The place of Sikyon in the development of these stories deserves consideration. The author of the *Corinthiaca* had dealt firmly with Sikyon. It was not allowed a lineage more ancient than that of the Corinthians. The Sikyonians on their side enlisted the Samian poet Asios, perhaps of the early sixth century.[22] For him Antiope was the daughter of Asopos (in agreement with *Odyssey* 11.260), probably identified as the Peloponnesian, not the Boiotian river. Her twin sons have two fathers, Zeus and Epopeus, just as Alkmene bore Herakles and Iphikles by Zeus and Amphitryon, respectively. This version clearly disagrees with that found in Apollodorus, which I have suggested represents the tradition of the *Europia*, where Antiope is the daughter of Nykteus; it also disagrees with that of the *Cypria*, where she is presumably the daughter (unnamed) of Lykos, Nykteus's brother; and it disagrees most of all with the *Corinthiaca*. It was, in effect, a Sikyonian answer to that poem and perhaps not far from it in date.

---

21. Kinkel, *Epicorum Graecorum Fragmenta*, pp. 187–92 and Jacoby, *Fragmente der griechischen Historiker* 451; doubts on the attribution to Eumelos, Pausanias 2.1.1; T. J. Dunbabin, "The Early History of Corinth," *JHS* 68 (1948) 66–68; Huxley, *Greek Epic Poetry*, 61–68. A more amiable Epopeus may have been presented by Euripides, cf. Hyginus 7 and 8. For an exploration of the cultic and mythic implications of Epopeus, Antiope, *et al.* at Thebes and Sikyon, see Walter Burkert *Homo Necans* (Berlin, 1972) 182–89, and in English translation (Berkeley, 1983) 185–90.

22. Kinkel, *Epicorum Graecorum Fragmenta*, pp. 202–5; Huxley, *Greek Epic Poetry*, 89–98, esp. 92, who, however, minimizes the differences between Asios and the Apollodoran version.

A contrast between Corinthian and Sikyonian versions occurs also in the events of later generations, but here we have no attributions to authors who can be linked to either city. The infant Oidipous is either set adrift in a chest on the Corinthian Gulf or is exposed on Mt. Kithairon, and is then rescued and reared by Polybos, who is described as the king of either Sikyon or of Corinth. The child is brought to the Sikyonian king by herders of horses, who in Greek legend surely tend their charges on plains, not on mountains. This may suggest that they belong with the version that has Oidipous in a chest that comes to shore. The herdsmen who receive Oidipous on Kithairon are not horsetenders, and based on geographical considerations one would expect Corinthian rather than Sikyonian herdsmen to meet Thebans on Mt. Kithairon.[23]

The persistent mention of Sikyon, first in connection with Antiope and then with Oidipous, makes it possible that Sikyonian tradition or even a Sikyonian poem was influential. But, as no early Sikyonian poets were remembered, the better attested Corinthian poetry was more likely the vehicle. Not every Corinthian poet who was heir to the legends and cults at the east end of the Corinthian Gulf may have wished to suppress the Sikyonian connections. The drastic hand seen in the *Corinthiaca* is another matter, but there is no reason to think that that work concerned itself with the Theban stories. It is

plausible then that a poem or poems from this area told the story of Oidipous, and it would be economical to suppose that such a poem also dealt with his ancestors, the earlier kings of Thebes, who, I have suggested, were subjects of the *Europia*.

Placing Labdakos in a poetic context has taken us onto uncertain terrain. To summarize the argument, early Corinthian and possibly Sikyonian poetry dealt with some parts of the Kadmeian line before Oidipous and so probably dealt with Labdakos. Unlike the Thebans themselves, Corinthians and Sikyonians would have caught the alphabetic allusion in his name immediately (Sikyon's *lambda* was no different from Corinth's). If Eumelos was in fact the author of the *Europia*, the coining of Labdakos's name would have occurred under Bakchiad rule, that is, before circa 650 B.C. and in the vicinity of the first Messenian War, the presumed date of the poem for Delian Apollo. This is the period, late eighth or early-seventh century B.C., that one would have expected for Labdakos's appearance, and it is close in date to the birth of Labda.

III

The pattern of the Oidipous story has often been seen as belonging to folktale rather than heroic myth. The story of Labda and her son Kypselos may equally be more of a folktale than the history it purports to be.[24] The stories share the theme of the child who threatens the ruler or the rulers and miraculously survives attempts on his life. Kypselos's rise is paralleled by that of Cyrus the

---

23. Nowhere in this myth was the existence of Megara, astride the Isthmos between Kithairon and Corinth, acknowledged, a silence certainly in accord with the Corinthian point of view.

Discussions of the various versions of the Oidipous myth start with Euripides, *Phoenissae* 22–30 and Schol. on 28 (cf. Schol. *Od.* 11.271 with material from Androtion, Jacoby, *Fragmente der griechischen Historiker* 324 F 62). See Erich Bethe, *Thebanische Heldenlieder* (Leipzig, 1891) 67–75; Robert, *Oidipus* 1.70; Ludwig Deubner, "Oedipus-probleme," *Abhandlungen Berlin Akademie* 4 (1942) 38–42; Edmunds, "The Cults and Legends of Oedipus," *HSCP* 85 (1981) 221–38 (on the connections with Sikyon, 227, n. 23). Neither in this note, nor elsewhere in this study, do I convey adequately the complexity and the ingenuity of scholarly speculation on the origin and development of these myths.

24. Oswyn Murray, *Early Greece* (Sussex and New Jersey, 1980) 142–43, suggests a Mesopotamian origin for this type of story, appropriate to the Greek city "most receptive to oriental artistic influence." On the oracles to Aetion, see Roland Crahay, *La Littérature oraculaire chez Hérodote* (Paris, 1956) 235–41, who compares the stories of Labda and Oidipous; and Joseph Fontenrose, *The Delphic Oracle* (Berkeley and Los Angeles, 1978) 116–17. On Oidipous, see, for example, M. P. Nilsson *Göttinginsche gelehrte Anzeigen* (1922) 36–46 = *Opuscula Selecta* 1 (Lund, 1951) 338–48, and

Great (Herodotos 1.108ff.). A daughter of the ruler(s) marries an outsider; their son, it is prophesied, will overthrow the ruler(s); he survives attempts to kill him; he comes to manhood and fulfills the prediction. Oidipous's story has the pattern characteristic of comedy—the foundling proves to be the legitimate heir—not tragedy.[25] One might expect a happy ending. But the theme is inherently ambivalent.

Did the story become attached to the Kypselids at the time of their rise and popularity? That is suggested in Herodotos's account (5.92.β-ε) of the exciting and heart-warming incident of the baby Kypselos smiling at the first of the ten Bakchiad delegates sent to kill him and being passed in turn to each of the ten and back to his mother, and then escaping discovery hidden in a beehive when the executioners, having come to their senses outside the house, return to kill the child.[26] But the overthrow of the despotism of the ruling group results in the tyranny of one man. This is seen more convincingly in the case of Periandros, Kypselos's son, than with his father.[27] It is worth noting that the occasion for the whole account in Herodotus is the Corinthian warning to the Spartans against supporting the Athenian tyrant Hip-

pias. Even the story of Cyrus, whose rise is a triumph for the Persians and a calamity for the Medes, can be seen as ambivalent. Reversals have unpredictable consequences. The Oidipous story, as perfected by Sophocles in the *Oedipus Tyrannus*, offers one apparently successful escape after another to culminate in the most complete disaster.[28]

The theme of lameness in the Theban and Corinthian stories signals and reinforces the ambivalent destinies of the heroes. The deformed and the handicapped are at the least extraordinary, at the worst monstrous and ominous. At their most benign they are well suited to be the heroes of reversals of fortune. The despised Labda, whom no Bakchiad will marry, becomes the mother of their nemesis. The lame foundling becomes king of Thebes, for a time. An oracle of Apollo, "Beware the lame kingship," is brought out against the succession to the Spartan kingship of the lame Agesilaos in 399 B.C. It is interpreted successfully by the influential Lysandros as a warning against an illegitimate, not a physically lame, heir, and for Xenophon at least Agesilaos proved to have heroic dimensions.[29] In more plebeian circles, Aesop, the fabulist, who was said to be extraordinarily ugly and maimed, turned the tables on his enemy, another slave by the name of Agathopous ("good-foot").[30]

But the sinister implications of lameness are also clear. The succession to the kingship of Kyrene by Battos IV, who was lame and not *artipous* ("sound of foot") and who was descended by one account from an original Battos, a bastard with a speech impediment, prompts consultation of the Delphic oracle, and in the end he turns out to be the last king of that name.[31] Some Spartans, too, clearly

The Mycenaean Origin of Greek Religion (Berkeley, 1932) 104–5.

25. Cf. Richmond Lattimore, *Story Patterns in Greek Tragedy* (Ann Arbor, 1969) 8–9.

26. Also in Nikolaos of Damaskos, *Fragmente der griechischen Historiker* 90 F 57, simplified and rationalized, as Jacoby remarks. On Kypselos's name and his hiding place, see Georges Roux in *REA* 65 (1963) 279–89.

27. Herodotos is alone in depicting Kypselos as an unmitigated tyrant. Contrast Aristotle *Politica* 1315B 27–29. Among the many discussions of the Kypselid tyranny, see Antony Andrewes, *The Greek Tyrants* (London, 1956) 43–53; Claude Mossé, *La Tyrannie dans la Grèce antique* (Paris, 1969) 25–37; Will, *Korinthiaka*; Oost, "Cypselus the Bacchiad," who carries furthest a not uncommon view that Kypselos was a Bakchiad and sees him reviving a Bakchiad kingship. Historically, Kypselos may indeed have exploited his ties with the old ruling elite, but it should be stressed that that is not what Herodotos understood and that it is essential to the Labda story that she was cast out. Aetion's Lapith ancestry is used to set Kypselos apart from the previous rulers.

28. Cf. J.-P. Vernant, *Mythe et tragédie en Grèce ancienne* (Paris, 1973) 99–131.

29. Xenophon, *Hellenika* 3.3.3, Plutarch, *Lysander* 22.12, Pausanias 3.8.8–10.

30. *Vita Aesopica*, p. 81 and *Vita Xanthi Philosophi*, p. 35, in B. Parry, *Aesopica* 1 (Urbana, 1952). I owe these references to the kindness of Jack Winkler.

31. Herodotos 5.161.1, 162.4; 155.1–3. βάττος meaning "stammerer" is also quoted from Hesychius.

took Agesilaos's lameness to be ill omened. Tenedos once had a lame king with the unpropitious name of Amauros, "The Weak."[32] Bakchis, the first of the Bakchiads, was said to have been lame.[33] The lameness of his descendant Labda brought an end to their reign but in time it could be seen as ominous for all the Corinthians. Labdakos initiates a crippled line that spells eventual disaster for Thebes. In the unbalanced abnormal physique and gait of the lame there may also be implications of sexual perversion and of disturbance in the normal succession of generations, as has been argued recently, and this can be exploited in depicting the essentially asocial and perverse role of the tyrant.[34] More generally one might say that in Greek society attention is always on the moral and

religious health of the leadership, be it that of king, tyrant, or Perikles as "demagogue." Lameness is one way of marking the anticipated break-up of order and the failure of rule.

Nothing survives to tell us what part Labdakos's lameness played in his own story. As for Oidipous, his lameness is likely to have been more explicit in earlier versions than in Attic tragedy, which, nonetheless, makes great play with the theme of feet.[35] It has been suggested that he was club-footed from birth and that this fact served originally as a token by which he was recognized.[36] We need not suppose that it was Greek distaste for deformed heroes that shifted the original lameness of Oidipous and Kypselos to their forebears, Labdakos and Labda.[37] Labda's lameness explains her being cast out (or is a description of her outcast status),[38] and the historical Kypselos was not known to be lame. Rather, the tell-tale defect appears early in the descent line. Transference of significant features within a story is familiar. It serves to color what follows and to confirm what preceded. For the Greeks, of course, the unity of a line of descent was strongly felt.

The Greek poetry that followed on the heroic epic we see in the *Iliad* and in the *Odyssey* admitted more freely the magical and the monstrous, the trivial and the gross, and, not least, violence within the family.[39] It was perhaps the resurgence of a more popular, folkloric imagination. Taste and society were changing, and a different culture was emerging with Archaic Corinth as one of its major centers. While trade and colonization expanded, the Bakchiad rulers at home enforced endogamy on their members, froze the size of family properties and the number of citizens, limited the political power to

---

Herodotos believed the name was derived from the Libyan word for king, 5.155.2.

32. Heracleides Ponticus, *Fragmenta Historicorum Graecorum* 2, p. 213, 7.2 (also ap. Aristotle Fr. 611.23).

33. Ibid., pp. 212–13, 5 (Aristotle, Fr. 611.19). But he was handsome, he ruled well, and he had ten children. Oost, "Cypselus the Bacchiad," 23, sees Bakchis's lameness as an insertion used by Kypselos to emphasize his membership in the *genos* via his lame mother. This is to misunderstand the implications of lameness.

34. Vernant, "From Oedipus to Periander: Lameness, Tyranny, Incest in Legend and History," *Arethusa* 15 (1982) 19–38: a rich and wide-ranging study I was fortunate enough to see before completing the present paper. Vernant's study and the discussions of Marie Delcourt, *Stérilités mystérieuses & naissances maléfiques* (Liége and Paris, 1938) esp. 110–12, and *Oedipe ou la légende du conquerant* (Liége and Paris) esp. 26–29 are the most rewarding comparisons of the Oidipous and Labda stories. The theme of lameness is related to that of "monosandalism," as in Jason's single sandal. See Angelo Brelich, "Les monosandales," *La Nouvelle Clio* 9 (1957) 469–84; he discusses the trait as applied to Dionysos's enemy Lykourgos, who, as we have seen, appeared in the *Europia* (483–84).

Vernant apparently takes Laios's name from λαιϝός, "left," in agreement with Claude Lévi-Strauss, *Structural Anthropology* (New York and London, 1963) 214. (I do not know of earlier proposals for this derivation.) "Gauche" is an attractive name for a character with Laios's misadventures and kin. But I find no ancient awareness of the possibility and no formation from λαιϝός among the Greek names referring to left-handedness, and I see a difficulty in the formation of Λᾶϊος from λαιϝός. The usual derivation is from λᾶϝός, "people," cf. *Publius*; so Fick and Bechtel, *Die griechischen Personennamenz*, 429; Delcourt, *Oedipe*, 27.

35. See Vernant, "From Oedipus to Periander," 36, n. 24.

36. Robert, *Oidipus* 1, 63.

37. As argued by Delcourt, *Stérilités*, 111, and *Oedipe*, 21.

38. Louis Gernet, *Anthropologie de la Gréce antique* (Paris, 1968) 350.

39. Cf. Jasper Griffin *JHS* 97 (1977) 39–53.

themselves and within the group gave the office of *prytanis* or *basileus* to the eldest descendant of the founder of their line (not to the eldest son of the previous holder), thus guaranteeing a gerontocrat within an oligarchy.[40] The picture of a tense and rigid upper crust on top of an exceptionally energetic society is clear even if the details are uncertain. Whatever its precise cause or the nature of its support, Kypselos's coup in the mid-seventh century B.C. was a predictable explosion, and it altered Corinthian leadership permanently. It is to this world, before and after the revolution, that belong, I suggest, the stories of Labdakos and his descendants as well as the stories of Labda and her descendants. These are stories concerned with a fearful and doomed leadership and with violent reversals bringing new dangers, and they share the allusion, sophisticated for its time, to the unbalanced *lambda*.[41]

June 1983

40. On the character of the Bakchiad regime, see Will, *Korinthiaka*, 298–362, and Oost, "Cypselus the Bacchiad." The appointment of the eldest descendant of the founder may have been superseded by the selection of an annual official, unless one was *basileus*, the other *prytanis*.

41. The representations of poetic subjects in the art of the seventh century are very restricted. The absence of Theban subjects does not tell against the suggestions made here. See Hans von Steuben, *Frühe Sagendarstellungen in Korinth und Athen* (Berlin, 1968), and Klaus Fittschen, *Untersuchungen zum Beginn der Sagendarstellungen bei den Griechen* (Berlin, 1969), with discussion of a fragment of a Cycladic relief vase from Thebes showing Europa on the bull, p. 197. For the dominance of Trojan War themes, see Richard Kannicht, "Poetry and Art: Homer and the Monuments Afresh," *Classical Antiquity* 1 (1982) 76–84.

Some comparisons between Corinthian "history" and Theban legend: Telestes, the last Bakchiad king, was deprived of his throne during his minority (Diodorus Siculus 7.9.5) as was Laios (Apollod. 3.40, Hyginus 9.1); mother-son incest—rejected by the Bakchiad Diokles who retires to Thebes with his lover Philolaos (Aristotle, *Politica* 1273.31–42, a Theban guide's story about two graves?), alleged of Periandros (Aristippos ap. Diog. Laert. 1.96); Amphion, Labda's father, has the name of the builder of the walls of Thebes (was the Corinthian, or his father, responsible for the heavy defensive wall of the first half of the seventh century? A. N. Stillwell, *Corinth* XV, i, 14–15, R. Carpenter, *Corinth*, III, ii, 82–83).

3. Corinth and the Cult of Aphrodite

CHARLES K. WILLIAMS, II

AMERICAN SCHOOL OF CLASSICAL STUDIES, ATHENS

The specific subject of this paper is a discussion of the cult of Aphrodite on Akrokorinthos, but before this can be done a certain number of observations should be made generally concerning Aphrodite in relation to the city of Corinth in the pre-Roman period.[1]

A number of literary and epigraphical sources mention the cult on Akrokorinthos; it is identified as Ourania.[2] It is, however, only one of a number of shrines to the goddess that must have been scattered throughout the city. There are references to a temple of Aphrodite at each of the ports of Corinth. At Kenchreai a temple with stone statue sat on the mole of the harbor and, although not stated, probably was part of a seamen's cult.[3] It need not interest us here, for the harbor constructions are all of Roman date, as the recent excavations have illustrated; thus the temple on the mole and its cult there probably both date to the Roman period. At Lechaion, the western harbor of Corinth, one knows of a temple of Aphrodite in use at the time of Periander; unfortunately, little can be said about that sanctuary. Archaeologically it still is unknown.[4] A sanctuary of Aphrodite Melainis was to be found at the northeastern edge of the city, apparently close to classical graves, one of which was that of Lais. This cult apparently emphasized the chthonic aspects of the goddess, also indicated by her cult activities in other cities.[5] Other archaeological evidence for the goddess is to be found scattered in different parts of the city, but of special interest is a sherd inscribed in Corinthian epichoric with the name Astarte (figure 1A). The sherd was found at the southwest corner of what was to become the Roman forum, in a general fill of the later fifth century B.C., over the earliest floor of a pentagonal building of unidentified function.[6] The sherd takes on special signifi-

1. I offer the following pages to Professor Amyx in thanks not only for the scholarly expertise that he has showered on the Corinth excavations and on Corinthian scholars but also for the most enjoyable times that he and his family have shared with us during the years that he has worked at Corinth.

A first draft of this paper was presented at a Massenzia colloquium in Rome in January 1982. The paper, in its present, expanded form was given at a seminar at the Swedish School in Athens in February 1982. I thank Professor Kyle Phillips, Director of Massenzia, and Dr. Robin Hagg, Director of the Swedish School in Athens, as well as the participants of both sessions, for their observations and discussions that helped put this paper into its final form. To Professor R. S. Stroud and Dr. N. Bookidis, who have read these pages, I admit a great indebtedness, having benefited over the years from their broad knowledge of things Corinthian. Thus the chance to correct mistakes has been offered me by numerous skilled and active minds; the mistakes of the text that remain, therefore, I must own, are mine.

2. Pindar, fr. 107 (Bowra). For other occurrences of this cult, see L. R. Farnell, *The Cults of the Greek States* vol. 2 (Oxford, 1896) 749, n. 105.

3. Pausanias 2.2.3.

4. Plutarch, *Sept. sap. conviv.* 2, p. 146 D (Paton-Wegehaupt).

5. Pausanias 2.2.4; Farnell, *Cults*, vol. 2, 652. For Thespiae, see Pausanias 9.27.5; for Mantinea, see Pausanias, 8.6.5.

6. C-75-65; concerning the pentagonal building, see C. K. Williams, II, "Corinth, 1974: Forum Southwest,"

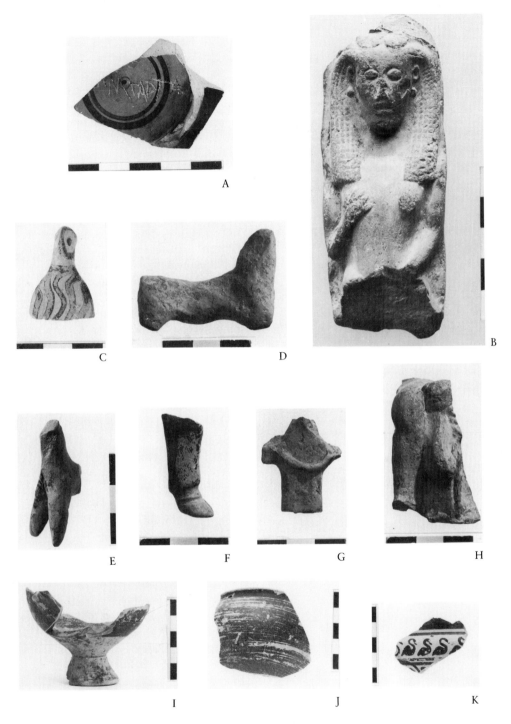

Figure 1. All items are from Old Corinth, Museum. A. Inscribed Sherd from Forum SW, inv. no. C-75-65; B. Terracotta Figurine, inv. no. (4039); C. Mycenaean "Phi" Figurine from Akrokorinthos, inv. no. MF 747; D. Fragmentary Animal Figurine, inv. no. MF 710; E. Fragmentary Animal Figurine, inv. no. MF 718; F. Leg of an Animal Figurine, inv. no. MF 748; G. Fragmentary Female Figurine with Necklace, inv. no. MF 750; H. Fragmentary Figurine of a Boy on a Stool, inv. no. MF 726; I, J, K. Geometric Sherds from Akrokorinthos.

cance when one considers that a building lying about 20 meters due east of the pentagonal building served as a commercial center in which were found over 4½ tons of discarded amphoras. Over two tons of amphoras were of western Punic forms, now thought to be from Morocco.[7] The construction of this building is dated within the fifth century B.C.; its destruction and abandonment have been fixed between 430 and 420 B.C. The proprietor of the establishment appears to have been an importer of good wines from the Aegean (Chios, Mende, etc.) and of fish from the western Mediterranean or from the warm waters of the Atlantic. This man received produce from Punic fishermen over

a period of about a half of a century, or slightly less; he apparently dealt in bulk.

One can only wonder at the full significance of the material, and at the relationship that might exist between the building and the sherd inscribed with the name of Astarte. It does seem less likely, when one compares the figurines found in deposits in the area with material found within the building, that this sherd belongs to a house cult rather than to a neighborhood shrine.

Other physical remains exist at Corinth that might suggest an early knowledge of Astarte or an eastern Aphrodite. One seventh century figurine suggests Astarte (figure 1B).[8] A plaque from the Heraion at Perachora portrays a female rising from a "sack"; she has painted hair and eyes, and dots on the jaw that may indicate a "beard." Payne suggests that we have at Perachora a "Grecized version of the bisexual Aphrodite of the Orient and Cyprus being born from the severed genitals of Ouranos, an incident that took place in Cyprus."[9] This plaque is dated Early Daedalic by style; that is, it is dated in the first half of the seventh century, probably in the second quarter.

Evidence of Aphrodite in the later Greek period is easier to come by, including figurines from house debris, from various votive dumps, and from the Demeter Sanctuary. One votive dump outside Shrine A of the Potters' Quarter contained no figurines that can be said, definitely, to portray Aphrodite, but an inscribed bronze phiale (figure 2C) dedicated to the goddess was found in the fill along with a number of appropriate terracottas.[10] No figurines of the Greek period that portray Aphrodite were found in the Corinthian Asklepieion, although marble statuettes of the Roman period were found there.[11]

Hesperia 44 (1975) 7–9. The sherd was found in the fill between the first and second phase floor, stratum dated to the second and third quarters of the fifth century B.C., and perhaps to the fourth quarter. Also found in the fill was a fragment of a Cypriot bichrome closed jar, C–1975–349. See, also, C. K. Williams, II, "Corinth, 1975: Forum Southwest," *Hesperia* 45 (1976) 108. For figurines from the immediate vicinity of the pentagonal building see C. K. Williams, II, "Corinth, 1974," p. 8. These are mostly types associated with heroes: horse and rider, snake stele, banqueting hero. For a deposit more appropriate to Aphrodite or Astarte, found circa 30 m north of the pentagonal building, see C. K. Williams, II, "Corinth, 1974," n. 17 on p. 8. Part of this deposit is published by G. R. Davidson, *Corinth* XII, *The Minor Objects* (Princeton, 1952) deposit 8, pp. 18, 23.

The deposit of figurines that is most appropriate for Astarte, which was found to the southeast of the pentagonal building is published by H. S. Robinson, "Excavations at Corinth, 1960," *Hesperia* 31 (1962) 113, pl. 41. The deposit is dated within the second half of the fifth century B.C. Of special interest is the female protome with hands holding breasts, MF 10083 (figures 2A, head, and 2B, hand holding breast). Part of the head is illustrated by Robinson, pl. 41b and c. The Robinson deposit, with perforated disc, animal figurines, and other votives, is close in content to the Aphrodite deposit of the Potters' Quarter. See A. N. Stillwell, *Corinth* XV, ii, *The Potters' Quarter, the Terracottas* (Princeton, 1952) 22; see both Aphrodite deposit and deposit in stele Shrine A.

7. M. L. Zimmerman Munn, "Corinthian Trade with the Atlantic Coasts of Spain and Morocco in the Fifth Century B.C." Paper given at the Archaeological Institute of America Meeting, 1981; Y. Maniatis, R. E. Jones, I. K. Whitbread, A. Kostikas, A. Simopoulos, C. Karakalos, C. K. Williams, II, "Punic Amphoras Found at Corinth, Greece: An Investigation of Their Origin and Technology," *JFA* 11 (1984) 205–22.

8. Davidson, *The Minor Objects*, 29, pl. 6, no. 85.

9. H. Payne, *Perachora* 1, *The Sanctuaries of Hera Akraia and Limenia* (Oxford, 1940) 231–32, pl. 102, no. 183. Of interest is the back of the plaque painted with a Pegasos and a dog.

10. Stillwell, *Corinth* XV, i, *The Potters' Quarter* 115, pl. 47, no. 1.

11. C. Roebuck, *Corinth* XIV, *The Asklepieion and*

At this point one other general fact might be mentioned concerning Aphrodite at Corinth, even though the fact is of Roman date. When describing the west end of the forum of Roman Corinth, Pausanias mentions that he saw a statue of Aphrodite (probably in a temple) made by Hermogenes of Kythera. At Kythera itself, Pausanias saw:

> The sanctuary of Aphrodite Ourania which is most holy and it is the most ancient of all the sanctuaries of Aphrodite among the Greeks. The goddess herself is represented by an armed image in wood.[12]

Whether there was a conscious intent with the Roman reestablishment of the city of Corinth in 44 B.C. to have a sculptor from Kythera carve a statue of Aphrodite in the manner of the famous armed cult statue of his home or whether the selection was coincidental now is impossible to tell. If there was a wish to revive the cult of Aphrodite Ourania with an appropriately recognizable cult statue, one could do no better than to draw from the oldest of her sanctuaries in Greece for authenticity. In using this argument, one has, however, a problem with the cult statue of Aphrodite on Akrokorinthos itself, which was known from archaic times to be the seat of Corinthian Aphrodite Ourania. Pausanias himself says that the statue that he saw in the second century after Christ was armed.

Ἀνελθοῦσι δὲ ἐς τὸν Ἀκροκόρινθον ναός ἐστιν Ἀφροδίτης ἀγάλματα δὲ αὐτή τε ὡπλισμένη καὶ Ἥλιος καὶ Ἔρως ἔχων τό-ξον.[13]

(For one mounting Akrokorinthos there is a temple of Aphrodite. The statues are armed Aphrodite, Helios and Eros with bow.)

But Roman coins show her draped from thigh to floor, armed only with a shield, and in her Akrokorinth temple. Variations exist

between coins, with most showing her holding the shield on her right side. Sometimes she has her shield supported by a column or by an Eros. In the later coins she holds the shield free.[14]

The statue type is discussed by Furtwängler in detail and again discussed by O. Broneer.[15] Furtwängler sees in the Capua Aphrodite the closest parallel now known to a Skopan original. In this the goddess looks at her reflection in the shield; without further argumentation the statue is assigned to Corinth. Broneer assumes that the Aphrodite of Capua and the Corinthian Aphrodite are two distinct and independent works, seeing the Capua statue going back to an original Nike of the late fifth century, garbed with chiton and outer garment. Only after the fifth century did the Nike lose her shirt, leaving her upper body nude; thus was the statue converted into an Aphrodite. In either case, we come back to the main problem. A cult statue of one of the most important Corinthian state goddesses would not be carved naked in the fifth century B.C. in Greece, and certainly not in the sixth century B.C. A radical change in the concept of the early cult statue probably should not be expected before the Hellenistic period. One might consider that the cult statue might have undergone a radical iconographical change in the Hellenistic period, but the logical break in tradition is at the beginning of the Roman colony, when Corinth's warring days were over.[16] I would assume that, when Pausanias

---

Lerna (Princeton, 1951) 144–45, pl. 59, nos. 8–10.
12. Pausanias 3.23.1.
13. Pausanias 2.5.1. See, also, Strabo 8.6.20.

14. F. Imhoof-Blumer and P. Gardner, *A Numismatic Commentary on Pausanias*, Reprint from *JHS* (1885–1887) 25–27, pl. G. 121–25, 134; FF, 13.
15. A. Furtwängler, *Masterpieces of Greek Sculpture* (ed. E. Sellers, London and New York, 1895) 384ff. O. Broneer, "The 'Armed Aphrodite' in Acrocorinth and the Aphrodite of Capua," *University of California Publications in Classical Archaeology* 1 (1930) 65–84.
16. Occasion for a radical change in type of cult statue is most logical, if not in the Roman period, then as the result of a Macedonian takeover of the citadel of Corinth, that is, in the Hellenistic period. Under foreign control the citadel and the access to it would have been restricted; Corinthians well might have found the temple unavailable and inaccessible for the practice of ritual and feasts. Under such conditions one can imagine

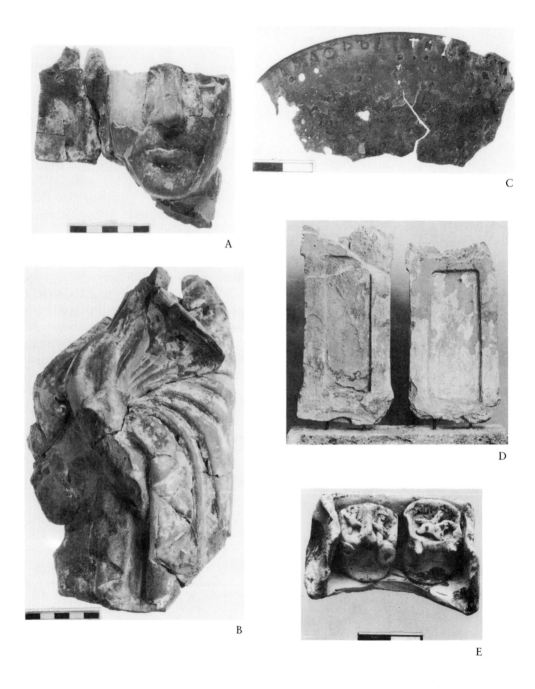

Figure 2. All items are from Old Corinth, Museum. A, B. Fragmentary Female Figurine, inv. no. 10083; C. Inscribed Fragmentary Bronze Phiale, inv. no. KMI; D. Stelai of the Potter's Quarter; E. Miniature Terracotta Stelai-Shrine; inv. no. KT-64-4.

refers to Aphrodite *Hoplismene*, he is applying a cult epithet and that, in the Roman period, Aphrodite with shield alone is enough to justify the epithet.

One of the most important questions having to do with the cult of Aphrodite *Hoplismene* or Ourania concerns the date of its introduction into Corinth. Much literature has been written arguing the fact that Aphrodite evolved on Greek soil in prehistoric times.[17]

Other literature considers her a Cypriot goddess even in the Neolithic period; there are facets of the goddess to be found throughout the Near East and Anatolia.[18] The literary tradition, as stated by Pausanias, is that the earliest appearance of Aphrodite in Greece is at Kythera.[19] Hesiod implies primacy of Kythera even over Cyprus.[20] Some scholars assume that the cult spread from Kythera northward to Corinth, the theory being derived, in most cases, from a late author, Alkiphron.[21] Aphrodite also made an early appearance at Thebes and at Athens, but it was at Corinth where she became, straightforwardly, the armed protectress of the city, the equivalent of Athena Polias at Athens and in many other mainland cities. At Corinth she is called Aphrodite Ourania and Kypri;[22] only here in Greece does she maintain an entourage of sacred prostitutes. The closest parallels lead to Astarte in the Near East for this aspect of her cult, and to the city of Askalon. In fact, Pausanias mentions, when talking about Aphrodite Ourania in Athens, that the cult of Aphrodite Ourania

---

a surrogate cult statue dedicated in the lower city to serve the needs of the state. The above argument does not support the theory that a semi-draped Aphrodite with shield is developed for Corinth before the very end of the fourth century B.C.; rather, it must be set up within the Hellenistic period, perhaps when Aratus gives over the Acropolis to the Macedonians.

A parallel may be imagined in Corinthian Helios. A minor deity of Greece, but important to Corinthian mythology, Helios shares the summit of Akrokorinthos with Aphrodite. Pausanias mentions altars to him at the foot of the hill, below the Demeter Sanctuary that now is largely excavated (Pausanias 2.4.6–5.1). The altars of Helios have not been found nor does archaeological evidence exist for the construction date of these altars. One must, however, explain their position well below the summit and as easily accessible to the city; the altars may have been set up there by Corinthians who were barred from access to the acropolis.

17. The introduction of Aphrodite and her cults into Greece is a complex problem. Many scholars have argued the fact that Aphrodite evolved on Greek soil in prehistoric times. See J. C. van Leuvan, "Mycenaean goddesses called Potnia," *Kadmos* 18 (1979) 122, esp. n. 31. Although Aphrodite is not recorded in Linear B, and Aphrodite, at least by that name, may well not be a Mycenaean goddess, van Leuvan sees in Linear B tablets certain aspects of her in Potnia (pp. 120–29).

In opposition to the view of an indigenous Aphrodite, see T. J. Dunbabin, "The Early History of Corinth," *JHS* 68 (1948) 66ff. "So it may be that the Corinthians who set up at Posideion and elsewhere at the eastern end of the Mediterranean learnt there to use these cults, and brought them home together with a number of myths and legends." Farnell also argues against Aphrodite as an aboriginal goddess; he, too, sees her as an import from the east. Farnell, *Cults*, vol. 2, 618–19.

In any case it seems best to assume that if Astarte, in her aspect of protectress of the city, had existed in the Mycenaean period, such a concept would have become extremely diluted between the fall of the centralized Mycenaean government and the Late Geometric period. The new drive at the end of the Geometric period for synoikismos would then have been a stimulus for the reintroduction of her cult at Corinth to serve as a focal point for the newly emerging concept of urbanism.

It is interesting to note that Athens has a different set

of myths surrounding its period of synoikismos. There Aphrodite appears, but on a goat and as Pandemos. See R. E. Wycherley, *The Athenian Agora*, vol. 3, *Literary and Epigraphical Testimonia* (Princeton, 1957) 224–25.

J. G. O'Neill, in *Ancient Corinth* (Baltimore, 1930), presents the theory that temple prostitution developed locally because of Corinth's being a commercial town "and, consequently, just the place where lewd rites, once introduced in order to cater to a sea-faring center, might be expected to grow and flourish" (p. 101). See also, H. Conzelmann, "Korinth und die Madchen der Aphrodite," *Nachrichten der Akademia der Wissenschaften in Göttingen* 8 (1967) esp. p. 260.

18. For Aphrodite as eteocypriot, but with Syrian, Anatolian, and Cretan characteristics, see O. Masson, "Cultes indigènes, cultes grecs et cultes orientaux à Cypre," *La religion grecque ancienne*, Colloque de Strasbourg, 1958 (Paris, 1960) 129–42, esp. 132–33. See, also, F. G. Maier, "The Paphian Shrine of Aphrodite," *Acts of the International Archaeological Symposium "The Relations between Cyprus and Crete, ca. 2000–500 B.C."* (Nicosia, 1979) 228–34.

19. Pausanias 1.14.7.

20. Hesiod, *Theogonia*, lines 190ff.

21. Alkiphron 3.24 (Schepers).

22. Pindar, frag. 107 (Bowra); Simonides *ap.* Athenaeus, *Deipnosphistae*, vol. 13, 573; also 574.

at Kythera was introduced there from Askalon.[23]

But when was the cult of Aphrodite Ourania introduced to Corinth? Our earliest testimonia indicate only that Ourania was an official state cult at Corinth before the Persian Wars, by which time she already had a priestess and a staff officiating at her altar. It is reported that the sacred prostitutes of Aphrodite made sacrifices for deliverance of Greece during the Persian invasion and that, after the Greek victory, a stele was erected to record the names of the hierodouloi and priestess who prayed to the goddess.[24] Thus Ourania was well established in Corinth by circa 500 B.C.

Certainly Ourania arrived after the high Mycenaean period and after the Bronze Age centers of population in the Corinthia had shifted with the collapse of the Mycenaean culture. This point seems secure, for the first trace of habitation on the top of Akrokorinthos seems to be Protogeometric or, possibly, even late Mycenaean 3C, but not earlier. Such a date is attested by the ceramic remains recovered in the American School excavations of 1926 on Akrokorinthos.[25] From these excavations comes one Mycenaean "phi" figurine, datable in the 3A period (figure 1C).[26] Two fragmentary pots may be My-

cenaean 3C; at least one deep bowl with conical foot can be dated to the Protogeometric period, with a relatively higher proportion of Geometric sherds, most of which are one-handled, monochrome cups with striped handles (figures 1I, 1J, and 1K). No indication exists, as of the moment, that there was canonical Mycenaean inhabitation on Akrokorinthos, at least in the area where the Aphrodite cult was established. In fact, none of the prehistoric sites in the Corinthia, such as Aetopetra, Agios Yerasimos, Korakou, Chiliotomylos, or even Tsoungiza and Zygouries, preserves archaeological evidence for continuity of a Bronze Age cult into classical times. If continuity does exist it is only because the inhabitants took with them their Bronze Age gods from the earlier sites and reestablished them in the new areas.[27]

Only for Demeter might one imagine the possibility of site continuity because of the archaeological remains. Her sanctuary at Solygeia is close to Mycenaean tombs and may, in some way, be connected with them.[28] The Demeter Sanctuary on the north slope of Akrokorinthos has Mycenaean 3C and Proto-

23. Pausanias, 1.14.7.

24. Athenaeus, *Deipnosophistae*, vol. 13, 573.

25. C. W. Blegen, R. Stillwell, O. Broneer, A. R. Bellinger, *Corinth* III, i, *Acrocorinth* (Cambridge, Mass., 1930) 1–28. On p. 28 Blegen recognizes Geometric as the earliest material from the site. The earliest temple is "a small building of the sixth or even the seventh century B.C." (p. 3), or as early as the end of the seventh century B.C. (p. 4). The following pottery has since been inventoried from excavation at the summit: C–1929–63, Protogeometric cup with conical foot (figure 1A); C–1926–65, Geometric one-handled cup, body sherd (figure 1J); C–1926–64, Early Corinthian (?) kylix sherd, possibly referred to by Blegen on p. 28, row of long-necked birds going r., glazed inside (figure 1K). Corinth pottery lots 1926–1 through 1926–14.

26. MF 747. The "phi" figurine has neither polos nor plait; eyes are not applied. Black glaze line that represents the neckline of a dress runs horizontally around the whole of the base of the neck. For the type see E. French, "The Development of Mycenaean Terracotta Figurines," *BSA* 66 (1971) 117–20. This terracotta was found 1.10 m below the surface in disturbed fill. Corinth notebook 89, p. 14.

The other figurines recovered from the summit include MF 710, body of handmade animal (figure 1D); MF 718, front portion and two legs of handmade animal (figure 1E); MF 748, leg of animal, probably handmade leg of bull with cloven hoof (figure 1F); MF 750, handmade female figurine with necklace (figure 1G); MF 726, left leg, hand of boy on stool, drapery hanging from left side, almost as a bag (figure 1H), mouldmade (this type appears in the Corinth Demeter Sanctuary); similar to MF 750, although not from same the mould, MF 11100, 13452–3, 13455, MF 68–357; MF 752, mouldmade figurine, white paint, unidentified fragment, perhaps Hellenistic rider on horse?

27. E. Will, *Korinthiaka, Recherches sur l'histoire et la civilization de Corinthe des origines aux guerres médiques* (Paris, 1955) 227, also n. 5 of same page and n. 5 of p. 231. For additional bibliography about cult continuity, see J. Rutter, "The Last Mycenaeans at Corinth," *Hesperia* 48 (1979) 349, n. 2.

28. N. Verdelis, in "'Αναϭβαφὴ εἰς τὴν 'Αρχαίαν Σολύγειαν" (1958) 135–45, pls. 109–16. Verdelis suggests that this is a sanctuary of Hera, offering the alternative (note 1 of p. 136) identification of Demeter and Kore. With the close parallels between finds of the Demeter Sanctuary at Corinth and those at Solygéia, the latter identification seems more likely. Earliest votive pottery is Late Geometric.

geometric levels associated with it, but even here continuity cannot be put back as far as the Mycenaean 3B period, if one opts for continuity at all.[29] The ceramic remains of the Demeter site on Akrokorinthos are, in fact, no earlier than those around the Aphrodite shrine at the very crown of Akrokorinthos.

If, as is postulated for the Demeter shrine on Akrokorinthos, one also assumes that the earliest pottery of the summit is domestic and not cultic, then when is it most logical to expect the appearance of Aphrodite on the mountain? Boardman suggests that Aphrodite was imported at the beginning of the orientalizing period, in the first quarter of the seventh century B.C. by Corinthian contact with the North Syrians.[30]

One can perhaps be more precise than that, however, concerning the introduction of Aphrodite Ourania to Corinth. Corinth probably had no need or desire for a city goddess, especially on the top of Akrokorinthos before its synoikismos. The sanctuary may have been established to give a political focus to the newly centralized amalgamation of villages. In fact, it may have been Bacchiad policy to set up a state cult and a protecting goddess, borrowing a city goddess and her cult from a powerful and admired state in the Near East or Cyprus, thereby obtaining the most powerful protectress available in the Mediterranean. Roebuck makes a good argument that "we should credit the Bacchiad aristocracy with the political synoe-

cism of Corinth, that is, with the creation of an effective state, in the latter half of the eighth century B.C."[31]

The pottery from the summit implies occupation or activities of some sort at the top of Akrokorinthos from as early as 1125 B.C.[32] The area is a logical place for inhabitants desiring secure homestead. It is high, with a view, and isolated for protection, yet it is well watered with natural springs; even today the hill affords good pasturing.

One cannot tell from excavated finds, unfortunately, when the cult of Aphrodite itself found a place at the summit. In fact, archaeologically, very few finds there point definitely to cult activity. Only seven fragmentary figurines were recovered in the 1926 excavations. One is Mycenaean, the rest are archaic to Hellenistic, including a handmade standing female, two portions of animals, one boy on a bench, and one unidentifiable fragment. Very few votive pots were recovered. One is a skyphos, one a krateriskos, and one a ritual "dish." The glazed wares are those customarily found in domestic contexts. The best preserved material is that datable between 320 and 260 B.C. This material includes fish plates, kantharoi, and powder pyxides. No graffiti nor any overwhelmingly high percentage of any certain type of pottery points to dedications for this sanctuary. In fact, one has the impression that this hill was not a place for major dedications. Lack of significant votives might be explained in a number of ways, including the following: the rites of prostitution may have served as an act of dedication, with the money given becoming sacred to Aphrodite and thus received at the temple as the major cult offering; dedications may have been offered in the city below rather than at the temple on the summit (this might be especially so in the

29. Rutter, "Last Mycenaeans," 348–92, esp. 389ff.

30. J. Boardman, *The Greeks Overseas* (Harmondsworth, 1964) 93–94. The Astarte-type figurine from Corinth, published by Davidson, see above, note 8, is considered by Boardman as an import. The clay does not appear, by examination with the naked eye, to be very different from that of other figurines of the period which are accepted as Corinthian. Boardman considers the earlier material, such as eighth century faience from a Geometric grave at Corinth and that from Perachora as "casual imports" (p. 129). See Davidson, *Minor Objects*, no. 1763 (MF 6137), probably Phoenician; T. J. Dunbabin, ed., *Perachora* 2, *The Sanctuaries of Hera Akraia and Limenia* (Oxford, 1962) 462–63. See, especially, discussion of three scarabs in *Perachora* 1, 76–77, not later than third quarter of the eighth century B.C.

31. C. Roebuck, "Some Aspects of Urbanization at Corinth," *Hesperia* 41 (1972) 127.

32. The earliest pottery, in Corinth pottery lots 1926–1 through 1926–14, contains mostly small fragments, but all seem to be monochrome and can be paralleled by similar material from the Demeter Sanctuary on the north slope of Akrokorinthos.

Hellenistic period when Akrokorinthos was held by a Macedonian garrison); or, possibly, dedications on Akrokorinthos may have been perishable, that is, dedications of cloth, wood, hair, or foodstuffs.[33]

I hope that the above points emphasize the many problems that exist concerning the cult of Aphrodite Ourania as official protectress of Corinth. I would assume her cult statue on Akrokorinthos to have been that of a canonically armed goddess, at least through the classical period. Either in the Hellenistic period or in the Roman refounding of the city, the cult received its first semi-draped cult statue. I would further postulate that the cult originally came directly from Phoenicia, rather than via Kythera, and that it was brought to Corinth by the Bacchiads when the synoikismos of Corinth was taking place. The cult was employed as a symbol of unification to various groups or villages, serving as a state cult, designed for the security of the community. A Phoenician goddess was selected because she supported the major and most powerful maritime state of the time. In the selection of Astarte, Corinth also received a few cultic side effects, such as sacred prostitution, which could not be isolated from the cult when it was imported; nor could the practice be ignored; Corinth could only modify it.

One first should consider the different possible categories of ritual into which temple prostitution can be divided. In the eastern ritual of Astarte, service was done by dedication of a girl's virginity to the goddess. Dedication was general, including girls from the best families, and done before marriage. When sacred prostitution was transmitted to Corinth, the ritual was changed to make it compatible with Greek mores. Dedication of the sexual act was achieved through a general class of women who were dedicated to the goddess. These were neither freeborn

Corinthians nor were they girls offering their virginity to the goddess. They were slaves who were bought and dedicated to the goddess and who thereafter served the goddess.[34]

A number of facts are missing from this picture. For example, do all prostitutes working at Corinth in pre-Roman times fall under the protection of Aphrodite Ourania and are they all sacred to her? Or is it only a special class of persons, girls who are dedicated to her, who are called hierodouloi, who serve her? Hand in hand with this comes the problem of fees. It appears that the sacred slaves of the goddess accepted money in exchange for services. This arrangement makes the girls equal to temple endowment. Revenue for the temple of Aphrodite Ourania thus would be obtained in this manner, and, although Herodotos was shocked by this ritual, it is best that he be quoted at this point.

> The foulest Babylonian custom is that which compels every woman of the land once in her life to sit in the sacred compound of Aphrodite and to have intercourse with some stranger. . . . When a woman has once taken her place there she does not go away to her home before some stranger has cast money into her lap and had intercourse with her outside of the sacred compound. . . . The woman will never refuse, for that were a sin, the money being by this act made sacred . . . and thereafter there is no bribe however great that will get her. There is a custom like this in some parts of Cyprus.[35]

Finally the question arises as to whether or not prostitution in Corinth was performed in the temple compound. In the Near East it seems that the commitment was made on sacred ground but that the act was done elsewhere. With the acceptance of the cult of

33. *The Greek Anthology* (Loeb ed., 1916) vol. 6, 210. Sandals, a lock of hair, a bronze mirror, a belt, and other womanly things were offered at the temple of Cypris by a courtesan.

34. Xenophon of Corinth vowed and dedicated more than a hundred girls to the goddess after his double victory at Olympia in 464 B.C. Pindar, frag. 107, 11 18ff. (Bowra). In the time of Strabo at least a thousand girls served the goddess. Strabo 8.6.20.

35. Herodotos 1.199. A general collection of the literary evidence concerning prostitution is to be found in E. M. Yamauchi, "Cultic Prostitution. A Case Study in Cultural Diffusion," *Orient and Occident, Essays Presented to Cyrus H. Gordon on the Occasion of His Sixty-fifth Birthday* (H. A. Hoffner, Jr., ed., Neukirchen-Vlyn, 1973) 213–22.

Aphrodite to Greece, it seems likely that prostitution was not made part of the activities of the temple sanctuary on Akrokorinthos. Only the "gold" would have returned to the temple. To this last question can be offered a bit of archaeological evidence. The temple built at the end of the seventh century B.C. is a small, simple affair.[36] The second temple, perhaps fifth century B.C. in date, can have been prostyle or amphiprostyle. It is either about 13 or 16 m long. Its cella is about square, ten meters to a side, with two side aisles. To the north of the area identified as the site of the temple is a Christian church. The area around the temple slopes downward from the temple site and indicates no large area for one hundred or, in Strabo's time, a thousand girls. Unless a series of insignificant, small, and now indistinguishable, buildings were erected on the slopes around the temple, one might better think of the hierodouloi as having conducted their activities within the heart of the city.

Broneer suggests that the second floor of the South Stoa was a place for Corinthian courtesans, once the Corinthian League no longer used the stoa. "The building itself, erected to serve a more sublime purpose, was well adapted to become the locale of the world's most celebrated entertainers."[37]

Is it possible that the hierodouloi had their own quarters? If so, were they built and maintained under the control of the priestess of Aphrodite, but in the center of the city? It seems to be a logical solution, but no evidence, neither literary nor archaeological, exists at the moment to support the theory.

Other possible facets of the cult of Aph-

rodite focusing around the goddess as protectress of the city may exist around the walls of Corinth, but there is little except archaeological fact upon which to base conclusions. One possible case, however, of Aphrodite as protectress of the city walls might be seen at the Potters' Quarter. The following theory is offered as possible; it is not proven fact.

In the northwest corner of the city lies the Potters' Quarter; evidence exists here for the making of Corinthian ceramics from the Late Geometric period down into the last quarter of the fourth century when, apparently, this tongue of city plateau was abandoned. In this same area one also has evidence for the manufacture of terracotta figurines.

The Potters' Quarter was enclosed by a defense wall by the last quarter of the seventh century B.C. or, perhaps, by as early as in the first half of the same century.[38] The wall with a socle of uncut stones set into a deeply cut bedrock trench ran along the edge of the cliff southward to the acropolis. Except for a roadway along the inside of that defense line the area seems to have been laid out in city blocks or, by other interpretations of the remains, by stoas or long buildings used by the potters and makers of figurines to store, to display, and to distribute their wares. In the late 430s or in the 420s B.C., the early defense wall was deemed either too old-fashioned to serve Corinth during the dangers of what looked like a war in which Athens might attack the city of Corinth itself, or else the walls may have been damaged by earthquakes in 420 B.C., perhaps with part of the cliff and wall falling away, thus demanding reconstruction of those walls on a line further back from the cliff edge. In any case, the early defense line along the cliff edge was abandoned and a new wall of cut block socle and of horse-shoe towers was built generally more than six meters in back of the earlier wall.

The land between the earlier and later city wall became a sort of no-man's-land with the

---

36. Blegen et al., *Acrocorinth*, p. 4

37. O. Broneer, *Corinth* I, iv, *The South Stoa and its Roman Successors* (Princeton, 1954) 157. Although the South Stoa may have housed girls serving Aphrodite at some time in its life, the stoa definitely was not built to serve as housing for the sacred slaves. If such a structure were to be expected in the lower city, its form surely would be more that of a house or a sacred compound with a central court and a place for sacrifice, even if not equipped with a cult statue. See above, note 16; also, O'Neill, *Ancient Corinth*, 52, also note 75. O'Neill concludes that the hierodouloi did not live on Akrokorinthos.

38. A. N. Stillwell, *Corinth* XV, i; 11, 14–15. See below, note 50.

construction of the later fortification. What was protected in the sixth century B.C. found itself outside and unprotected in the later fifth and fourth centuries B.C. One would expect, once the new wall was built, a prohibition to be made against constructing houses or against building within the no-man's-land, for any such construction would hinder the most effective use of the new fortifications. This, however, is not exactly true, for a number of small, rectangular shrines were constructed over the ruins of the destroyed buildings within this zone.

At this point, it is perhaps best to describe one or two of these shrines. In the Potters' Quarter the constructions are rather rude, with roughly squared poros orthostates for enclosure walls. Sometimes the enclosure wall is of rubble, perhaps with some mud-brick superstructure. The form is always rectangular and hypaethral.[39] The enclosure wall should not be restored as being much above the level of the shoulder of a grown man. In every case the shrines seem to have been built over a destroyed building, and in most cases the wall foundations of one of the rooms of that building are used for the enclosure wall of the shrine. The shrine always has at least one stele in it, placed against its west wall, facing east. Sometimes there are two stelai side by side, and in one case a single stele is carved with two panels on it, making it, in fact, a double stele.

It is on these stelai that the shrines focus. A quick look at the stelai themselves, therefore, is not amiss. The stelai of the Potters' Quarter are thin poros slabs; each is designed with a rectangular panel recessed into its broad, front face (figure 2D). Rarely may a stele have two panels rather than one. The crowning frame always is horizontal, with a rectangular, shallow shelf along the front face, and this shelf is determined in width by the width of the panel below it. If the stele

carries two panels, two shelves crown the stele, one over either panel.

A terracotta miniature of a stelai shrine was found in the Corinthian Potters' Quarter excavation (figure 2E).[40] It illustrates quite clearly the use of the shelf at the top of the stelai, shelves being used as a place to deposit one's votive figurines. In the model one sees a horse and a rider on one shelf, a female figurine on the other.

The present discussion concerns, however, one specific shrine within the no-man's-land. This is Shrine A, built within the walls of the long south building, a structure that existed contemporaneously with the first fortification wall.[41] Shrine A was not part of the original design of that building, but, rather, it seems to have been constructed either within the building as an alteration or over its ruins, apparently around 500 B.C. This shrine was destroyed after the mid-fifth century, probably in connection with the construction activities that took place when the defenses of the city were being altered in this area. Shrine A was not rebuilt when the new defenses were finished; instead, a replacement was erected slightly to its south, this time outside the line of defenses. A second shrine, named "Erosa" from an inscribed sherd found in the area, was built at the same time, again outside of the new city wall and still further to the south, over the southeast corner of an earlier house.[42]

When excavated, Stele Shrine A was found to have in it a large number of skyphoi buried in upright stacks of three to seven, and others with their mouths against the stelai, all in a fill approximately 60 cm deep, starting at circa 10 cm from the top of the stelai. In places the fill overlapped the wall. The material must have been put into the shrine as a final offering or as part of an offering ritual. In all, 55 votive figurines were found,

39. For a fuller account of this type of shrine, see C. K. Williams, II, "The City of Corinth and Its Domestic Religion," *Hesperia* 50 (1981), pp. 412–18.

40. Stillwell, *Corinth* XIV, ii, 208, pl. 45, KT–64–4, group 33, 1.

41. Stillwell, *Corinth* XIV, i, 22–23.

42. C. K. Williams, II, "Corinth and Its Domestic Religion," 413–15, fig. 2.

along with 162 pots and 215 miniature pots.[43]

The votives are mostly female, both seated and standing; some carry doves. The deposit has at least four horses and riders. There is a wide range of animals, including one dog, one ram, three doves, and a sphinx.[44] One stele with two snakes crawling upward on it was found; also found were one terracotta votive mirror, seven shields, and a circular, perforated decorated plaque.[45] The composition of votives suggests a female goddess and, with the reclining banqueters, horses and riders, and the snake stele, possibly an accompanying hero.

Outside Shrine A was found a second deposit, this one not only containing vases and figurines but also one phiale of bronze with a dedicatory inscription on its lip: τᾶς Ἀφροδίτας ἐμί (I belong to Aphrodite). This deposit has over fifteen figurines and two lamps. Six female figurines, one male figurine, and a second male, a grotesque "orator," a cut-out disc, two horses, a dove and one other animal, and a shield follow the pattern of votives found within the shrine.[46] Only one terracotta boat model expands the terracotta subject matter into different areas.

The important fact about the second deposit is that we have a dedication to Aphrodite from it. This is a bronze phiale (figure 2C). Because of the high percentage of female figurines found within and just outside of the sanctuary and because of the inscription, dated by Jeffery to between 500 and 475 B.C., one might say that the shrine was dedicated, at least in part, to Aphrodite.[47]

But since two stelai stood within the shrine, one should assume that Aphrodite shared the enclosure (figure 2D). Enough evidence does not exist, however, by which one can identify the second deity or hero. In fact, various ways of interpreting the votives themselves can add confusion to the subject, not clarification. For example, certain types of terracotta votives may have been felt to be more appropriate to Aphrodite in one of her aspects than in another.[48] Thus it would be more appropriate to offer terracotta shields to her as protectress of the city than to her as goddess of marriage or of industry. One might equally well argue that the shields are votives not to Aphrodite but to the accompanying god or hero of the shrine.

It has been argued elsewhere that the Corinth stelai shrines are a special variety of sanctuary and that they "would, under certain conditions, be built at Corinth over a destroyed house, and that it would be upon the initiative of a private citizen to construct such a shrine, where a family or group could continue to honor heroes or gods that were honored in the destroyed house."[49]

The terracotta shields, the boat, and the date of 500 to 475 B.C. for the erection of stele Shrine A demand consideration in the following theory for the history and the identification of this specific shrine. Can this shrine be to Aphrodite Ourania and a consort, built as it is close to the city wall where Aphrodite can be encouraged to protect the defenses and the community close by? The sanctuary, it will be noted, was constructed circa 500 B.C. and survived until it was replaced because of the construction of the new

---

43. Stillwell, *Corinth* XV, i, 23.

44. For the lion-sphinx as emblem of the goddess Astarte in Phoenician religion, see R. D. Barnett, "Some Contacts between Greek and Oriental Religions," *Éléments orientaux dans la religion grecque ancienne*, Colloque de Strasbourg, 1958 (Paris, 1960) 146–47. Such figurine may thus be related to Aphrodite and appropriate in this deposit.

45. Stillwell, *Corinth* XV, ii, 22, deposit in Stele Shrine A.

46. Ibid., Aphrodite Deposit.

47. L. H. Jeffery, *The Local Scripts of Archaic Greece*

(Oxford University Press, Cambridge, 1961) 132, no. 35.

48. Stillwell, *Corinth* XV, ii, 8; W. H. D. Rouse, *Greek Votive Offerings* (Cambridge, 1902) 390–91. Against this there exists the possibility that gifts do follow a rational pattern as made by dedicants; it may be a misunderstanding, a lack of knowledge today of the exact function of a god or goddess or a present lack of knowledge of the local function or functions of a cult that suggests the apparent random choice of votive gifts.

49. C. K. Williams, II, "Corinth and Its Domestic Religion," 421.

defense system.[50] In other words, the sanctuary may have been established at the time of the Persian War, when the Corinthians were dropping back to the Isthmos in preparation for their defense against the invaders; at that time they would have planned to rely on their own city wall as well. This defense system was renewed when Athens was emerging as a danger to Corinth and when there was a distinct possibility that Athens could attack the city itself during the Peloponnesian War. At both times it would not have been inappropriate for the community at the Potters' Quarter to call on Aphrodite Ourania for support.

50. The initial interpretation of the chronology of the Corinth city walls is discussed in C. K. Williams, II, "The Early Urbanization of Corinth," *Annuario della scuola archeologica di Atene e delle missioni italiane in Orient* 60 N.S., 44 (1982) 12–19. This article also gives arguments for a reinterpretation of dates maintained by Carpenter, Parsons, and Bon in *Corinth* III, i, *The Defenses of Acrocorinth and the Lower Town* (Cambridge, Mass., 1936) 83–84, 115–25.

4. Pausanias and Tree-Worship in Corinth

DARICE BIRGE

DEPARTMENT OF CLASSICS, COLUMBIA UNIVERSITY

Pausanias briefly mentions a pair of statues dedicated to Dionysos in his description of the city of Corinth (2.2.7).[1] He tells how the Delphic oracle ordered the Corinthians to find the tree in which Pentheus died and to worship it *isa tōi theōi*. The wooden statues that Pausanias saw were made from that tree according to the Corinthians' interpretation of the oracle's command. This construction of *xoana* (as Pausanias calls them) as an expression of piety toward a tree represents the establishment of a local Dionysiac cult. The foundation of this cult as reported by Pausanias, however, differs from accounts concerning the introduction of Dionysiac worship elsewhere in the Greek world.[2] Worship of a tree, moreover, is atypical of Greek religion in general.

In this paper I will examine the appropriateness of Pausanias's verb *sebein* for an activity directed toward a tree and, briefly, the logic of the Corinthians' assumption that the oracle intended for them to construct statues and the extent to which Greeks considered Dionysos a tree-god, and so deserving of worship involving trees.

After Pausanias lists the features of the Kraneion grove on the outskirts of Corinth, and before he describes the topography of the city's agora, he mentions statues of two deities, Artemis Ephesia and Dionysos. The *xoana* of Dionysos, called Lysios and Baccheus, are gilded except for their faces, which have been colored red. After the maenads tore Pentheus apart on Mt. Kithairon, the oracle at Delphi decreed that special attention be paid to the tree in which he was caught. The Corinthians were to find that tree and, apparently, worship it in the same way as they would the god (*isa tōi theōi sebein*).[3] Because of the oracle, says Pausanias, they carved two statues from its wood.

Pausanias's brief description raises several questions that cannot be answered here. The

---

1. Pausanias 2.2.7: "There are, then, in the agora . . . wooden statues of Dionysos, gilded except for their faces. Their faces are decorated with red paint. They call the one Lysios and the other Baccheus. I also record the things said about the wooden statues. They say that Pentheus, acting outrageously toward Dionysos, ultimately dared to go to Kithairon to spy on the women and, climbing up a tree, to gaze upon what they were doing. The women, when they discovered him, immediately dragged Pentheus down and tore him limb from limb while still alive. Later, as the Corinthians say, the Pythia declared to them in an oracle that they were to find that tree and revere it equally with the god. From it, for this reason, they have made these likenesses."

For Darrell Amyx with respect and affection. Thanks to Evelyn Bell and Edward Kadletz for helpful comments on this paper.

2. Compare, for example, Apollodoros 3.5.1–3; Euripides, *Bacchae* 20–50; Strabo 10.3.12–16; *Iliad* 6.130–40. See also J. G. Frazer, *Apollodorus: The Library*, vol. 1 (London, 1921) 146–47, for various citations of the myth of the daughters of Proitos.

3. The oracle is catalogued in H. W. Parke and D. E. W. Wormell, *The Delphic Oracle: The Oracular Responses* (Oxford, 1956) no. 547 and J. Fontenrose, *The Delphic Oracle: Its Responses and Operations with a Catalogue of Responses* (Berkeley, 1978) L149.

names of the statues[4] and the coloring of their faces,[5] the connections between Corinth and Thebes (the closest important center of Dionysiac worship to Corinth), and the history of *xoana* in general[6] are all significant but involve aspects of the cult other than those with which we are specifically concerned here. The primary concern of this paper is Pausanias's use of *isa tōi theōi sebein* for the oracle's pronouncement.

A brief examination of the verb *sebein* in Greek literature shows that with the passage of time the word may have come to be used more extensively in religious contexts than in secular ones.

We begin with its use in the Homeric poems. In the *Odyssey sebein* conveys astonishment, and (where inanimate objects are not involved) the people who feel astonishment and those who are its source are approximately equal in status.[7] In the *Iliad* forms of *seb-* describe shame and the act of following one's conscience.[8] The gods in the *Homeric Hymn to Athena* (number 28) were struck with wonder at Athena (line 6), and the flower that attracted Kore in the *Homeric Hymn to Demeter* aroused *sebas* (line 10), not because it was supernatural but because it was an entirely new, unique creation. In this poem *sebas* also connotes religious awe and refers to humans' relationships with the gods in general.[9] This use transcends the ideas of amazement or respect produced and

felt among equals that one normally finds in epic contexts.

Likewise, Pindar used forms of *seb-*, compounded (as in *eusebia*) or not, in contexts that involved religious awe and in cases where humans are astonished at their peers.[10] Aeschylus employed words based on *seb-* to indicate respect toward humans (for example, *Choephori* 704, *Persae* 694 and 695 [toward Darius's ghost] and 945) and reverence paid to the gods (as in *Supplices* 396 and 671 and, perhaps, *Eumenides* 885, if Peitho is deified).[11] Other forms also occur in contexts in which things are revered in the same way that gods might be (wealth: *Persae* 166; the Nile: *Supplices* 1025).

Plato carried the use of *sebein/sebesthai* a step further in passages involving both respect paid toward abstractions and piety in the traditional sense.[12] In Greek literature after his time, however, *sebein* seems to stand more for religious fear than for secular respect. For example, Plutarch employed it to a greater extent for gods, heroes, creatures, and places associated with religion[13] than for people worthy of respect.[14] In the *Onomasticon* of Pollux the group of synonyms for *sebein* includes categories of words with religious usages, for example, oracles, divine epithets, and ways of approaching a divinity. Furthermore, his *seb-* compounds, if they do not reinforce or negate the meaning of the base, include the base *theo-*, indicating that Pollux understood *-seb-* terms in a religious sense.

---

4. See Pausanias 2.7.6 for Sikyonian statues with the same names.

5. J. G. Frazer, *Pausanias's Description of Greece*, vol. 3 (London, 1913) 20–22.

6. For wooden statues and the origins of Greek sculpture and a history of the use of the word *xoanon*, see Alice A. Donohue, *Xoana* (Ph.D. diss., Institute of Fine Arts, New York University, 1984).

7. S. Jäkel, "*Phobos* und *Sebas* im frühen Griechischen," *Archiv für Begriffsgeschichte* 16 (1972) 143–44.

8. For examples, Proitos's avoiding the murder of Bellerophon (6.167) and Achilles's restraining himself from stripping the corpse of Eetion (6.417). Jäkel, "*Phobos* und *Sebas*," 144, thinks cultic fear is the cause.

9. Awe: Metaneira of Demeter, l.190, along with *deos* and *aidōs*; toward the gods in general: l.479.

10. For example, *Olympian* 3.41; 6.79; 8.8; *Pythian* 6.25; *Isthmian* 5.29, 8.40.

11. S. Jäkel, "*Phobos* und *Sebas*, *Pathos* und *Mathos* im Drama des Aischylos," *Eirene* 13 (1975) 45.

12. Abstractions include beauty: *Phaedrus* 252A; shame: *Laws* 1.647A; piety: *Laws* 9.917B.

13. For example, of the gods in general: *de liberis educandis* 7E; of Herakles: *Amatorius* 754D; of dogs in Egypt: *Quaestiones Convivialum* 703A; for Etna as the place of Kore's abduction: *Quaestiones Naturales* 917F; for the woodpecker, guardian of Romulus and Remus: *Romulus* 4.2.

14. Such as parents: *Coriolanus* 36.2; the wealthy: *quomodo ... audire debeat* 36E; messmates: *Quaes-Conviv* 643D.

Pausanias's use of *sebein* clearly continues a literary usage in which forms of *seb-* signify reverence toward deities. Pausanias also describes reverence toward a god's instrument or possession or a non-deified religious object with the same term. Thus in 2.2.7 the oracle's pronouncement concerns not a god per se, but his representation and cultic equipment, emphasized with *isa tōi theōi*. Elsewhere Pausanias uses forms of *sebein* for descriptions of divine worship that might be considered typically Greek, for example, worship of Aphrodite (1.14.7), Athena (8.26.6), local Attic deities (1.26.6), and the heroized dead at Marathon (1.32.4), as well as for objects with religious significance: a statue of Hygeia at Titane (2.11.6) and stones at Pharai in Achaia (7.22.4) and Orchomenos (9.38.1). Pausanias's language is ambiguous, especially with regard to the stones at Pharai, but these objects seem to belong to gods and are not themselves divine. Nonetheless, these instances imply a religious action, whether it is directed toward an anthropomorphic deity or a sacred object.

One might argue, however, that Pausanias's use of *sebein* regarding objects implies animism or veneration of objects as sources of divinity. Religious historians have now turned away from animism as an element of Greek religion, although in the early years of this century scholars identified many examples of object-worship in Greek cults.[15] Examples of trees used in supposed animistic cults are pertinent here; Tylor considered the oak at Dodona, hamadryads, and metamorphoses of people to trees all to be examples of tree-worship, a form of animism. That is to say, certain trees were intrinsically sacred and possessed of their own spirit and were not possessions of deities who existed separately from these trees. If one examines literary works that mention these various examples, one finds, without speculating on the earliest stages of worship, that in Greek literature the trees at Dodona or Daphne were not necessarily objects of worship.[16] Daphne was not herself divinely powerful, and her tree does not appear to have supernatural powers. Zeus's power might on occasion work through the oak at Dodonaean; the tree was a vehicle of a discrete divine force. Hamadryads and their myths perhaps approach the idea of tree worship more closely than Zeus's oak; they may die when their trees do, but in their own lifetimes they exist apart from trees.[17] However, none involves a tree that is completely inseparable from a spirit; therefore these should not be used as examples of animism.

On the one hand, Pausanias's reports of stones such as those at Pharai and Orchomenos are admittedly obscure. Single trees that he mentions, on the other hand, are clearly important because they are remarkably ancient survivors of the heroic age[18] or because they are prominent features of shrines.[19] All are recognized because they are landmarks, drawing attention to a sacred place or a sacred time. They are not divine in themselves. We may compare Theokritos's "Revere (*sebeu*) me, I am Helen's tree" (18.48). This tree is to be worshiped not because it is Helen but because it belongs to her.

---

15. See Sir E. B. Tylor, *Religion in Primitive Culture* (New York, 1958; reprinted from the second edition of *Primitive Culture*, London, 1873) 10–11, 58–80, 246–69, 305–6, and elsewhere for a definition of animism and illustrations of its existence in Greece, and J. G. Frazer, *The Worship of Nature* (London, 1926) 6–9.

16. Dodona: for example, Aeschylus, *Prometheus Vinctus* 830–32 and scholia, Sophocles, *Trachiniai* 1168, and Lucian, *Gallus* 2; Daphne: (near Antioch, where the nymph was transformed) Strabo 16.2.6 and Philostratos, *Vita Apollonii* 1.16, which implies, perhaps, skepticism.

17. See A. Henrichs, "'Thou Shalt not Kill a Tree': Greek, Manichean and Indian Tales," *Bulletin of the American Society of Papyrologists* 16 (1979) 85–108 for an examination of Greek stories of hamadryads and their eastern counterparts.

18. Trees at Aulis (9.19.7) and Kaphyai (8.23.4–5) date to the time of the Trojan War.

19. For example, the myrtle at Boiai (3.22.12), connected with Artemis and the city's foundation legend and revered (*sebousi*) as the goddess's instrument, and the spring and plane tree of Dionysos of the Kynaithians (8.19.1–2).

Pausanias's Corinthian informants, then, would have understood *isa tōi theōi sebein* as a religious act because of the common implications of the verb as well as its modifying phrase. Since trees were not worshiped per se, the Corinthians' response was to construct images of a god from the wood of the tree. These *xoana* honored an anthropomorphic god by adorning his shrine. To worship a tree equally with a god one does not consider the tree a god but rather the possession of a god.

The Greeks may not have believed that their gods took the form of trees, but their deities did have close associations with trees in myth, cult, and art. A brief glance at Dionysos, the god to whom Pausanias's *xoana* are dedicated, is valuable at this point. We might first note in passing that numerous deities have tree-epithets, although no evidence exists to show they were themselves considered to be trees. Examples are Apollo Myrtoos, Apollo Platanistios, Athena Kyparissia, Demeter Karpophoros, and Helen Dendritis.[20]

Prominent among these gods is Dionysos, called, for example, *endendros*[21] and *dendritēs*.[22] He was worshiped with rites called *dendrophoria*.[23] Attic vase paintings show the god's mask or statue, perhaps akin to the *xoana* at Corinth, intertwined with or supported by tree branches or trunks.[24] Diony-

siac myths such as those involving the hanged Erigone, the ship's mast become vine, and, of course, Pentheus and the pine on Mt. Kithairon, show the god's association with vegetation.

Epithets, artistic representations, festivals, and myths all yield evidence for Dionysos's concern with trees and plants.[25] It is not surprising, therefore, to find a foundation legend that includes a tree associated with a cult of Dionysos. The Corinthian reaction to the Delphic oracle is likewise reasonable. A pronouncement concerning Dionysos might well stipulate worship of a tree equally with him. To the Greeks of Pausanias's time, for whom venerable objects were attributes of anthropomorphic gods, such a command implied that the tree represented symbolically a distinct, separable divinity. The sacredness of the statues emanated not from the wood of the tree but from the god who possessed them.

20. Apollo Myrtoos: Kyrene *CIG* 5138.4; Apollo Platanistios: Troizen, Pausanias 2.34.6; Athena Kyparissia: Kyparissiai in Messenia, Pausanias 4.36.7: Demeter Karpophoros: Athens, *IG* II², 4587. 3; Ephesos, Dittenberger, *Sylloge Inscriptionum Graecarum*³ 820, 5–6; Tegea, Pausanias, 8.53.7; Helen Dendritis: Rhodes, Pausanias 3.19.10.

21. Hesychios, s.v. Dionusos en Boiōtiai.

22. Plutarch, *QuaesConviv* 675F.

23. Strabo 10.3.10; similarly, Artemidoros 2.37.

24. For lists of Attic black-figure and red-figure vase paintings of such figures, see A. Frickenhaus, *Lenäenvasen* (*Programm zum Winckelmannsfeste der Archäologischen Gesellschaft zu Berlin* 72 [Berlin, 1912]) catalogue, pp. 33–39; L. R. Farnell, *The Cults of the Greek States* (Oxford, 1909) 5.241–42; J. D. Beazley, *Attic Red-Figured Vases* (Oxford, 1963)² index s.v. Dionysos, festival of; U. T. Bezerra de Meneses, "Une représentation probable de Dionysos Dendritès," *BCH* 87 (1963) 309–21; H. F. Gaugh, "Dionysos in Greek Vase Painting," in *The Greek Vase*, S. L. Hyatt, ed. (Latham, New York, 1981) 43–61.

25. For the character of Dionysos as god of the vital, flourishing force of nature see W. H. Roscher, *Ausführliches Lexikon der griechischen und römischen Mythologie*, vol. 1 (Leipzig, 1884–1886) cols. 1059–63; S. Wide, *Lakonische Kulte* (Leipzig, 1893) 166–68; W. F. Otto, *Dionysos: Mythos und Kultus* (*Frankfurter Studien zur Religion und Kultur der Antike* 4 [Frankfurt, 1933]) 138–45; H. Jeanmaire, *Dionysos: Histoire du culte de Bacchus* (Paris, 1951) 11–18; Bezerra de Meneses "Dionysos Dendritès," 313–15.

5. The Torch-Race at Corinth

Sharon Herbert

Classics Department, University of Michigan, Ann Arbor

The torch-race with its ritual—the carrying of sacred fire from one altar to another—was a popular event in many Athenian festivals of the fifth and fourth centuries B.C.[1] Its presence in the Panathenaia, Hephaisteia, and Prometheia is documented epigraphically.[2] Herodotos tells of a λαμπάς in honor of Pan instituted after the battle of Marathon.[3] Plato, in the beginning of the *Republic*, mentions a torch-race on horseback to Artemis-Bendis,[4] and black-figure fragments from Brauron that show girls running with torches suggest a torch-race to Artemis at Brauron.[5] It seems quite likely that a torch-race was part of the Anthesteria; van Hoorn in his *Choes and Anthesteria* collects the contemporary vase evidence,[6] and there is an inscription of the Roman period that definitely attests to a torch-race in the Anthesteria at that time.[7] Another indication of the popularity of the torch-race in Athens in the fifth and fourth centuries is its constant appearance in the metaphors and similes of that

period: Herodotos compares the Persian mail system to it; Clytemnestra likens her signal fires to it; Plato has life passed on like a torch, and Aristophanes mentions the event several times.[8] In addition, numerous representations of the torch-race and its victory ceremony on red-figure vases testify to the frequent occurrence of the event in classical Athens.[9]

Although the torch-race proliferated throughout the Greek world in Hellenistic times,[10] evidence for its performance outside

1. For general information on the character of the torch-race, see J. Juthner, "Λαμπαδηδρομία," *RE* (1924) 569. J. R. S. Sterret, "The Torch-Race," *AJP* 22 (1901) 394. P. E. Corbett, "Attic Pottery of the Later Fifth Century," *Hesperia* 18 (1949) 346ff.

2. Cf. *IG*, I², 84, for the regulations for the Hephaisteia in 421/420 B.C., which mention also the torch-race at the Panathenaia and Prometheia as well.

3. Herodotos, 6.105.

4. Plato, *Republic*, 328a, and 354a.

5. Lily G. Kahil, "Autour de l'Artemis attique," *Antike Kunst* 8 (1965) 20–33.

6. G. van Hoorn, *Choes and Anthesteria* (Leiden, 1951) 33.

7. *CIL* 3, 93.

8. Herodotos 8.98; Aeschylus, *Agamemnon* 312–14; Plato, *Laws* 776b.; Aristophanes, *Frogs* 129ff., 1079ff., *Wasps* 1203.

9. For a list of torch-race scenes from attributed Attic vases see T. B. L. Webster, *Potter and Patron in Classical Athens* (London, 1972) 200–201. For the ceremony after the torch race, see H. Metzger, *Les représentations dans la céramique du IV siècle* (Paris, 1951), pp. 351–55.

10. Alexander instituted torch-races in many of his festivals: Asklepios at Soloi, Herakles at Tyre, and several others (Arrianus, *An.* 2, 5, 8; 2, 24, 6. For a full list see Sterret, "The Torch-Race," p. 418, n. 4). There was a torch race to Apollo at Delos, circa 95 B.C. (G. Fougères, "Fouilles au gymnase de Delos," *BCH* 15 [1891]: 263). An Apulian mug in the Karlsruhe Museum with running torch racers (C. Blumel, *Sport der Hellenen*, 134, no. 115) and Tarentine coins of the third century B.C. with a torch race on horseback (N. Gardiner, *Greek Athletic Sports and Festivals*, 426, fig. 170) show that the torch race had spread to South Italy. There is epigraphical evidence for torch races in Athens in the second century B.C. at the Theseia (*IG*, I², 444–50), the Epitapheia (*IG*, I², 465–71), and the Hermeia (*IG*, II, 1223). Harpokration (s.v. λαμπάς) mentions a torch race at the Apatouria. For a torch-race in honor of Melikertes at Isthmia in Roman times see W. R. Biers and D. J. Geagan, "A New List of Victors in the Caesarea at Isthmia," *Hesperia* 39 (1970), 91.

Figure 1. Fragment, Corinthian Red-figure
Bell-Krater, Old Corinth, Museum,
inv. no. C-31-329.

Figure 2. Fragment, Corinthian Red-figure Bell-Krater,
Old Corinth, Museum, inv. no. C-37-254.

Figure 3. Fragment, Corinthian Red-figure Bell-Krater,
Old Corinth, Museum, inv. no. C-37-250.

Attica in the classical period is scarce. The scenes on three Corinthian red-figure bell-krater fragments found in the Corinth excavations[11] may offer contemporary evidence for a torch-race at Corinth in the fifth and early fourth centuries B.C. (figures 1, 2, 3). There can be little doubt that the painted fragment in figure 1 represents a torch-race procession, most probably a victory celebration. The high, spiked wreath on the youth to the right and the handguard on the torch, both of which Giglioli has shown to be characteristic of the torch-race,[12] allow the scene to be identified with confidence. The painter of the fragment shown in figure 2 is less skillful; his depiction of the wreath and particularly the handguard, which is rendered by a simple circle of applied white with yellow wash to indicate the customary bronze disc, is rudimentary but nonetheless identifiable. The presence of a winged Nike on this fragment places us securely in a victory procession. The little remaining of the krater shown in figure 3 preserves only the torso and the

legs of a youth and his left hand holding a torch, but the handshield on the torch he carries is identical with that shown in figure 2 and should be from the same sort of scene. The fact that the youth with the torch is partially clothed and the presence of another youth directly in front of him again indicate that a procession rather than the race itself is being depicted.

Another Corinthian red-figure vase, a large skyphos in the National Archaeological Museum in Athens, pictured here in figures 4 and 5, depicts two mantled youths.[13] On one side of the skyphos, shown in figure 5, the youth on the left carries a torch that can be justly described as the crudest piece of torch-race equipment yet to come to light. The reserved circle around the lower part of the torch is recognizable as a hasty attempt at a handguard resembling those in figures 2

11. No. 1, C–31–329; no. 2, C–37–254; no. 3, C–37–250. These fragments first came to my attention while I was working on Corinthian red-figured pottery at Corinth from 1970–1973. I would like to thank C. K. Williams, II, for his permission to study and to publish the Corinth material. A more detailed description of these fragments is published in *Corinth* VII, 4, nos. 35, 59, 21.

12. G. Q. Giglioli, "La corsa della facciola ad Athene," *Rendiconti della R. Accademia dei Lincei* no. 5, vol. 31 (1922) 330.

13. Athens National Archaeological Museum, no. 1405. *Corinth* VII, 4, no. 161. I wish to thank Dr. Barbara Philippaki and the Greek Archaeological Service for permission to publish this vase.

Figure 4. Corinthian Red-figure Skyphos, Athens, National Museum, inv. 1405.

Figure 5. Second view of Skyphos in Figure 4.

and 3. An enormous, sodden sponge hanging from the right wrist of this same youth completes his athletic paraphernalia in the same spirit. The other side of the skyphos, shown in figure 4, shows a Bacchic scene with a youthful Dionysos and companion dancing.

These four vases cover the entire life span of the Corinthian red-figure pottery industry that began in imitation of hard-to-get Attic red-figure during the Peloponnesian War and that continued to be produced by a handful of local artists until the middle of the fourth century B.C. The torch-race scenes furnish a representative sample of the best to the worst of Corinthian red-figure vase painting; the hands of four of the six identifiable Corinthian red-figure painters can be recognized.[14] Figure 3 represents the earliest of the Corinthian artists, the Pelikai Painter, who begins to work around 425 B.C. and continues until the final decade of the fifth century. Figure 2 represents a more skillful student of the Pelikai Painter, the Pattern Painter, whose work continues well into the first quarter of the fourth century. The painter of figure 1 is the best of the Corinthian red-figure artists, the Hermes Painter, a contemporary of the Pattern Painter and a member of the same work-

shop. Figures 4 and 5 represent the latest of the Corinthian red-figure artists, whom I have called the Student Sketch Painter, and this fragment can be dated by shape and by style to late in the second quarter of the fourth century.[15]

The torch-race equipment—spiked wreaths and torches with handguards—on these four Corinthian red-figure vases, which were most probably manufactured specifically for the Corinthian home market, provide contemporary evidence for the running of the torch-race in Corinth in the fifth and early fourth centuries B.C.[16] They do not provide any new information about the running of

14. For a detailed discussion of the individual Corinthian red-figure vase painters and the development of the industry, see *Corinth* VII, 4, chapter 2.

15. Cf., the skyphos, New York Metropolitan Museum, no. 06.1021.201, G. M. A. Richter and L. F. Hall, *Red-figured Athenian Vases in the Metropolitan Museum of Art* (New Haven, 1936) pl. 165.

16. Because the mineral content of Corinthian clay is not suitable to first-class reproduction of the Attic red-figure color scheme (see discussion *Corinth* VII, 4, chapter 1), Corinthian red-figure vase painters never achieved a pottery of consistent export quality. Very little Corinthian red-figure has been found outside the Corinthia. The impetus for the development of Corinthian red-figure circa 430–420 B.C. seems to have been trade difficulties caused by the Peloponnesian War. I have argued elsewhere (*Corinth* VII, 4, chapter 1) that, since the Corinthians did manage to import large quantities of Attic red-figure during the war, the appeal of the inferior local product lay in the buyer's opportunity to "special order" scenes appropriate for specific occasions. If this argument is accepted, the illustrations of torch-races on Corinthian red-figure would indicate that it was a local event.

the race, whether it was always a relay or occasionally an individual event. In any case, the torch-race, however it was run, was not primarily an athletic event but rather a religious ritual in which the sacred fire was transferred from one altar to another. As such, the most interesting question about the torch-race at Corinth, as at other places, is what god or gods were being honored by the race?

The Corinthian vases themselves give little help in answering this question. The field may be legitimately limited, however, to the gods for whom we have classical torch-race testimonia from Athens, the city whose torch-race is most fully documented. The Athenian torch-race gods are Pan, Hephaistos, Prometheus, Athena, Artemis-Bendis, and probably Dionysos.[17] Considering the ceramic evidence alone, Dionysos is clearly the best candidate from this group for the Corinthian torch-race. The possible presence of a satyr in figure 1[18] and the scene in figure 4 of Dionysos holding a kantharos and thyrsos and his companion dancing with an extinguished torch both point to a Dionysiac connection for a Corinthian torch-race. The connection is strengthened by another Corinthian vase in the fifth century outline style depicting two revelers, one with a kantharos, the other with a torch.[19] Their rather entangled position has been described as the classical equivalent of an egg-and-spoon race. It could be a torch-race relay at the moment of passing the torch.

At this point we should examine both the literary and archaeological evidence for a sanctuary or a cult building dedicated to one of the torch-race gods in Corinth, particularly in the area around the race course where two of the fragments under discussion

and many other Corinthian red-figure athletic vases were found.[20] Once again Dionysos is a very strong candidate. While there is little indication of the worship of Hephaistos, Prometheus, or Pan in the areas under discussion,[21] a good case can be made for Dionysos as the god of the Sacred Spring. Campbell Bonner first made this suggestion.[22] C. K. Williams's recent reinterpretation of Pausanias's route through Corinth places a Roman monopteron to Dionysus very near the Sacred Spring, and he suggests that this may be an instance of the Romans continuing a Greek cult near its original location.[23]

However, the one piece of literary evidence for a torch-race at Corinth in Greek times suggests that the deity is female. Pindar in *Olympian* 13 mentions that a certain Xenophon of Corinth won seven times in the Hellotia.[24] The major scholia on this poem (BCEDQ) all identify the Hellotia as a festival of Athena at Corinth in which young men run carrying torches.[25] There are three variant explanations of Athena Hellotis and her festival. First is the tradition identifying the Corinthian Hellotis with the Athena of the Marathonian marshes, connecting the word ἕλους with hellotis. The second explanation derives Hellotis from ἑλοῦσα and reasons that the festival was in honor of Athena's taming of Pegasos for Bellerophon. The third explanation is that the festival is named after Hellotis, a daughter of the Corinthian Timander, who was burned to death within the temple of Athena where she was taking refuge from attacking Dorians. Athena, as

---

17. See above, notes 2–10.

18. Note the vestigial tail on the left figure. He does not, however, have the typical pug nose of a satyr, and his ear is not preserved. Perhaps he is a youth in a satyr costume.

19. C–34–362. M. Z. Pease, "A Well of the Late Fifth Century at Corinth," *Hesperia* VI (1937) 310, fig. 40.

20. Nos. 2 and 3 are from a drain in the South Central Forum Area covered by the South Stoa terrace (*Corinth* VII, 4, deposit 5). No. 1 is from the Asklepieion.

21. Robert Lisle, "Cults of Corinth," Ph.D. diss. submitted to the Classics Department of Johns Hopkins University, 1955, pp. 99–125.

22. C. Bonner, "A Dionysiac Miracle at Corinth," *AJA* 33 (1929) 368–75.

23. C. K. Williams, II, and Joan E. Fisher, "Corinth, 1974: Forum Southwest," *Hesperia* 44 (1975) 28.

24. Pindar, *Olympian* 13.56.

25. A. B. Drachman, ed., *Scholia Vetera in Pindari Carmina* vol. 1 (Leipzig, 1903) 367ff.

Figure 6. Fragmentary Corinthian Red-figure Bell-Krater, Old Corinth, Museum, inv. no. C-71-220.

Figure 7. Second View of Bell-Krater in Figure 5.

usual, incensed by the violation of her sanctuary, sent a plague that could not be lifted until the Corinthians built a temple to Athena Hellotis and instituted a festival called the Hellotia.

There is some difficulty in reconciling the tradition of the scholia with the archaeological remains now available. Indications of a classical cult to Athena around the race course are scarce. There has been speculation about the possibility of a female goddess of the Sacred Spring,[26] and some illustrations of a female patron of athletes have been found on Corinthian red-figure vases of the early fourth century B.C. One side of a small bell-krater, shown in figure 6, illustrates the best preserved example of this goddess from Corinth.[27] On the other side of this small bell-krater, shown in figure 7, a mantled youth, possibly a victorious athlete, hangs his prize taenia on a temple-like building. To the right is a roughly drawn doorpost, and above this a fascia projects to the left with a sketchily drawn triglyph. In figure 6, apparently within the building, elevated on a plinth-like block and looking toward the youth, is an elaborately dressed female figure, her hair

pulled up in the popular late-fifth-century B.C. lampadion style and holding a tympanon in her left hand. A Corinthian red-figure pelike in Athens provides the most convincing connection of this figure with athletics (figure 8).[28] On the Athens vase she wears the same type of dress complete with embroidered wave border and rosettes on the bodice; her hair is up in the lampadion and she sits very much in the same position facing an athlete to her right on the same side of the pelike. The athlete is nude and carries a discus. One interesting difference between the female figures on the two vases is that the woman in Athens holds in her left hand not a tympanon but a strigil, an instrument not altogether appropriate to her dress but possibly explained as a prize. One thing that can be said with certainty about the identity of this Corinthian patroness, as she is represented on these two vases, is that whoever she is, she is definitely not Athena, unless the Corinthians had a radically different conception of Athena than the rest of the Greeks.

The question now is whether this notably feminine athletic patroness can be reconciled with Artemis-Bendis, the only other torch-race goddess for whom we have fifth century

26. The discovery of a number of earrings in the area of the Sacred Spring gives some support to this theory. For the earrings, see C. K. Williams, II, "Excavations at Corinth, 1968," *Hesperia* 38 (1969) 62, no. 16.

27. C–71–220. *Corinth* VII, 4, no. 85.

28. Athens National Archaeological Museum, no. 16025. I thank the Greek Archaeological Service and Dr. Barbara Philappaki for permission to publish this photograph.

Figure 8. Corinthian Red-figure Pelike, Athens, National Archaeological Museum, inv. no. 16025.

documentation, and whether there is evidence for a suitable Artemis cult in the area under discussion. At first glance the maenad-like figure on the Corinthian red-figure vases would seem as much unlike the huntress Artemis as the aegis-bearing Athena. But in the late fifth century, representations of Artemis, unlike those of Athena, do become more feminine with more emphasis on elaborately decorated dress than on weapons. A good example of the beginning of this tendency is the Lambros pelike by a late-fifth-century painter near the Kadmos Painter.[29] On this vase Artemis stands to Apollo's right wearing an embroidered peplos and holding a torch and oinochoe. The only feature other than her connection with Apollo that definitely identifies her as Artemis is the very tip of a bow appearing over her right shoulder. The figure on the Corinthian vases can be recon-

ciled with this later type of Artemis, and the personage in figure 6, holding a tympanon, fits particularly well with what is known about the rites of Bendis, the Thracian Artemis, which were orgiastic and involved the participation of maenads with tympana.[30]

Although there are no direct literary or epigraphical indications of an Artemis-Bendis cult at Corinth,[31] there is a strong literary tradition for the worship there of Kotyto, whose rites Strabo links with those of Bendis.[32] Eupolis's *Baptai*, according to Hesychios, ridicules the Corinthians' worship of Kotyto, whose rites appear to have been orgiastic with an initiation rite requiring water.[33] This leads Robert Lisle to suggest Kotyto as the goddess of Temple B, the apsidal building connected with the Sacred Spring.[34] It is significant that this same Kotyto appears as the sister of Hellotis in the Pindaric scholiasts' aetiological myth on the origin of the Hellotia.[35]

In light of the connection between Hellotis, Kotyto, and Artemis-Bendis, it would be profitable to examine more closely the scholiasts' reasons for assigning the Hellotia to Athena. To begin with, some doubt is thrown on their credibility by an earlier source; Athenaeus identifies the Hellotia at Corinth as a festival commemorating the return of the bones of Europa.[36] Within the scholia them-

---

29. *ARV²*, 1187, 1. *CVA*, San Francisco, fasc. 1 (U.S.A. fasc. 10) 41–44.

30. The connection between the Thracian goddess, Bendis, and various cults of Artemis seems certain. Hesychios defines Bendis as the Thracian Artemis (s.v. βενδεῖς) and Herodotos (5.7) makes the two goddesses one.

31. An unusual number of terracotta figurines of the Artemis-Bendis type were found in a third/second century B.C. deposit in the area of the Peribolos of Apollo (G. R. Davidson, *Corinth* XII, 42, nos. 228–35). The type is recognized and best described by Agnes Stillwell, *Corinth* XV, 2, 124; XVII, 17 (KT 12–7).

32. Strabo 10.3.16.

33. Lisle, Cults of Corinth, p. 116, notes 155–68, assembles the references to Kotyto in connection with Corinth. Her rites at Corinth are discussed in detail by S. Srebrny, "Kult der thrakischen Goettin Kotyto in Korinth und Sicilien," *Melanges Cumont*, vol. 1, 423–47.

34. Lisle, Cults of Corinth, 116.

35. Drachman, *Scholia Vetera*, 368.

36. Athenaeus, *Deipnosophists* 15, 678A and B. The

selves only one of the three variant explanations—that deriving Hellotia from ἑλοῦσα and connecting it with the taming of Pegasos—need be linked with Athena alone. And since Athena was certainly worshiped for this deed at Corinth as Χαλινῖτις,[37] it seems the least believable of the three explanations. The connection of Athena from the Marathonian marshes with the Hellotia could be applied equally to Artemis Ἐλεῖα from Messene.[38] Finally, it need hardly be mentioned that the story of the death of Hellotis within the temple of Athena is a common type of aetiological myth applied to any number of gods, temples, and festivals throughout the Greek world. The presence of Kotyto in the story does point to Artemis-Bendis rather than Athena as the vengeful goddess. I would suggest that we have in the scholia to Pindar a not unprecedented substitution of the more familiar deity, Athena, for the esoteric Bendis.[39] The most pertinent example of this type of substitution occurs in the scholia of the *Republic*. When Socrates says he is going to see the new rites "τῇ θεῷ" some scholiasts identify the god as Athena.[40] Later it becomes unmistakably clear from the text itself that the goddess in question is Bendis.[41]

There is also reliable evidence for the worship of Artemis under other epithets in fourth-century B.C. Corinth. Xenophon in the *Hellenika* mentions the festival of Artemis Eukleia near the agora, which lasted several days and included a dramatic contest.[42] The cult of Artemis Eukleia has an interesting connection with the torch race. The origin of the torch racers' spiked wreaths is often traced back to the laurel that Euchidas wore when he carried the sacred fire from Delphi to Plataia after the battle of Plataia. This same Euchidas, who died immediately after delivering the sacred fire to Plataia, was buried there in the sanctuary of Artemis Eukleia.[43] Surely, then, a torch-race would be appropriate at the Eukleia.

Clearly, with the evidence now available, a strong argument can be made for Artemis, under one of her more Bacchic aspects or a combination of epithets, as the deity for whom the torch-race represented on the Corinthian red-figure krater fragments was run. But given the numerous festivals in Athens at which the torch-race was run in the fifth and fourth centuries B.C., the chance survival of one confused reference to a torch-race at the Hellotia in Corinth should not lead us to ignore the possibility of contemporary torch-races in honor of other gods at Corinth. As has been seen above, a good case can be made from the archaeological evidence for a torch-race to Dionysos, and the argument against torch-races in honor of the other eligible gods could be overturned at any moment by a new discovery. The study of Corinthian red-figure vases does leave us at the least with rare contemporary proof for the running of the torch-race, to whatever god, outside of Attica in the fifth and fourth centuries B.C., and does throw doubt on the Pindaric scholiasts' identification of the Hellotia at Corinth as a festival to Athena.

Etymologicum Magnum 332 and 340 also give Ἑλλῶπς as another name for Europa, as well as an epithet of Athena, honored at Corinth with a torch-race.

37. Pausanias 2.4.1. The existence of a cult of Athena may account for the scholiast mistakenly linking Athena to another Corinthian cult, the Hellotia.

38. L. Farnell, *Cults of the Greek States*, vol. II (Oxford, 1986) 559, 5.

39. G. H. MacCurdy, "The Origin of a Herodotean Tale," *TAPA* 43 (1912) 79 ff., assembles a number of examples of the substitution of Athena for Artemis.

40. Plato, *Republic* 1, James Adams, ed. (Cambridge, 1902) p. 1, n. 2.

41. *Republic* 1.354a.

42. Xenophon, *Hellenika* 4.4.2.

43. Plutarch, *Aristides* 20.4.5.

6. Xenophon at Corinth

JOHN K. ANDERSON

CLASSICS DEPARTMENT, UNIVERSITY OF CALIFORNIA, BERKELEY

Xenophon, according to Diogenes Laertius,[1] settled at Corinth when he was forced to leave Scillus in the aftermath of the Battle of Leuctra, and he perhaps died there at an advanced age. The archaic glories, on which the scholar whom we honor is the greatest living authority, had long departed from Corinth, and Xenophon's residence there makes only the smallest footnote to the city's history. Indeed, some of those who have most recently discussed Xenophon's own career and works have either passed the matter over[2] or, while accepting the tradition, have apparently attached little importance to it.[3] After all, the repeal of the decree that had exiled Xenophon from Athens; his renewed interest in Athenian affairs, as demonstrated by the *Poroi* and the *Hipparchicus*; and his sons' service in the Athenian army seem, as they seemed in antiquity, to be the truly important features of the last part of Xenophon's career. Yet the impracticability of some of the advice offered in the *Poroi* may perhaps be due to the fact that the author was writing from a distance.[4] Moreover, though other reasons can be given for Xenophon's failure to make an impression on Athenian intellectual life (if we are to judge by the silence of his fellow-Socratic Plato and his fellow-demesman Isocrates), they can be reinforced by the suggestion that even after the repeal of his banishment he was only an occasional visitor to Athens.

Professor Delebecque[5] provides insights into Xenophon's stay in Corinth (as into so many aspects of Xenophon's career), though some points remain debatable.[6] He remarks[7] that Xenophon's neglect of the naval victories won by Athens during the period covered by *Hellenica 5* is better explained by the supposition that Xenophon was not in close touch with Athens when he wrote the book than by his supposed wish to please the Spartans, whose impiety and treachery he attacks

---

pare G. L. Cawkwell's review of the above, *Classical Review* 29, no. 1 (1979) 19, allowing that Xenophon's absence from Athens might have something to do with the impracticability that Cawkwell ("Eubulus," *JHS* 83 [1963] 47–67, especially 63–64) had already noted as characteristic of parts of the *Poroi*.

1. Diogenes Laertius, *Vitae Sophistarum* 2.53; 2.56. His visit to Elis no doubt represents a vain attempt to persuade the Eleans not to evict him. Lepreum, where he rejoined his sons, was a suitable rallying point for friends of Sparta, but nothing more.

2. W. E. Higgins, *Xenophon the Athenian* (Albany, 1977).

3. H. R. Breitenbach, s.v. "Xenophon," *RE* (Stuttgart, 1967) col. 1573; R. Nickel, *Xenophon* (Darmstadt, 1979) 8.

4. P. Gauthier, *Un commentaire historique des Poroi de Xenophon* (Geneva and Paris, 1976) 64 accepts the possibility that Xenophon was writing at Corinth. Com-

5. E. Delebecque, *Essai sur la vie de Xenophon* (Paris, 1957) 312–41.

6. Thus Delebecque, *La vie de Xenophon*, 329–31 believes the last chapter of the *Constitution of the Lacedaemonians* to have been a postscript, written at Corinth, to a work whose other parts date from before the battle of Leuctra. I personally consider this chapter to be an integral part of the original, following A. Momigliano, "Per l'unita logica della *Lakedaimonion Politeia* di Senofonte," *Rivista di Filologia e d'Istruzione Classica* NS/14 (1936) fasc. 2, 170–73 (reprinted in *Storia e Letteratura* 108 [1966] 341–45).

7. Delebecque, *La vie de Xenophon*, 318–24.

without mincing words.[8] Yet Book 5 was written after the capture of Plataea and Tanagra by the Thebans,[9] and it contains allusions to the Battle of Leuctra itself.[10] It is unlikely that Xenophon found time to compose history in the interval between the battle and his own departure from Scillus. Therefore, even if the ancient tradition of his life had recorded no more than the repeal of his banishment from Athens, we might have guessed at a lengthy stay in some place of refuge on the way.

It would even have seemed likely that this refuge was in the northeast Peloponnese. From the winter of 370/369 B.C. on, the Isthmus of Corinth becomes, as between 394–387 B.C., the center of the military operations described in the *Hellenica*.[11] It is easy to accept the suggestion that the historian himself, now in his sixties but still viewing with a professional eye the battles in which he was too old to take part, watched from the walls when the Corinthian light infantry, hurling stones and javelins from the tops of the grave monuments, repulsed the Theban attempt to surprise the Phlius Gate of Corinth.[12] Even more readily we can imagine Xenophon's keen personal interest in the brilliant action that the cavalrymen sent by Dionysius of Syracuse fought in the Corinthian plain, and we can suppose that it was not so much the battle as the spectator's view of it that faded away when the Thebans and their allies drew off toward Sicyon.[13]

But the argument that when Xenophon writes vividly he writes as an eyewitness can be pressed too far. For example, we might suppose that he took advantage of the Olympic festival of 364 B.C. to revisit a countryside that he knew and loved so well. The journey, whether from Athens or from Corinth, should have been well within the pow-

ers of a healthy man in his sixties. So he could conceivably have been a witness of the Battle in the Altis,[14] which he describes in as much circumstantial detail as any of the actions near Corinth. But this is obviously the merest conjecture.

To return to the neighborhood of Corinth, Xenophon's interest in the affairs of Phlius and his admiration for the courage and the loyalty of its people provide material for some of the best chapters of *Hellenica* 7. His narrative, as Delebecque justly points out, is constantly enriched with details that must have been observed by an eyewitness.[15] After the defeat of the enemy, who had surprised the acropolis of Phlius, "one could see the men clasping hands to congratulate each other on their safety, and the women bringing them something to drink and weeping for joy all the while."[16] When, with the help of Chares, the men of Phlius surprised the half-built fort on Thyamia, "they caught the enemy in the fort, some washing, some cooking, some kneading, some making up their bivouacs."[17] But need the eyewitness have been Xenophon himself? And need the close topographical knowledge that Xenophon's chapters on Phlius constantly reveal have been acquired at this time? If we are to suppose that between 368 and 366 B.C. Xenophon made journeys to and from Corinth and Phlius, and perhaps as far as Sicyon,[18] we must also ask the purpose of these journeys. Phlius, desperately short of provisions and compelled, at great hazard, to escort its own "useless mouths" to find refuge in Pellene,[19] would hardly have welcomed an el-

8. Xenophon, *Hellenica* 5.4.1.
9. Xen. *Hell.* 5.4.14, 49.
10. Xen. *Hell.* 5.4.1, 33.
11. Delebecque, *La vie de Xenophon*, 315.
12. Xen. *Hell.* 7.1.18–19.
13. Xen. *Hell.* 7.1.20–21. Compare Delebecque, *La vie de Xenophon*, 317.

14. Xen. *Hell.* 7.4.28–32.
15. Delebecque, *La vie de Xenophone*, 331–34.
16. Xen. *Hell.* 7.2.9.
17. Xen. *Hell.* 7.2.22.
18. Delebecque, *La vie de Xenophon*, 333. See also W. K. Pritchett, *Studies in Ancient Greek Topography: Part II, Battlefields* (Berkeley and Los Angeles, 1969) 96–111, especially 96, n. 8. The countryside through which Xenophon passed on these journeys (if they ever took place) has been recently described by J. R. Wiseman, *The Land of the Ancient Corinthians* (Goteborg, 1978).
19. Xen. *Hell.* 7.2.1; 7.2.10; 7.2.17–18.

derly noncombatant, however distinguished and friendly to the "best people," who had come merely to make historical inquiries. Of course, Xenophon was not as old as his friend Agesilaus, who had still many distinguished years of service ahead of him. Conceivably the veteran general was in charge of the convoys that brought up provisions from Corinth to Phlius. But it strains the imagination—to say nothing of the evidence—less to suppose that he was a good listener as well as a good observer and that, remaining in Corinth, he had plenty of opportunity to hear first-hand stories from the front. After all, the mingled tears and laughter of the women of Phlius are less remarkable than the reaction of Agesilaus and the Spartan elders to the news of Archidamus's victory in Arcadia.[20] And this Xenophon certainly did not see for himself.

In short, the evidence of Diogenes that Xenophon established himself at Corinth fits in well with what can be guessed from his own writings, and there is no need to go further. But why did he settle at Corinth? We may note Xenophon's developing sympathy for the Corinthians as the *Hellenica* progresses. At the end of the Peloponnesian War, Corinth supports the Thebans in demanding the total destruction of Athens,[21] and when Corinth and Boeotia later refuse to join Pausanias's expedition against the Democrats in the Piraeus or to march with Agis against Elis,[22] it is clear that their real motive is dislike of Sparta rather than love of its enemies. Disappointed in their war aims and frustrated in their desire for revenge, the Corinthians, whose leaders have been suborned with Persian gold,[23] lend their support to the alliance against Sparta that forces Agesilaus to abandon his war of liberation in Asia. At first their part is still passive; once again they refuse to join the Spartans when Pausanias invades Boeotia.[24] But by 391 B.C. their own

country has become the seat of war; their existence as a nation is threatened by the enforced union with Argos; the leaders of their aristocracy are massacred without regard to either the holiness of the day or the altars of the gods. At this point Xenophon shows not merely his usual sympathy with "the best people" but also a knowledge of details that proves him to have drawn information from at least one close acquaintance. He knows the omen of the fallen column capital that induced the survivors of the massacre to descend from Acrocorinth and the details of the conspiracy by which the Long Walls connecting the city with Lechaeum were betrayed to the Spartan commander at Sicyon.[25] No Corinthian stands out as an individual in the *Hellenica* as do Stasippus, the leader of the "best men" at Tegea,[26] and the more fortunate Procles of Phlius. But among the Corinthian aristocrats, Pasimelus[27] is named twice, once for the forethought that preserved the younger members of his party from the massacre and once as one of the conspirators who admitted the Spartans within the Long Walls. Years later he makes a final appearance, as a mediator between the Spartans and Euphron of Sicyon. Perhaps Xenophon and Pasimelus became friends while Xenophon was still in the Spartan service, before the "King's Peace" of 387 B.C.

At all events, that peace freed Corinth from the Argive connection and left it governed by the "best people," on whom Sparta and Xenophon could rely when disaster struck. In the later books of the *Hellenica*, Xenophon treats the Corinthians with sympathy, and something more. Cliteles of Corinth is applauded by the Athenian when he represents his city as the innocent victim of Theban aggression after Leuctra.[28] Corinth gives essential support to Phlius in its hour of need and provides a base for Athenian forces under Iphicrates, Chabrias, and

20. Xen. *Hell.* 7.1.32.
21. Xen. *Hell.* 2.2.19.
22. Xen. *Hell.* 2.4.30; 3.2.25.
23. Xen. *Hell.* 3.5.1.
24. Xen. *Hell.* 3.5.17, 23.

25. Xen. *Hell.* 4.4.1–13.
26. Xen. *Hell.* 6.5.6–10.
27. Xen. *Hell.* 4.4.4, 7; 7.3.2.
28. Xen. *Hell.* 6.5.37.

Chares. In 366 B.C., the Corinthians set an example to the rest of Greece by refusing the terms sent down by the Great King, acting in support of Thebes.[29] Even when stress of war compels the Corinthians to expel the Athenian garrisons and make a separate peace with Thebes, they act with dignity and good faith.[30]

At this point we may return to the question of whether Xenophon himself continued to live in Corinth until his death, "sending" his sons (as Diogenes puts it)[31] to serve with the Athenians in the support of their Spartan allies and of course visiting Athens himself from time to time. As I have already indicated, this view commends itself to me as helping to explain Xenophon's apparent failure both to establish himself in Athenian intellectual circles and to come face to face with the realities of Athenian finance and politics. We may imagine him lonely at Athens, barely recognized by the friends of his youth and out of touch with those of his adult career; distressed by the sight of his family's home in other hands. These are good, though conjectural, reasons for his failure to take full advantage of the repeal of his banishment. Yet it must be allowed that Diogenes quotes only Demetrius of Magnesia for the story that Xenophon died at Corinth,[32] whereas the previous statement, which says no more than that he settled there after losing Scillus, is prefaced by "they say" and so presumably rested on the consensus of the authorities. To Delebecque,[33] Corinth appears as a temporary refuge, from which Xenophon soon began to turn his eyes in the direction of Athens and which he had quitted by 365 B.C. at the latest in order to establish himself and his family in his true country. This may well be correct; yet if Xenophon remained at Corinth we may perhaps see (once again letting imagination carry us far beyond the evidence) a special significance in Xenophon's story of the forced march by which the Athenian cavalry saved Mantinea: "Starting from Eleusis, they took their dinner at the Isthmus, and, passing through Cleonae also, they happened to have arrived at Mantinea and been billeted within the walls in the citizens' homes."[34] We know well enough (though not from Xenophon)[35] that among those brave men, as they were shortly to prove themselves, the bravest was Xenophon's own son Gryllus. We may conceive the father hurrying out to the Isthmus for a last brief meeting at this wayside halt and returning home to seek on his son's behalf the protection of the gods whom he had so piously respected throughout his own career. At Corinth then (we may suppose) the tidings of the death of Gryllus came to Xenophon when he was engaged in sacrificing. "And at the news, he took off his chaplet. But when the messenger added that he had fallen valiantly, he replaced it on his head." In that act of pious commemoration we may leave him.

29. Xen. *Hell.* 7.1.40. Delebecque, *La vie de Xenophon*, 333.
30. Xen. *Hell.* 7.4.4–11.
31. Diog. Laert. *Vit. Soph.* 2.53.
32. Diog. Laert. *Vit. Soph.* 2.56.

33. Delebecque, *La vie de Xenophon*, 325, 342.
34. Xen. *Hell.* 7.5.15.
35. Diog. Laert. *Vit. Soph.* 2.53; Pausanias 1.3.4.

7. Celts in Corinth

ISABELLE K. RAUBITSCHEK

DEPARTMENT OF ART, STANFORD UNIVERSITY

The discovery of distinctly foreign objects in a panhellenic sanctuary like Isthmia raises at once questions about the origin of the finds and the circumstances of their deposit. There are additional questions concerning date of manufacture and the chronological context of excavation.

In the case of Celtic objects that have been found in Greece and in Asia Minor, the tendency has been to connect them directly or indirectly with the "Galatian" invasion of the early third century B.C. However suggestive this connection may be, one should be careful in dating Celtic objects found in Greece solely on the basis of their assumed association with the well-known invasion of Brennus.

It occurred to me while working on bronzes from Isthmia that the date and the circumstances of deposit of two such objects, heavy, cast bronze women's anklets (IM 821, IM 822), should be reexamined because they have become important in dating other similar anklets of uncertain date.

In the first publication, J. Caskey[1] dated the anklets found in a well near Isthmia to the second half of the fourth century B.C., since most of the other objects in this well could be dated to that period. The anklets, however, have been, ever since, used as evidence for a date in the third century B.C., and it has been assumed that the Celtic invasion under Brennus penetrated Greece as far as Isthmia.[2]

1. *Hesperia* 29 (1960) 168–76, pls. 54–56.
2. W. Krämer, *Germania* 39 (1961) 32–42, pls. 15–16.

The anklets (figure 1) have an inner diameter of 7 and 7.5 cm, respectively. They consist of eight smooth, hollow bronze nuts and are made in two pieces of six and two nuts each, the smaller parts being attached to the larger on each side by carefully made toggle latches. This type of anklet is well known from La Tène graves excavated in the Danube basin.[3] Thus, the origin of these anklets is not in dispute, but scholars of Celtic art disagree about their date. Although Krämer pointed out[4] that many of the tombs with "Hohlbuckelringen" belong chronologically near the La Tène B period, he suggested that the anklets from Isthmia date in the early third century B.C. Yet Jacobsthal had already established a date in the second half of the fourth century B.C. for the Waldalgesheim style, which included anklets of the Isthmia type.[5] Evidently, fascination with the connection with the historically well attested, ill-fated invasion of Brennus in 279 B.C. (Diodorus 22.9.1–3; Pausanias 10.19.5) persuaded some scholars to date the Celtic anklets from Isthmia in the third century B.C.[6]

3. J. Déchelette, *Manuel d'archéologie préhistorique celtique et gallo-romaine*, vol 2 (1914) 3, 1220, fig. 517, 12; Krämer, *Germania*, 41–42, gives a list of 37 examples from Bavaria, Austria, Czechoslovakia, Hungary, and Jugoslavia.
4. Krämer, *Germania*, 37–41.
5. P. Jacobsthal, *Early Celtic Art* (Oxford, 1944) 135, 141, 190, 207.
6. F. Hodson, *Bulletin of the Institute of Archaeology, University of London* 4 (1964) 123–41, especially 134 (I owe this reference to F. A. Winter); J. V. Megaw, *Liber J. Kostrzewski dicatus* (Warsaw, 1968) 189; M. Szabo, *BCH* 95 (1971) 503 (but see his earlier article mentioned in footnote 7); U. Schaaf, *Germania* 50

Figure 1. Celtic Bronze Anklets in the Isthmia Museum, inv. nos. IM 821 and 822.

It is highly unlikely, however, that any Celts reached the Corinthia at this time, since the survivors, warriors and camp followers alike, fled after their defeat at Delphi from Greece through Thermopylae.

Since the dating of Celtic objects is so greatly dependent on datable Greek objects and on events attested by the Greek historical record, the evidence of the contents of the Isthmia well should be carefully considered. Among the various instances related by ancient historians of encounters by Greeks with Celts in the fourth century B.C., the most significant for our purposes is the victory of the Corinthian Timoleon in 340 B.C. at the river Crimisus in Sicily over the Carthaginian army, which included Celtic mercenaries (Diodorus 16.73.2; Plutarch, *Timoleon* 28.6).[7] Notable is the fact that Timoleon ordered the spoils of armor to be brought to Corinth and to be dedicated at the temple of Poseidon, that is, at Isthmia (Diodorus

16.80.5; Plutarch, *Timoleon* 29). The Isthmia anklets are not pieces of armor, but the Celtic women accompanied their men into battle, and they wore pairs of such anklets.[8]

Celtic dedications of the fourth century B.C. are known from another Corinthian sanctuary, Perachora. Of the five bronze bracelets found there, four have incised decorations like those on similar objects from a fourth century B.C. grave in Switzerland.[9] Although four bracelets have smooth surfaces, the fifth consists of sixteen solid cast knobs separated from each other by vertical ribs.[10] Since the Perachora bracelets may have been acquired by trade, they do not prove the actual presence of Celts in the Corinthian area, just as the anklets from Isthmia may not necessarily prove the presence of Celts in the area. It is unlikely that the anklets were worn by Greek women, and there is a strong presumption that they belong to the booty cap-

---

(1972) 97; M. Maier, *Germania* 51 (1973) 476–77 (I owe this reference to K. Kilian who cautioned me in regard to my conclusions).

7. For a list of contacts of Celts with Greeks and of occasions when Celts may have been present in Greece during the fourth century B.C., see M. Szabo, *Acta Antiqua (Academiae Scientiarum Hungaricae)* 16 (1968) 174–76. Szabo at first accepted Caskey's date for the Isthmia anklets in the fourth century B.C. and anticipated the conclusions reached here, but in 1971 he reverted to the communis opinio; see note 6.

8. H. Lorenz, "Die Kelten in Mitteleuropa," *Salzburger Landesausstellung* (1 May–30 September 1980) 133–35, fig. 1.3. In this exhibition a pair of anklets identical with those from Isthmia were shown (no. 103, p. 256) that had been excavated from grave 47 in Hallein-Durnberg and dated between 320–220 B.C.

9. *Perachora* 1, 175, pl. 78, 1–3, 5. For the Swiss examples from grave 5 in Andelfingen see, Krämer, *Germania*, 35, pl. 16, 5.

10. This bracelet too has a parallel from grave 5, Andelfingen; see *Perachora* 1, 175–76, pl. 78, 4, 6; Krämer, *Germania*, 35, pl. 16, 4.

Figure 2. Celtic Bronze Fibula in the Isthmia Museum, inv. no. IM 1149.

tured by Timoleon and brought back to Corinth.[11]

Another Celtic object from Isthmia is a hitherto unpublished fibula (IM 1149). It is a bronze object 9.5 cm long with two pins formed from the same piece of metal as the triply coiled spring (figure 2). This element once fitted into one end of the piece of bronze from which the lanceolate bow is made. The catchplate is made of one piece with the bow, which has a strengthening rib underneath the leaf. The fibula cannot be dated from its place of discovery, the starting line of the archaic stadium, where the accumulation contained objects dating from the Geometric to the Hellenistic periods. But the origin and the date of similar fibulae have been established by Rolley.[12]

Years ago, C. Blinkenberg had considered such fibulae as Thessalian.[13] However, the excavation of a large number of graves at Gostilj near Lake Skutari (ancient Scodra) in Albania during the 1970s has revealed similar fibulae found with coins dating from the end of the third to the beginning of the sec-

ond century B.C.[14] None of the various fibulae found at this Illyrian site is exactly like the one from Isthmia. Some fibulae have bows in the shape of an ivy leaf, other fibulae with lanceolate bows have two pins like the Isthmia example, but the catchplate is shovel-shaped, forming an extension of the bow, rather than bent underneath the bow as on the Isthmia fibula.[15] Other fibulae from Gostilj with one pin and a simple rod have catchplates like the Isthmia one. Rolley regards these variations as having been made in the course of a short time within the second century B.C.[16] The double pin type is said by Garašanin to be a loan form from the Celts.[17] We know that one Celtic tribe, the Scordisci, appeared in the Balkans as early as the third century B.C. (Strabo 7.3.11; 5.2) and became mixed with the Illyrians.

Illyrian fibulae of the Isthmian type with two pins have come in small numbers from several sites in Greece: four from Delphi, one from Medeon in Phocis, one from Dodona, one from Thisbe in Boeotia, and one possibly from Cyprus (now in the National Museum, Athens, inv. no. 18600).[18]

In Corinth itself, one Illyrian fibula of the

11. This is also the conclusion drawn by R. J. Talbert, *Timoleon and the Revival of Greek Sicily 344–317 B.C.* (Cambridge, 1974) 76–77. For the inscription mentioned there, see A. G. Woodhead, *Durham University Journal* 37 (1976) 210, who also refers to the *Supplementum Epigraphicum Graecum* 22.218, 23.172, 25.335.

12. *BCH* Supp. 4 (1977) *Études Delphiques*, 443–50, figs. 1–23. I am most grateful to Claude Rolley for identifying the fibula from Isthmia and for discussing with me the problems associated with it.

13. *Fibules grecques et orientales* (Copenhagen, 1915) 15, no. 1, fig. 2, type 6.

14. Rolley, *BCH* Supp. 4 (1977) 446–48, figs. 14–18.

15. The five Illyrian fibulae with two pins found at Olympia are all of this type; H. Philipp, *Bronzeschmuck aus Olympia, Olympische Forschungen* 13 (Berlin, 1981) 322–24, nos. 1146–50, pls. 22, 71. She has dated no. 1150 circa 400 B.C. because of its find-spot while admitting that no stratigraphical observations were made at the time of its discovery. No corroboration for a fifth century B.C. date is to be gained from the Corinthian fibula, Corinth Museum MF 11465, since it was found in fill 4 of manhole 8 along with sherds of the middle of the second century B.C.; see H. S. Robinson, *Hesperia* 38 (1969) 11, 19–20, no. 37, pl. 6.

16. The contemporaneity of the various types of Illyrian fibulae is also posited by R. Vasić, *Archaeologia Iugoslavica* 16 (1976) 14–16.

17. M. Garašanin, *Prehistory of Serbia* (in Serbo-Croatian with a French summary) (1973) 653–54. I owe this reference to N. G. L. Hammond and the use of the book to my colleague, Wayne Vucinich.

18. Rolley, *BCH* supp. 4 (1977) 443–46, figs. 1–10. Vasić, *Archaeologia Iugoslavica*, 16, note 19 adds only one fibula to Rolley's list, a fragment in the museum at Eretria that I have not seen. I owe this reference to H. Vetters.

Isthmian type, but with only one pin, has been found in a manhole in West Corinth (Corinth Museum, inv. no. MF 11465) along with pottery dating in the second century B.C.[19] Another fibula like it has been found in the Agora of Athens (Agora inv. no. B 772).[20] Two fibulae of the same type from western Macedonia are now in the National Museum, Athens (inv. nos. 16879, 16880). The "Megarian" red bowls found with them confirm their date in the second century B.C.,[21] and the single-pin Illyrian fibulae that were found at Ithaca and Dodona may belong to this group.[22] We may assume with Rolley, on the one hand, that they had been worn by Illyrians who wandered into Greece during and after the Second Macedonian War.[23] On the other hand, the fibulae may have been acquired by Greek merchants in Illyria and brought home, for many Greek objects dating from the seventh to the second centuries B.C. have been found in Illyria, testifying to its contact with Greece.[24]

Fibulae of the same Illyrian type were found in several places in Asia Minor, in sanctuaries, in graves, and in houses.[25] This implies that the fibulae were used sometimes as offerings, but they were also used sometimes as articles of clothing. These fibulae were often found in pairs, and it is probable that the second pin of the two was used to attach a second article of clothing, a scarf or a cape, to the main garment.

The bronze anklets and the fibula from Isthmia were probably offerings that were deposited there, the anklets in the second half of the fourth century B.C. and the fibula in the first half of the second century B.C. before the sanctuary's destruction in 146 B.C. The anklets were doubtless made in the heartland of the Celts, the Danube basin, while the fibula came from Illyria where Celtic workmanship was imitated.

---

19. Robinson, *Hesperia* 38 (1969) 11, 19–20, pl. 6.

20. F. Maier, *Germania* 51 (1973) 472–73, pl. 30.3.

21. Rolley, *BCH* Supp. 4 (1977) 451, note complémentaire.

22. For Ithaca, see S. Benton, *BSA* 35 (1934–1935) 69, fig. 18e. For Dodona, see C. Carapanos, *Dodone et ses ruines* (Paris, 1878) 94, pl. 51.7 and Megaw, *Liber J. Kostrzewski dicatus*, 185–86, fig. 2.

23. *BCH* Supp. 4 (1977) 451, note 22.

24. A comprehensive account of these objects is presented by M. Parovic-Pesikan in *Archaeologia Iugoslavica* 5 (1964) 61–81. I owe a copy of this article to H. Vetters.

25. H. Polenz, *Bonner Jahrbücher* 178 (1978) 181–216, illustrates fibulae from Kayseri, Priene, Mersin, and Bogasköy in figs. 1–4. K. Bittel informs me, by letter, that fibulae from Kussary, Sinope, Cannakkale, Pergamon, and Finike are of the same type.

8. Corinth and Comedy

WILLIAM S. ANDERSON

CLASSICS DEPARTMENT, UNIVERSITY OF CALIFORNIA, BERKELEY

Although Professor Amyx has earned his reputation by his distinguished studies of Corinthian pottery, he also has an interest in Corinth itself. I, who dare not say anything about pottery, dedicate this little survey of Corinth and comedy to him. "Non cuivis homini licet esse hac arte perito" (Not every man can be expert in this field).

I was tempted to conclude my dedication with a direct citation of a hexameter from Horace: "non cuivis homini contingit adire Corinthum" (Not every man happens to arrive at Corinth).[1] However, apt though the line at first sight seems in expressing Professor Amyx's remarkable ability in arriving at his special mastery of Corinthian pottery, closer consideration of Horace's epistle reveals that he practices an irony that is totally out of place for our present occasion. In Horace's context, "to arrive at Corinth" symbolizes the dubious success of winning the favor of powerful and wealthy patrons in Augustan Rome. The art of the slick courtier, full of study and effort, no doubt, differs strikingly from that of a scholar (or of a poet like Horace).[2] Furthermore, as the Roman audience knew only too well, Horace was playing with a familiar Greek saying that applied strictly to an ignoble art of Corinth—to her

notoriety as a center of prostitution. Since this Greek saying may have been uttered first in an Athenian comedy and marked an important stage in Corinth's long involvement with comedy, I revised Horace's Latin to be more fitting, but I shall continue for a while with the original Greek, having at last "arrived at Corinth" and comedy.

The Greek, οὐ παντὸς ἀνδρὸς ἐς Κόρινθον ἔσθ' ὁ πλοῦς (It is not for every man to voyage to Corinth), constitutes a good trimeter, a metrical form that could, of course, have been employed in comedy over a long period from the fifth century B.C. onward, but a form that could also have served an entirely nondramatic function. A trimeter puts an idea in a potentially memorable way. The earliest writer to cite the line was an almost exact Greek contemporary of Horace. Strabo, both in his description of Corinth itself (8.6.20) and in his account of a dissolute Armenian city named Comana (12.3.36), quotes what he regards as a proverb, without concern for its ultimate author or source, and applies it specifically to a notorious problem that confronted travelers to Corinth: its many hetairai demanded such exorbitant fees that they ruined many a fool. Hence, not every man had the means or the wits to cope with a visit there. Strabo guarantees that the proverb was current before his and Horace's time, but we cannot go far back with him. However, the next writer to cite the Greek, Aulus Gellius, embellishes it a little with an anecdote about Demosthenes

---

1. *Epist.* 1.17.36.
2. Lewis and Short, but not the recent *Oxford Latin Dictionary*, propose as the primary reference of the proverb the difficult navigational approach to the harbor of Corinth. That erroneous interpretation can be traced back through Erasmus to an alternative explanation of Apostolius 13.60.

and the famous Corinthian hetaira Lais.[3] That link might be a clue to the original date and the context of the trimeter. After these two early imperial authors, we find the proverb in a series of late compilers of sayings, such as Zenobius, Diogenianus, Apostolius, Photius, Eustathius (in Greek), and Pseudo-Acro commenting on the line in Horace's epistle.[4] They all seem to depend on Strabo, and, similarly, none specifies a source for the Greek.

A single late writer, the lexicographer Hesychius, credits the trimeter to Aristophanes: he simply names the Athenian comic poet, adding no details, no title, no dramatic context of the comedy from which it supposedly came.[5] Not many people have taken him seriously. Commentators on Horace, such as Kiessling-Heinze or E. P. Morris, ignore Hesychius and Aristophanes completely and talk of the trimeter as an ordinary proverb, referring us to someone like Zenobius for meaning. Leutsch and Schneidewin, who collected the material for the *Corpus Paroemiographorum Graecorum*, in the mid-nineteenth century, also ignore Hesychius. Editors of Aristophanes either did not know of Hesychius's attribution or scorned it until rather recently. Kock did at least note it and list the line as doubtfully Aristophanic.[6] Hall and Geldart, in their Oxford text of 1901, number it identically among the doubtful fragments of Aristophanes.[7] J. M. Edmonds did the same in 1957.[8] Liddell and Scott exhibit the same minor trend: in their lexicon editions of the late nineteenth century, the

line appears as a proverb of unknown provenance, but in more recent editions the entry under Corinth refers readers to Aristophanes, fragment 902a (without, however, warning that the fragment is doubtfully assigned). In view of a sole witness, Hesychius, and the frequent interpolations of his manuscript, it would seem that Aristophanes' authorship of the trimeter remains very questionable.

Two other kinds of evidence should also be considered, namely, a possible dating of the trimeter and the likelihood that Aristophanes might produce such a witty reference to Corinth's notorious prostitutes. As I noted earlier, Gellius links the common saying "illud frequens apud Graecos adagium" (that familiar Greek proverb) to the exorbitant prices charged by Lais, for which he cites the authority of Sotion, and he summarizes an anecdote about Lais and Demosthenes, who prudently decided that he could not afford the cost of the dazzling hetaira. If the anecdote is a fact, and if the saying did originate in relation to Lais, then we may safely conclude that it came into existence in the mid-fourth century B.C., long after the death of Aristophanes. However, a complication must be recognized: there were two outstanding hetairai named Lais in Corinth, the elder of which lived in the time of Aristophanes; this elder Lais had a well-chronicled affair with Aristippus, the Cyrenaic devotee of intelligent pleasure, which offers moralists the material for an anecdote similar to that about Demosthenes and the younger Lais.[9] The same Sotion also wrote about this Lais and Aristippus, according to Diogenes Laertius. Perhaps this duplication proved a trap irresistible for the not very reliable Pseudo-Acro; at any rate, in his comment on Horace's hexameter version of the proverb, he applies it to the relationship of the elder Lais

---

3. Gellius, *Noctes Atticae* 1.8. A red-figured vase, seen in Rome in a private collection in 1847, preserved a prose version of the Greek proverb as follows: OU PANTOS ESTI KORINTHOS (Corinth is not for everyone). Thus, the proverb goes back at least to the fifth century. Cf. *AZ* 5 (1847), Beilage 2, 21–22.

4. Porphyrio, the earlier and more reliable commentator on Horace, says nothing about the Greek origin of the proverb.

5. Hesychius, s.v. οὐ.

6. Kock, Aristophanes (dub.), fr. 902.

7. Fr. 902 a.

8. *Remains of Greek Comedy*, vol. 1, Aristophanes fr. 902.

9. Diogenes Laertius 2.75; cf. also Athenaeus, *Deipnosophistae*, 13.588d and 599b. To a critic of his involvement with Lais, Aristippus replied, "I possess her; I am not possessed."

and Aristippus. That would date it to the life-time of Aristophanes.

Independent evidence also proves that Aristophanes mocked Corinthian prostitution in general and the elder Lais in particular. In his last extant play, the *Plutos*, the comic poet used Corinthian hetairai to represent the mercenary ways of all prostitutes, who regularly and predictably favor the rich as preferred customers and scorn the poor (*Plutos* 149). At *Plutos* 179 the speaker asks about the love affair of Lais and a certain Philonides, who is also mentioned at 303. In commenting on these three passages, the scholia mention Lais each time even though Aristophanes has named her only once. They assume that Philonides is the rich man and Lais the high-priced whore of 149. In a still later comedy, the *Kokalos*, Aristophanes introduced a character who, given a new verb, declared: "I am acting the part of a Corinthian" (*korinthiazomai*).[10] This character, a male, identifies himself as either a customer of a hetaira or a pimp. According to one tradition, the *Kokalos* deserves credit as the first comedy to exhibit some of those hallmarks of New Comedy, a rape and a recognition.[11] A prostitute's lover or a pimp would also have been an expectable role.

All this circumstantial evidence does not add up to solid proof that the trimeter was a comic trimeter or that it was written by Aristophanes. My personal inclination is to claim it for comedy but to deny Hesychius's attribution to Aristophanes and rather date it to the fourth century, to Middle or New Comedy. But whether or not this particular proverb about Corinthian hetairai originated in a particular comedy of the fifth or fourth century, it is clear from the *Plutos* and from the fragment of the *Kokalos* that Corinthian hetairai furnished material for comedy during the lifetime of Aristophanes.

In the remaining portion of this article, I shall trace the subsequent involvement of Corinth with comedy down to the time of

Terence. It might be expected that the hostility between Corinth and Athens during the Peloponnesian War would have spawned sneers at Corinth on the public stage during performances of Old Comedy. In fact, though, except for these two late plays, neither of which is regarded as a pure specimen of Old Comedy, Corinth was not a particular target for Aristophanes, nor for other comic poets of the period.[12] If one wanted to refer to prostitutes, then Corinth might stand for the whole profession; but, after all, prostitution was normal in Athens, too, and Aristophanes at least finds more comic interest in what he and his audience considered more amusing aspects of erotic intercourse that were well illustrated by certain Athenians.[13]

Corinth itself had a theater by 415 B.C., and the excavators have been able to distinguish a second phase of building at the end of the fourth century, which introduced typical modifications to accommodate New Comedy and Hellenistic theatrical performances.[14] Although the architectural evidence indicates a continuous theatrical history, little survives to suggest that Corinth itself, like Athens, originated much literature, let alone comedy. There is a vague tradition that the writer Machon, who staged comedies in Alexandria in the third century, may have been born in Corinth (but probably in Sicyon); other than him, I can find no Corinthian comic poet.[15] Thus, we may imagine that the Corinthians had frequent opportu-

12. Plato comicus referred to Lais (scholia on *Plutos* 179); Strattis listed her in a group of Corinthian women, probably hetairai (Athenaeus, *Deipnosophistae* 13. 589a); and Cephisodoros wrote an *Anti-Lais* comedy (Suidas)—all probably in the same period as Aristophanes' late plays. Hesychius states that Eupolis in his *Baptae* vented his hatred of the Corinthians (masc.). The play, which seems to have been a comic attack on Alcibiades, ridiculed the Athenian aristocrat and his friends as corrupt votaries of a disgraceful alien goddess. But no clear connection can be drawn with Corinth's notorious prostitutes. See G. Norwood, *Greek Comedy* (New York, 1963) 188–90.

13. See, in general, J. Henderson, *The Maculate Muse* (New Haven, 1975).

14. On the theater at Corinth, see Richard Stillwell, *Corinth* II (Princeton 1952), especially chapter 3.

15. Athenaeus, *Deipnosophistae* 6.241 and 14.664a.

10. Hall and Geldart, fr. 354.
11. *Vita Aristophanis.* 1.69.

nity in the late fifth, fourth, and third centuries to attend performances of comedies, but these comedies were imported from nearby Athens, and the audience had to endure jokes that had been designed for Athenian prejudices, as, for example, had been the humor regarding Corinth's notorious hetairai.

Aristophanes' son Philetairos wrote a so-called Middle Comedy whose title, *The Whoremonger* or *The Pimp* (*Korinthiastes*), exploited the neologism of his father in the *Kokalos*.[16] Epicrates entitled one of his comedies in this era *Anti-Lais*.[17] Anaxandrides included Lais in a list of Corinthian hetairai.[18] (Lists of hetairai seem to have been a popular topos of Middle Comedy, and the names are by no means exclusively Corinthian; indeed, more often the women are known on the streets of Athens.)[19] Athenaeus attributes to Eriphos, another comic poet of this age, a witticism that implied that Lais was equal to Corinth, the place of her practice, in wealth and in practical power.[20] Antiphanes wrote a *Korinthia*, and Klearchos entitled one of his plays *Korinthioi*.[21] Although we do not know for sure what the titles signified, it is probably safe to conjecture that Antiphanes and Klearchos, like Philetairos above, referred to those involved in Corinthian prostitution. Finally, Alexis in *Philousa* (The Girl Who Loves or Kisses) mentioned a special celebration for Aphrodite held by hetairai in Corinth.[22] For the sheer number of references to Corinthian prostitution, especially considering its en-

tirely fragmentary condition, Middle Comedy is remarkable.

If Middle Comedy developed, among other things, the characteristic contours of the hetaira as a comic type, it was New Comedy that incorporated the hetaira into a sentimental and highly successful generic plot. One of the typical situations features a beautiful young girl who, as the comedy opens, is either just involved or about to be involved with her first lover, a young man whom in fact she "honestly" loves and who "truly" loves her. The girl has a mother who is herself a retired hetaira, but who is now a bawd, and she is putting her daughter to the only practical career that seems open to her. Suddenly, in the denouement of the fourth and fifth acts, it turns out that this mother is only a foster parent, that the girl was kidnapped or exposed as a baby, and that by discovering her true father (and mother) she can recover her status and indeed become eligible for a legitimate love match in marriage with this first lover of hers. This might have been a plot type in which Corinth and Corinthian mercenary prostitution were typically used. However, such evidence as has survived proves that the playwrights of New Comedy made no special use of Corinth as a setting for such plots, nor did they single out Corinthians as typical bawds (or pimps, for that matter).

We possess the title of a play by Philemon, *Korinthia*, but no evidence as to how he presented this "woman from Corinth." On the analogy with such Menandrian titles as the *Samian*, *Andrian*, and *Perinthian*, we may doubt that Philemon exploited any prejudice against Corinth, and indeed we might suspect that this Corinthian woman (or girl) turned out to be the long-lost daughter of some Athenian, hence an Attic citizen, quite marriageable at the end.[23] Menander located his *Perikeiromene* in Corinth. The plot follows the lines of the type I have specified, and, at the end, Glykera, recognized as the

---

16. Athenaeus, *Deipnosophistae* 13.559a. The same title is given by Athenaeus, *Deipnosophistae* 7.313c, for a play of Poliochos, but he is not securely dated (despite Edmonds's guess that he wrote Old Comedy).

17. Athenaeus, *Deipnosophistae* 13.570b.

18. Athenaeus, *Deipnosophistae* 13.570d.

19. Cf. the list of Theophilos in Athenaeus, *Deipnosophistae* 13.587.

20. In a comedy entitled *The Peltast*: Athenaeus, *Deipnosophistae* 4.137d.

21. For Antiphanes' play, see Athenaeus, *Deipnosophistae* 3.95; for Klearchos's, see Athenaeus, *Deipnosophistae* 14.613b.

22. Athenaeus, *Deipnosophistae* 18.574b. The title suggests an affectionate hetaira.

23. For Philemon's play, see Stobaeus, *Florilegium* 108.7.

daughter of Pataikos (and no longer as the daughter of the dead bawd), is able to marry by her free choice the soldier whose violent passion has initiated the complications and given the play its title. But Menander makes nothing special of the mise-en-scène in Corinth. He also wrote the *Synaristosai* (Women at Breakfast), which Plautus adapted for his *Cistellaria*: a rather similar plot, involving an innocent *meretrix* (prostitute) and her recovery of parents and her consequent marriage with her lover Alcesimarchus, is enacted in Sicyon.[24]

Diphilos probably located the action of his *Merchant* in Corinth, to judge from the first line of a long fragment cited in Athenaeus 6.227e. Nevertheless, this and a second excerpt concentrate on the choice foods, especially fish, that could be bought in Corinth. We have no reason to suspect that Diphilos also featured a Corinthian hetaira. It is perhaps a mark of the declining relevance of Corinthian hetairai in New Comedy that Nicolaus in the second century could even parody the proverb that I earlier discussed. He substituted for Corinth (and hence for the allusion to Corinth's notorious prostitution) the word *table* and thereby shifted attention from sex to food: οὐ παντὸς ἀνδρὸς ἐπὶ τράπεζὰν ἐσθ' ὁ πλοῦς (It is not for every man to voyage to the dinner table).[25]

The Roman comic writers seem to have attached little special meaning to Corinth. Plautus, who adapted various Greek writers besides Menander, enjoyed making cracks about Greek decadence for the amusement of his chauvinistic Roman audience. He ridicules Greeks in general, however, and does not single out Corinth at all. If his originals did say anything about Corinth—and we have no reason to suspect that they did—Plautus has filtered it out. As for Terence, he refers to Corinth in two of his plays. In the *Hecyra* we hear of an Athenian *meretrix* who

has accompanied a soldier as his concubine and has lived two years in Corinth (85–87). Coals to Newcastle, if Corinth still had the reputation as the archetype of prostitution!

The usage in the other comedy, *Heautontimoroumenos* (The Self-Tormentor), is more interesting. Terence has adapted a play of Menander that varied the scheme I outlined of the young prostitute, supposed daughter of a bawd. In his innovative fashion, avoiding the normal Menandrian informative prologue, Terence only gradually gives us background information and thus creates a certain amount of misdirection and suspense. The first key details are reported by the father of Clinias, and he and we treat them as facts:

> est e Corintho hic advena anu' paupercula;
> eius filiam ille amare coepit perdite. (*HT* 96–97)
> (There is a poor old woman who came here from Corinth;
> he fell fatally in love with her daughter.)

A needy old woman has come from Corinth and has allowed, more likely has encouraged, her daughter to seduce Clinias. At any rate, he begins to live with her as a kind of wife (98). The concerned father obviously thinks of the girl as a *meretrix*, her mother as a *lena* (bawd). Is it also possible that the reference to Corinth automatically reinforces that suspicion in the mind of father and audience? Did Terence, and Menander before him, count on the general prejudice against Corinth? The answer, I think, is no. As we have seen, Menander exploited the bias in none of his surviving plays or fragments; and there is no reason for Terence to have inserted the point. Corinth here possesses importance only as a foreign city: the women are strangers in Athens, noncitizens, and the only real livelihood for them in the world of New Comedy is prostitution. The same bleak choice would face any other such young woman, for example, the one from Andros whom Terence describes in *Andria* 74ff. Fortunately the father has the facts wrong. We soon hear that the girl is unlike the typical

---

24. Menander refers incidentally to a business trip to Corinth in *Georgos* 6: it had nothing to do with hetairai.

25. Stobaeus, *Florilegium* 14.7.26.

grasping prostitute, that she is well and modestly brought up ("bene et pudice eductam, ignaram artis meretriciae" [well and chastely raised, unaware of the prostitute's art] [226]); moreover, that the old woman was not her mother after all (269). It is no surprise, then, that her true mother, an Athenian neighbor of Clinias, recognizes the girl, so that the loving young couple can get legally married.

As one surveys the evidence for the comic exploitation of Corinth's supposed notoriety as a haven for hetairai, from the late fifth century to the mid-second century, the conclusion seems inevitable that the greatest frequency of reference occurred during the period of Middle Comedy, from roughly 380 to 320 B.C. I cannot account for this fact, but the data seem unassailable. Perhaps this was the period when Corinthian prostitutes were especially infamous.[26] Perhaps Athenian playwrights were then more chauvinistic than at other times. Or perhaps, as they turned from the material of Old Comedy, they became particularly interested in the sensuous world of hetairai (as they did also in the gourmet world of cook and parasite). At any rate, we notice that the topic does not appear in Old Comedy before its last years, already in the fourth century, and it declines

rapidly in New Comedy, yielding, alas, to a preoccupation with Corinthian fish. If, then, we allow that the trimeter discussed earlier is the work of a comic poet, one of the many who ridiculed Lais in the fourth century, then it would follow that the unknown poet was a writer of Middle Comedy.[27]

Luckily, Corinth, especially early Corinth, had many other relevant areas outside of comedy and prostitution. Yet it is significant, I think, that, even for the comic poets, the topos of Corinthian prostitution was short-lived, confined to a relatively brief period in the fourth century. Not every man, after that fourth century, found Corinth a challenge to his amatory prowess and the capacity of his purse. Corinthian cuisine and Corinthian bronze were a steady and no doubt expensive lure. But only in modern times, with such scholars as Professor Amyx, have there appeared those rare individuals who have "gone to Corinth" for its pottery.

---

26. It goes without saying that the prostitutes of Corinth were well known much earlier. Athenaeus, *Deipnosophistae* 13.573c, reports two incidents, quite respectable, which involved them around 480: they participated in the religious rituals on behalf of the safety of Corinth at the time of Xerxes' expedition, and Pindar composed a poem for the Corinthian athlete Xenophon, who dedicated a hundred hetairai to Aphrodite after an outstanding triple victory at Olympia [Pindar fr. 122]. My concern is with the comic use of these prostitutes from the late fifth century on.

27. Since this was written, another early parody of the trimeter line has been discovered. In December 1984, at the meetings of the American Philological Association in Toronto, William Willis reported the existence of the *Comedia Dukiana*, fifty lines of trochaic tetrameter which extol the virtues of the river shad. To a skeptical companion, the principal speaker declares (extending the trimeter to a complete tetrameter by the addition of an insulting vocative): ὦ πονηρ’, οὐ παντὸς ἀνδρὸς ‹ἐσ› σιλουρόν ἐσθ’ ὁ πλοῦς (You fool, not every man can voyage to the river shad). Willis dates the papyrus to the second half of the third century B.C. and plausibly assigns the original Greek to an unknown Middle comedy. The parody, therefore, anticipates that of Nicolaus (see p. 48); and it exhibits superior wit, inasmuch as voyaging to a fish is metaphorically more apt than sailing to a dinner table. Moreover, if the *Comedia Dukiana* indeed comes from a mid-fourth-century Middle comedy, then parody of the original trimeter began almost immediately.

9. The Latin Epigram at Corinth

ARTHUR E. GORDON

CLASSICS DEPARTMENT, UNIVERSITY OF CALIFORNIA, BERKELEY

This slight tribute to Dick Amyx, from (I believe) his last living teacher, is intended to acquaint him with a Corinthian piece that he has been too busy with other Corinthiaca to notice. It is a stone in the Corinth museum (figure 1), inscribed with "the earliest and on the whole the most important published Latin inscription of Corinth";[1] not only that, it is also in verse, perhaps the only ancient Latin verse thus far found in Greece.[2]

It is an elegiac epigram in five couplets celebrating the feat of hauling a Roman fleet across the Isthmus of Corinth between 102 and 100 B.C., under the auspices of a proconsul, Mark Antony's grandfather, Marcus Antonius (consul in 99 B.C. and often called Antonius the Orator from Cicero's portrait of him in the *Brutus* and the *De Oratore*), and with the aid of a propraetor named Hirrus.

Antonius's name has been erased, either because of mistaken identity—confusion with his grandson—or, more probably, as part of the *damnatio memoriae* suffered by the grandson after the battle of Actium in 31 B.C. and the fall of Alexandria in 30,[3] but enough remains of the name to make it certain.[4] Hirrus, *(legatus) pro praetore* under Antonius, is thought to be a G. Lucilius Hirrus, otherwise unknown but probably a relative of both the satirist Lucilius and the *tribunus plebis* G. Lucilius Hirrus of 53 B.C.[5]

The unknown versifier probably served in the Roman fleet, and his verses[6] are "perhaps the first record found for the activity of such a poet on the scene of action. . . . As an honorary epigram," the poem "represents a comparatively unknown type in Latin epigraphic records. As a historical document, it provides new evidence for the obscure expedition of the orator Marcus Antonius against the pirates and for the use of the Diolkos [the slipway for the passage of ships across the Isthmus of Corinth] in the transportation of ships of war."[7]

The stone is a block of marble[8] found at

---

1. S. Dow, *HSCP* 60 (1951) 83, *init.*

2. It is not included in M. Šašel Kos's *Inscriptiones Latinae in Graecia repertae, Additamenta ad CIL* III (Faenza, 1979).

3. W. W. Tarn, *Cambridge Ancient History* 10.108, 112.

4. L. R. Taylor and A. B. West proved that the "M. Antonius" here was not Mark Antony but rather his grandfather, *AJA* 2, 32 (1928) 15–20.

5. West, *Corinth, Results of Excavations . . .* , 8:2, 4; T. R. S. Broughton, *The Magistrates of the Roman Republic*, vol. 1 (New York, 1951) 569, 570 n. 7, *Suppl.* 37.

6. "Doggerel," E. Badian, *JRS* 58 (1968) 242, on no. 151.

7. Taylor and West, *AJA* ser. 2, 32 (1928) 22; for Antonius and the pirates, cf. H. A. Ormerod, *Cambridge Ancient History* 9.351, and Broughton *TAPA* 77 (1946) 35–40. On the date of this inscription, cf. Broughton *TAPA* 77 (1946) 568f., and A. Degrassi, *Inscriptiones Latinae liberae rei publicae* (hereafter *ILLRP*) 1, 202, note on no. 342: Broughton favors 101 or, less probably, 100, Degrassi 102 B.C..

8. Not limestone, *pace* Taylor/West, West, Lommatzsch, and Degrassi. C. K. Williams, II, director of the Corinth excavations, in a letter of 19 July 1975, confirming Dow, *HSCP* 60 (1951) 81, *init.*, writes, "I would like to confirm the identification of S. Dow, that the inscription is on marble. . . . Taylor and West perhaps

Figure 1. Marble Latin Inscription, Old Corinth, Museum (reproduced by permission of Corinth Excavations, American School of Classical Studies, Athens).

Corinth in 1925. By 1926 it had broken into seven pieces. Its dimensions are: height 78.6 cm, width 1.175 to 1.20 m, thickness 22 cm. The letters are mostly about 3.2 cm tall, some a little taller. (These are my own measurements, made with my wife's assistance in 1973.) The epigram apparently contained no more than the present ten lines; most of it is on the largest one of the seven pieces of the block. One of the sides shows the remains of a "beautifully cut Greek inscription of the best period, possibly fourth century B.C. in date."[9]

Bibliography

First mentioned by B. H. Hill (Director of the American School of Classical Studies, Athens),

AJA ser. 2, 31 (1927) 79; first published by Lily Ross Taylor and A. B. West, AJA ser. 2, 32 (1928) 9–22 (with photos, commentary, translation); whence R. Cagnat and M. Besnier, RA 28 (1928) 353, no. 5 (no comm.), E. Diehl, Alt-latein. Inschriften[3] (Berlin, 1930 Kleine Texte f. Vorles. u. Üb. 38/40) 40, no. 306 (no. comm.), and E. Lommatzsch, CIL 1[2], 2, 2 (1931) 739f., no. 2662 (with textual suggestions of Ed. Fränkel and comm.); A. B. West, in Corinth, Results of Excavations . . . , VIII, 2, Latin Inscriptions 1896–1926 (Cambridge, Mass., 1931) 1–4 (with photo, drawing, comm.); E. H. Warmington, Remains of Old Latin 4, Archaic Inscriptions (Cambridge, Mass./London 1940) The Loeb Classical Library 132–135, no. 7 (text, transl., a few notes); S. Dow, HSCP 60 (1951) 81–96, 97–100 (the best text, with notes on it, photos of squeezes); A. Degrassi, Inscr. Lat. Liberae Rei Publicae 1[1] and 1[2] (Florence 1957 and 1965, repr. 1972) 201–203 no. 342, add. p. 327 (text, notes); A. Ernout, Studii Clasice 2 (Budapest[?], 1960) 73–76 (text, app. crit., notes, French transl.); A. Degrassi, ILLRP, Imagines (Berlin, 1965 CIL, Auctarium) 105, nos. 151 a-b (photos of Dow's main squeeze and of a plaster "copy" of the inscrip-

---

called it limestone because the front of the block is badly incrusted and has a calcium deposit over much of its face that makes the block look less like marble than it is."

9. Taylor and West, AJA ser. 2, 32 (1928) 9.

tion in Rome, with, however, some restorations—cf. E. Badian, *JRS* 58 [1968] 242, on no. 151); A. Deman, *Latomus* 25 (1966) 971, on no. 342 (suggests *[perpetu]av- [it]* at the end of line 1 of the test); A. De Rosalia, *Iscrizioni latine archaiche* (Palermo, 1972) 53f., 128f., no. 48 (text, app. crit., Ital. transl., notes); Degrassi and H. Krummrey, *CIL* 1², 2, 4 (forthcoming) on no. 2662 (*add. corr.* to Lommatzsch's 1931 ed.) (seen in galley proof by courtesy of H. K.); J. Wiseman, *Aufstieg und Niedergang des römischen Welt*, vol. 2, 7.1 (Berlin, 1982) 495f. There may be further bibliography that I have not seen; any such is probably listed in *L'Année Philologique*, currently in the section "Épigraphie latine." (The only independent texts, based on autopsy of the stone, are those of Taylor and West; West; Dow; and the present writer.)

Text (based on Dow and autopsy)

Quod neque conatus quisquanst neque
[¹⁹ ᶜᵐ AV-[it(?)]]
noscite rem, ut famaa facta feramus virei.
Auspicio [Ant]oni [M]arci pro consule classis
Isthmum traductast missaque per pelagus.
5 Ipse iter eire profectus (est) Sidam; classem Hirrus Atheneis
pro praetore anni e tempore constituit.
Lucibus haec pauc[ei]s parvo perfecta (sunt) tumultu
magna[a qu]om ratione atque salut[e¹¹·⁸(?)ᶜᵐ].
Q[u]ei probus est lauda[t], quei contra est in[videt actum(?)].
10 Invid[ea]nt dum q[uod ded(?)]ecet id v[ideant(?)].¹⁰

Line 1, *fin.* (1) [*adhuc meditatus*] Taylor/West, West (who credits it to R. K. Hack), and Diehl (with question mark), (2) [*concipere ausus*] F. E. Adcock, *ap.* West, (3) [*mente peregit*] S. R(einach), *Rev. Arch.* ser. 5, 35 (1932) 165, (4) [*post audebit*] Lommatzsch, Warmington, De Rosalia, (5) [*post agitabit*] Ed. Fränkel *ap.* Lommatzsch, (6) [*consumm]av[it*] Ernout, (7) [*perpetu]av[it*] Deman, (8) [---]*av[it?*] Dow, Degrassi, *ILLRP*. Of these, the first five are excluded by Dow's reading *AV* with a gap of 19 cm to the left (we measured 23 cm to the bottom of the V, space for 8 to 10 letters) and measuring space for two such letters to the right

as -*it*; he considered *AV[sus]* most unlikely because he found no trace of the first *S* where the surface is preserved; *concipere* he also found too long (p. 88f.). Numbers 6 and 7, which appeared after Dow's study, seem possible spatially, but (6) has a spondaic ending, which would be rare in a dactylic hexameter and does not occur in any of the forty-one similar line-endings collected for Dow by H. Bloch (p. 89f.; Ernout makes no defense of the ending), and the meaning of (7) seems wrong in the context. Dow himself suggests nothing positive.

Line 3. "The reading of the erased letters is the principal clue to the inscription. . . . There can be no reasonable doubt whatever as to the original text. . . . There is not quite enough room for *[ma]arci*," Dow, p. 90 (see fig. 3, photo of squeeze of the erasure).

Line 7. PAVCIS all editions before Dow, PAVC[ei]S Dow (p. 90f.).

Line 8, *init. magna [ac qu] om* Taylor/West, Diehl (has no underdot), West; *magna[a qu]om* Fränkel *ap.* Lommatzsch, Warmington, Dow (who underdots the O and shows that there is no space for a C), Ernout (who by oversight omits the last A in *magnaa*), De Rosalia; *magna [qu]om* Degrassi, *ILLRP* (by oversight? He follows Dow otherwise).

Line 8, *fin. salut[e simul]* Taylor/West, Diehl (no underdots), West; *salut[e bona]* Fränkel *ap.* Lommatzsch, Warmington, Degrassi *ILLRP* (with question mark), De Rosalia (Dow, p. 91f., makes no choice between *bona* and *simul*—so also Ernout—and finds "only a slight presumption against [*bonaa*].")

Line 9. *Q[u]ei probus est lauda[t], quei contra est in- [videt illum].* ("He who is upright praises; he who is the opposite looks askance at him.") Taylor/West (with ref. to Catullus 5, 12, and Cicero *Tusc.* 3.20, quoting Accius for the accusative *illum*), Diehl (has no underdots and questions the last phrase), Lommatzsch (no underdots and reads *in[videt*, not *inv[—]*, West ("Other restorations are of course possible"), Warmington (no underdots, reads *in[videt* like Lommatzsch, and translates the last phrase like Taylor/West, but suggests instead *illei*, "has envy against him"), De Rosalia (also reads *in[videt]*); *q[u]ei probus es̩t̩ ļauda[t], quei cont̩ra est in[videt actum]* Dow (p. 95) (". . . , whoever is the opposite feels envy on account of the accomplishment"), following N. Getty, but he quotes also J. P. Elder's *damnat* and A. H. Travis's *in[vidus damnat]*, Degrassi, *ILLRP* (questions the last phrase, but not in *CIL* 1², 2, 4; Ernout offers no text, but translates, "Le bon citoyen loue cet acte, le mauvais en est envieux" ("The good citizen praises this act, the bad is envious of it").

Line 10. *Invid̩[ea]nt, dum q[uos cond]e̩c̩et id v̩[ideant]* Taylor/West ("Let men look askance, if only those who should, look at this monument"), Diehl (no underdots), West (who also quotes F. E. Adcock's *v[aleant]* at the end); *Invid[ea]nt, dum q[uod cond]ecet id v[enerent]* Fränkel *ap.* Lommatzsch, Warmington ("Let men envy so long as they have reverence for what is seemly"), De Rosalia; *Invid̩[ea]nt dum q[ui cond]ecet id v[ideant]* Getty *ap.* Dow, p. 95 ("Let them envy, so long as they see how the feat is creditable"), but Dow notes the difficulty of *condecet*'s indicative mood in an indirect question (p. 94, cf. 100, note 13), so prefers either *q[uos add]ecet* or *q[uos ded]-ecet* ("Let them envy, provided whom it [the achievement] befits, this they see" or " . . . provided whom [namely, themselves] it [their envy] dishonors, this they see"); Degrassi, *ILLRP*, follows Getty and in *CIL* 1², 2, 4 quotes only Getty's text (but attributes it to Dow); *Invideant dum qu[od ded]ecet id v[ideant]* Ernout ("Qu'ils soient envieux pourvu qu'ils voient ce qu'il y a de malséant [dans leur envie"] or [below] "Qu'ils en soient envieux, pourvu qu'ils voient combien cela est malséant") ("Let them be envious provided they see what is unseemly [in their envy]," or "Let them be envious of it provided they see how unseemly it is").

"What no one has (ever before) attempted or carried out [? reading Ernout's spondaic ending *consummavit* despite what is said above], learn, so that we may celebrate a man's deeds. Under the auspices of Marcus Antonius, proconsul, a fleet was taken across the Isthmus (of Corinth) and sent over the sea. He himself (the proconsul) set out for Side (a coastal city in Pamphylia); Hirrus, propraetor, because of the season of the year, stationed the fleet at Athens. Within a few days this was accomplished, with little confusion (and) with great skill and good [or 'simultaneous'] success. He who is upright gives praise, he who is otherwise[11] is envious of the deed. Let them envy as long as they see what is unseemly."

Quisquanst (line 1) is doubly unusual: the *n* for *m* and (as also in *traductast*, line 4) the elision of the *e* of *est* indicated in writing, especially in an inscription[12]—are these here to save space? work? The use of an *(id) quod* clause picked up by *rem* enables the poet to fill out the line and avoid the succession *noscite ut*, impossible without hiatus. The *aa*'s are for long *a* (but only twice), the *ei*'s are for classical Latin's long *i*.[13] Line 3, the order *nomen, praenomen*, is obviously *metri causa*; also *metri causa*, to make a dactyl, the *s* of *profectus* (line 5) must be disregarded, as in Catullus 116, 8. Lommatzsch in *CIL* 1², 2, 2, p. 740, makes Hirrus the boastful hero of the epigram, but this seems wrong: the poet celebrates both men, but first Antonius, superior in command, and then the lower-ranking Hirrus, though no doubt the latter, as in all hierarchies, did more of the work involved.

11. A. H. Travis's objection to "any restoration which by putting a verb after *contra est* makes *contra* virtually a predicate adjective" (quoted by Dow, *HSCP* 60 [1951] 92) seems met by the examples cited by Dow from Cicero in note 8, p. 98, and also by the examples cited in *The Oxford Latin Dictionary* 433, col. 2, s.v. *contra*, sect. 10, b: "(used in pred. to indicate the reverse of a given word or phrase expressed in any grammatical form) otherwise, not, not so."

12. Aphaeresis: cf. Gildersleeve/Lodge, *Latin Grammar*³ 453, 719, 2, Exc.

13. For double *a*, cf. F. Sommer, *Handb. der latein. Laut- u. Formenlehre* (Heidelberg, 1914) 29, 7, or 4th ed. by R. Pfister (1977) 32, 7 (with ref. to the poet Accius [170\-ca. 86 B.C.] as quoted by the grammarian Terentius Scaurus [early second century A.D.], ed. Keil, *Gramm. Lat.* 7.18.12ff.). For spurious *ei* for long *i*, cf. Sommer, 73 *med.*, or 4th ed., 65, 2d par.

10. When Is a Kouros Not an Apollo?
The Tenea "Apollo" Revisited

ANDREW F. STEWART

DEPARTMENT OF ART HISTORY, UNIVERSITY OF CALIFORNIA, BERKELEY

For well over a century, connoisseurs of Greek sculpture have accorded the "Apollo" of Tenea (figure 1) an honored place in the annals of archaic sculpture.[1] And rightly so; its almost miraculous state of preservation, high quality, and air of restrained, insouciant elegance indeed include it among the most engaging statues of its class and period.

1. I owe a debt of gratitude to Kent Weeks for his help with matters Egyptian, to Nancy Tersini for ideas on social context, to Phillip Stanley for generous advice on economic issues, and to him, Anne Stewart, and Michael Tillotson for their patience in reading and criticizing this paper; if I have not followed their suggestions in every case, the responsibility is mine. V. Zinserling, "Zum Bedeutungsgehalt des archaischen Kuros," *Eirene* 13 (1975) 13–33, came to my attention when this essay was already in press. I regret the oversight, but I am pleased to see that her views coincide with mine in several respects, particularly as regards the supposed identification of the kouroi as Apollos, and their role as symbols of aristocratic *arete* and *kalokagathia*.

Fragments of Greek lyric poetry are cited where possible from the editions of D. L. Page, *Poetae Melici Graeci* (Oxford, 1962), and M. L. West, *Iambi et Elegi Graeci* (Oxford, 1972).

In the five years that this article has been in and out of press, a number of further contributions to the problem have appeared, of which the most important are W. Lambrinoudakis, P. Bruneau, et al., "Apollon," in *Lexicon Iconographicum Mythologiae Classicae* 2 (Zurich, 1984) 183–327, and A. M. d'Onofrio, "*Korai* e *kouroi* funerari attici," *Instituto Universitario Orientale. Annali del Seminario di Studi del Mondo Classico. Archeologia e Storia Antica* 4 (1982) 135–70. Bruneau's affirmation of the priority of the generic kouros type over individual manifestations as Apollo and d'Onofrio's stress on the heroic ambience of the Attic graves are both very much in accord with the views advanced in the present study.

When it was discovered in 1846, it was axiomatic that archaic males of this type represented Apollo. This identification was facilitated by the fact that only three other such statues were known: the colossal Apollo of the Naxians on Delos (*K* 12, first described in the early fifteenth century), an unfinished torso from Naxos (*K* 80n., discovered in 1835), and a quite well-preserved example from Thera (*K* 49, found in 1836).[2] Well-acquainted as they were with the Homeric hymns, where Apollo is described as youthful, athletic, and with long flowing hair, most observers were content to accept that all such pieces were indeed representations of the god.[3] A remark by Ludwig Ross (who had earlier rediscovered the Naxian Apollo) that the Theran statue had been found "near the rock-cut tombs on Mt. Exomytis" was simply ignored.[4]

In the following years, despite growing murmurs of discontent,[5] further discoveries within the sanctuaries of Apollo seemed to confirm the accepted identification. In fact, only after Arthur Milchhöfer took the

2. In the text, *K* followed by a number designates a catalog entry in G. M. A. Richter, *Kouroi*, 3d ed. (London, 1970).

3. *Hymn to Pythian Apollo* 270–71 (449–50); for bibliography and discussion, see W. Deonna, *Les "Apollons archaiques"* (Geneva, 1909) 9–11.

4. L. Ross, *Inselreisen* (Stuttgart, 1840–1843) i.8.

5. See Conze and Michaelis, *AdI* (1861) 80; Loeschke, *AM* 4 (1880) 304.

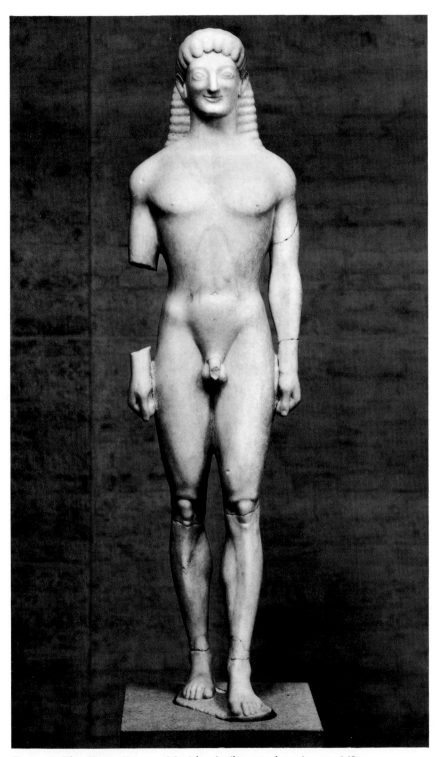

Figure 1. The Tenea Kouros, Munich, Antikensammlung, inv. no. 168 (photo: Koppermann 168, 1).

trouble during a stay at Corinth in 1880 to visit the actual findspot of the Tenea "Apollo," which turned out to be the cemetery of Athikia,[6] did widespread doubt begin to set in. By 1895 Leonardos could suggest "kouros" as a replacement for "Apollo,"[7] and by 1909 Deonna could state with full confidence in his definitive study of the subject that "just as the korai are impersonal representations of Woman, . . . so are these statues impersonal representations of Man, captured in the full bloom of his youth, unbearded, entirely nude, resplendent in the sheer glory of his beauty and bodily power."[8] Finally, in 1942 came the first edition of Richter's *Kouroi*, which all but made the new term a byword.

Yet the pendulum of scholarship is never still, and the recent appearance of two handbooks on archaic sculpture has re-opened the controversy once more. In 1977 B. S. Ridgway presented an eloquent and provocative case for believing that the type may have been understood as an Apollo after all and that its introduction may have been connected with the spread of his cult in later seventh-century Greece.[9] Yet simultaneously Burkert categorically regarded the identification as impossible from a religious point of view, and in 1978 Boardman independently restated Deonna's interpretation with equal force and cogency in his survey of archaic Greek sculpture.[10] Half a decade has now passed with no more extensive review

of the issue; where better, then, to take up the gauntlet than under the scrutiny of Dick Amyx, master of iconography.

First, let us briefly rehearse the facts, such as they are:

(1) The type was introduced circa 650 B.C., almost certainly from Egypt, which was only properly opened to Greek mercenaries, traders, and travelers under Psammetichos I (664–610). Produced in marble from the start, it soon replaced a homegrown type, the *kolossos*, posed like a guardsman "at attention" and sometimes apparently carved at large scale in wood. The kouros is first documented in two islands in the Naxian orbit, Thera and Delos, and somewhat later in Samos.[11]

(2) As normally defined, the type shows a nude, beardless youth walking with left leg advanced, feet flat on the ground and parallel to one another, arms by his sides, and head erect and facing to the front. It persists essentially unchanged for almost 170 years, though after circa 500 B.C. the hair, previously worn long, is either cut shorter or rolled up. Whether long or short, the hair may be bound by a fillet or, very occasionally, a *sakkos*.

(3) Canonical kouroi like these carry no attributes, though the type is sometimes adapted to indicate specific subjects. Mortals may hold offerings or other objects in the hands, with the arms flexed if necessary (see, for example, K 14 and 162, holding a ram and jumping weights respectively); Kleobis and Biton wear boots (K 12), perhaps to characterize them as farmers or travelers.[12] As for gods, so far only Apollo has been cer-

6. *AZ* (1881) 54.

7. *ArchEph* (1895) 75 n.1.

8. Deonna, *"Apollons"*, 15, quoting Lechat.

9. B. S. Ridgway, *The Archaic Style in Greek Sculpture* (Princeton, 1977) 49–59. She repeats this opinion in her article "Of Kouroi and Korai, Attic variety," *Hesperia* 20 (1982) 118–27, arguing in addition that the Akropolis korai were "not Athenian aristocratic girls, *ergastinai* or *arrephoroi*, but Nymphs or lesser deities in distinctive attire; they may have originally portrayed a major goddess, but their meaning became diluted into generality in the course of the 6th century in Athens" (pp. 126–27). As will become evident, I feel that this sequence of events should be reversed.

10. W. Burkert, *Griechische Religion* (Stuttgart, 1977) 225–26; J. Boardman, *Greek Sculpture: The Archaic Period* (New York, 1978) 22–23.

11. Discussion and documentation, Ridgway, *Archaic Style*, 23–24, 29–34, 46; most recent assertion of Egyptian origin, J. Boardman, *The Greeks Overseas* (London, 1980) 144.

12. C. Vatin has recently suggested that these two are the Dioskouroi: *BCH* 106 (1982) 509–25. If so, then boots would be appropriate to them as travelers, as Professor Amyx points out to me. Yet following a visit to Delphi in July 1983 my inclination, like that of the Berkeley epigraphists whom I have consulted, is to be skeptical.

tainly identified in this schema.[13] The gigantic dedication of the Naxians to Apollo on Delos (*K* 15) once held a cylindrical metal object, presumably a bow, in his left hand, and so probably represented Apollo,[14] while the Piraeus bronze (*K* 159bis) advances his right leg, lowers his head, and holds what appear to be the remains of a phiale and bow.[15] Pictures of kouros-like Apollos on coins and bases show other attributes, and texts add more.[16]

The Naxian Apollo wore a belt, a feature he shares with half-a-dozen other seventh-century marble kouroi from Thera and Delos (*K* 17, 18B-D and figs. 20–24; see figure 2) and a bronze statuette in Delphi (*K* figs. 14–16).[17] Since all but one were found in contexts connected with Apollo, it has sometimes been argued that the belt, too, should be taken as an identifying attribute of his.[18] A fifth-century vase depicting a cult statue of

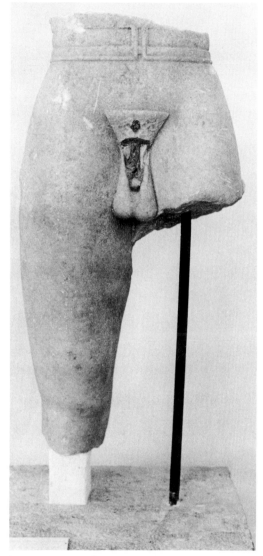

Figure 2. Kouros fragment, Delos, inv. no. A 333.

13. See I. B. Romano, *Early Greek Cult Images* (Diss., University of Pennsylvania, 1980), 391–98, 420–32; Lambrinoudakis, "Apollon," 189–90 and nos. 42–47, 335, 430–34.

14. The inscription (a renewal) reads only "The Naxians *to* Apollo"; the surviving line of the original dedication calls the statue an *andrias*, which could be taken to support its derivation from a generic, "canonical" kouros-type, not vice-versa. For the most recent discussion of *andrias*, see H. Philipp, *Tektonon Daidala* (Berlin, 1968) 106–7.

15. I take this statue to be sixth century and not archaistic, as implied, for example, by N. M. Kontoleon, *Opus Nobile: Festschrift zum 60. Geburtstag von Ulf Jantzen* (Wiesbaden, 1969) 91–98. Note that the lack of inlaid eyes is no argument; see, for example, Boardman, *Greek Sculpture*, fig. 122: a youthful head from Sparta, made circa 540.

16. Coins: Boardman, *Greek Sculpture*, figs. 126, 185; Lambrinoudakis, "Apollon," nos. 30, 51, 392, 395. Vases: K. Schefold, "Statuen auf Vasenbildern," *JdI* 52 (1937) 30–75, esp. 43–44, 46; Lambrinoudakis, "Apollon," nos. 5, 6, 272–73, 428. Reliefs and sealings: M. F. Boussac, "A propos de quelques sceaux déliens," *BCH* 106 (1982) 427–46; Lambrinoudakis, "Apollon," nos. 332, 390. Texts: Pliny, *Natural History* 34.75; Plutarch, *Moralia* 1136A (*De Musica* 14); see Romano, *Early Greek Cult Images*.

17. Anne Kuttner also draws my attention to the numerous Cypriot kouroi with bathing trunks. See, for example, J. L. Myres, *Handbook of the Cesnola Collection* (New York, 1914) 154–56, nos. 1040–47 and *AA* (1976) 29, fig. 3, etc.

18. Most recently by Ridgway, *Archaic Style*, 54–58.

Apollo with a belt[19] and the obscure cult of Apollo Zoster in Attica (Pausanias 1.31.1) have been taken as confirmation.

The question is complicated. The seven marbles are apparently not among the very earliest kouroi, which rather undermines the hypothesis that Apollo (belted or not) is the éminence grise behind the type. Also one

19. BM E 336: *ARV²*, 1010, no. 4; Schefold "Statuen," 43, fig. 7; Richter, *Kouroi*, fig. 1.

Figure 3. The "Auxerre" Kore, Paris, Musée du Louvre, inv. no. MA 3098 (photo: Louvre 79 En 6657).

(Thera, △, *K* 18D) was definitely found in a cemetery. In addition, at least three other vase-paintings show equally archaic-looking statues of Apollo,[20] but none wears a belt, and neither does the Piraeus Apollo (*K* 159bis). Finally, these belted kouroi seem to have had very restricted currency, and not merely in numbers: all eight pieces date from around 640–600 B.C., and the seven marbles are generally accepted as Naxian work. The statuette is more difficult to localize, but it may be Cretan.[21] The belt itself is Cretan in type, appearing on both earlier and contemporary draped figures from Gortyna, Prinias, and elsewhere, as well as on the Auxerre kore (figure 3).[22] Even more suggestively, it also turns up on a mid- or late-seventh-century bronze statuette of a kilted man in a kouros pose from Phaistos, now in Oxford (figure 4).[23]

In my view, all this tends to point to a passing fashion inspired by contact with nearby Crete, contact that prompted some Naxian sculptors to try to indicate clothing in an abbreviated way that would not compromise the nudity of their kouroi. This, together with the fact that the fashion was so short-lived even in the Cyclades and never caught on elsewhere, in turn suggests that nudity was regarded as a sine qua non of the kouros type, that it was, in a sense, an attribute.[24] I shall return to this point later.

(4) Canonical kouroi may serve equally as votives and as grave markers, like every other archaic statuary type, human, animal, or monstrous.[25] Yet in the case of votive kouroi

Figure 4. Bronze Statuette of a Kilted Man, from Phaistos, Oxford, Ashmolean Museum, inv. no. 1933-1569.

there is no close correlation with the sex of either the recipient divinity or the donor, and in the case of funerary kouroi there is no close correlation with the age of the deceased. While the great majority of votive kouroi do come from areas traditionally linked with Apollo (Naxos, Delos, Delphi, the Ptoion sanctuary, Didyma, etc.), where hard evidence exists, these kouroi cannot be connected with the first flourishing of the sanctuary;[26] furthermore, kouroi appear in

20. *ARV*², 203, no. 101, p. 599, no. 8, p. 1683, no. 31 bis.

21. C. Rolley, *Museum of Delphi. Bronzes* (Athens, n.d.) 19, no. 23.

22. Cf. Boardman, *Greek Sculpture*, 23 and figs. 28, 30, 32.

23. J. Boardman, *The Cretan Collection in Oxford* (Oxford, 1961) 119–21, no. 527; a wooden version with a tunic from Samos, Richter, *Kouroi*, fig. 17.

24. Cf. for a different emphasis Ridgway, *Archaic Style*, 53–54.

25. Noted by C. Karouzos, *Aristodikos* (Stuttgart, 1961) 30; cf. Ridgway, *Archaic Style*, 177. In terms of format, only the tall, narrow stele is confined to one function, namely, as a grave marker.

26. Best documented at the Ptoion: J. Ducat, *Les Kouroi de Ptoion* (Paris, 1971), 439–42.

the domains of other male gods (for example, in the sanctuary of Poseidon at Sounion) or even goddesses (for example, the Heraion at Samos).[27] As grave markers, kouroi do seem to have stood exclusively over the tombs of men, though the Midas Epitaph (*Anthologia Graeca* 7.153) reminds us that on at least one occasion a kore could serve the same purpose. In addition, and in stark contrast to the varied characterization of men on archaic gravestones, the funerary kouros was given no attributes regardless of whose tomb it crowned (see, for example, *K* 134, 136).

(5) The kouros is most unevenly distributed: it is thick on the ground in some areas (Boeotia, Attica, the Cyclades, Samos), all but unknown in others (the Peloponnese, Crete). Some prefer to use it as votive (Boeotians), others to stand it over their graves (Athenians), while still others employ it for both purposes alike (Therans, Samians).[28]

So, then, the true kouros has no attributes, no exclusive functions, and no easily explicable pattern of distribution. Indeed, the very fact that it has to be furnished with attributes to depict specific personalities like offering-bearers, athletes, or Apollo, indicates that no particular identity can be attached to the basic type.

What is one to make of this string of negatives? The answer, though inescapable, seems almost banal; the kouros is basically meaningless—or rather, its significance must lie in its only distinguishing characteristics, namely, its nudity, its youth, its beauty, its autonomy, and its immutability: in other words in its *form*. Hence, perhaps, its varied popularity. As a man for all situations yet obligatory in none, the kouros could be called on or not as the need arose, at the particular whim of the clientele, and for a variety of purposes. Clearly for the "true"

kouros meaning in the normal sense of precise signification is a secondary matter, acquired only (if at all) from context: in this it finds precise parallels in other motifs borrowed by the Greeks from Near Eastern sources, as, for instance the sphinx, the lion and the bull fight, and the battle between lion and man.[29]

Let us turn, then, to form. It is easy to misinterpret the nudity, youthfulness, and beauty of the kouros as manifesting a preoccupation with descriptive naturalism—a red herring if ever there was one. Indeed, for forty years the kouros has been considered, at least in Anglo-American scholarship, as primarily or even solely a vehicle for anatomical experiment and display. Yet, as Ridgway aptly notes, it is only in Attica that sculptors show "definite interest in musculature. . . . All other kouroi present abstract renderings of anatomical forms which may pass for natural but are rather simplifications or more or less convincing stylizations of the human body."[30] *Qua* image, the kouros was quite clearly numinous, even fetishistic, and anatomical exactitude was but one of the ways, and hardly the most important, by which sculptors could attain their goal. This, I believe, was the presentation of youthful beauty itself, of youthful *style*.

In this context, considering how expensive a kouros must have been and who its main clientele obviously was,[31] it is astonishing that it has so seldom been linked to that consuming obsession of archaic Greek upper-class thought, *arete*, and its constituent ele-

27. Sounion: *K* 2–5; Samos: B. Freyer-Schauenburg, *Bildwerke der archaischen Zeit und des strengen Stils* (*Samos* 11, Bonn, 1974), nos. 29–57; *BCH* 105 (1981) 860–61, fig. 175.

28. For a good summary, see Ridgway, *Archaic Style*, 46–49, 149–50.

29. Cf. J. Carter, "The Beginnings of Narrative Art in the Greek Geometric Period," *BSA* 67 (1972) 25–58, esp. 45–48; F. Hölscher, *Die Bedeutung archaischer Tierkampfbilder* (*Beiträge zur Archäologie* 5, Würzburg, 1972) 7–13, 100–104.

30. Ridgway, *Archaic Style*, 54.

31. Certainly other than aristocrats could commission kouroi (for example, Euthykartides the sculptor and Sombrotidas the doctor, *K* 16 and 134); note in this context the increasing complaints about the forwardness of the *plousioi* and *kakoi* (for example, Solon fr. 15 West, Anakreon fr. 388 Page, Theognis 149–50, 153–54, 183–92, 315–22, etc.): aping one's betters was as much a characterization of the parvenu in Archaic Greece as in any other society.

ments of personal autonomy and both moral and physical beauty and nobility, which to later generations became a catchword: *kalokagathia*.[32] Thus in Homer beauty, nobility, autonomy, and heroism are indivisible, as (in the person of Thersites, *Iliad*, 2.211–277) are their opposites. Two hundred years later Simonides is even more specific: opening a poem devoted to the problem of *arete*, he states bluntly that the noble man must be in "hand and foot alike foursquare / an ashlar cut without flaw" (fr. 542, 1–3 Page). Concomitantly, Theognis can preface his moralistic elegiacs to the handsome young aristocrat Kyrnos with the words:

> What is beautiful is loved, and what is not is unloved. (Theognis 17)

The message is aristocratic and exclusive, both literal and moral, replete with homosexual innuendo, and attributed by Theognis to the Graces.[33] A better commentary on the varied satisfactions offered by the kouros could hardly be imagined.

So what of the kouros's much-vaunted association with Apollo and his sanctuaries? Theognis himself calls Apollo "fairest (*kallistos*) of immortals" and anxiously prays to him for "due measure of youth" (5–7, 119–122). This is revealing: Greek culture was nothing if not a youth culture,[34] and, projecting its predispositions onto Olympos, the Greek people literally worshiped youth in the form of Apollo. As Burkert succinctly remarks, the fact "that youth itself, the kouros, become an ideal is what gives Greek culture its specific stamp; purified and elevated this ideal manifests itself in the Divine: the god of this culture is Apollo."[35] One need look

no further as to why Apollo, of all gods, is both honored with kouroi and himself appears in this guise by preference.[36]

This yearning for youth and the consequent drive to express and to perpetuate youthful beauty and nobility in sculpture may provide a key to the diverse local schools of kouros-making: each, in fact, pursues its own ideal of youthful *kalokagathia*. Naxos admires youths who are svelte, curvaceous, lean, and harmoniously proportioned; Parians prefer a powerful, barrel-chested athleticism; in Boeotia the going mode is vigorous, angular, almost brutal at times; and so on. From the mid-sixth century these styles begin to cross-fertilize each other, as sculptors and patrons alike discover merit in the ideals of other regions,[37] and here the Tenea "Apollo" is a perfect example.

In my view, its sculptor was probably trained on Paros.[38] His figure has the long torso with strongly oblique, V-shaped groin capped by two oblique pads of muscle, constricted waist, and swelling sides of Parian kouroi (cf. *K* 116: figure 5), as well as their rounded, heavy pectorals that swing out-

---

32. Archaic attitudes to *arete* and its constitutents are best summarized, in my opinion, in H. Fränkel's *Early Greek Poetry and Philosophy* (Oxford, 1975), index pp. 532–33; see also A. W. H. Adkins, *Merit and Responsibility* (Oxford, 1960).

33. Commentary, Fränkel, *Poetry and Philosophy*, 402, 418.

34. On this point, see esp. G. Devereux, *Symbolae Osloenses* 42 (1967) 76, 90–91; cf., for example, Alkman's celebration of the beardless Hagesidamos in fr. 10(b) Page.

35. Burkert, *Griechische Religion*, 226. John Board-

man reminds me that early Apollos in the islands are usually bearded—a further problem for those who would see him in these early kouroi; cf. Lambrinoudakis, "Apollon," 314 and e.g. nos. 625, 662.

36. It is legitimate to ask why Hera at Samos was honored with kouroi and Athena on the Akropolis was not: could it be because the former was worshipped at the Heraion in her roles as mother and bride (see H. Walter, *Das Griechische Heiligtum* [Munich, 1965] 20–22; H. Kyrieleis, *Führer durch das Heraion von Samos* [Athens, 1981] 13–18), while Athena was a virgin? Note the naked Astarte-type girls also dedicated to Hera on Samos: U. Jantzen, *Ägyptische und orientalische Bronzen aus dem Heraion von Samos* (*Samos* 8, Bonn, 1972), pls. 14–17; one can hardly imagine these on the Akropolis.

37. Cf. Ridgway, *Archaic Style*, 64.

38. Others, too, have seen varying degrees of island style in the piece: cf. Deonna, *"Apollons"*, 189, Ridgway, *Archaic Style*, 70. In this context I cannot resist mentioning that Prokesh Osten's quotation, in the first "publication" of the statue (*AdI* [1847] 503), of Pausanias's remark that the Teneans worshiped Apollo over all other gods because they traced their lineage back to captives from the Trojan War (Pausanias 2.5.4), led Migliarini to speculate that the piece was "in all probability imported from Troy" (*AdI* [1849] 159)!

Figure 5. Kouros from Paros, Paris, Musée du Louvre, inv. no. MND 888 (photo: Louvre 79 En 6656).

ward in front of the armpit to form in profile a prominent triangle, and their epigastric arch in the form of a parabola, its apex connected to the navel by a deeply modeled median line. The neck, too, is thick, and the skull is somewhat quadrangular, with a square chin and compact, though rather shallowly modeled, features.[39] Yet the massive build favored on Paros has been tempered somewhat: the hips and waist are finer, the chest juts rather less, the shoulders are

39. Dr. Francis Croissant tells me that terracottas from Paros are typically modeled in this style too.

narrower and slope a little more. The surface modeling is also somewhat softer, and the features are more delicate, imparting rather an East Greek flavor to the piece. All in all one's impression is of a youth who is muscular and well built, but at only five feet tall, he is no hulking strongman. Athletic yet graceful, he combines the best of both worlds with an elegance that is virtually unequaled in archaic sculpture.

The Tenea kouros was a grave-statue. As Karouzos has shown, such statues could be regarded as *agalmata*, gifts to delight the dead, who could perhaps find in such a gift some compensation for their fate.[40] In any case, the Tenea youth probably stands for the dead man, reminding him, his family, and the casual passer-by of the *akme* of his life on earth and thereby perpetuating it for all to see. Here its very lack of specificity except in the matters of youthfulness, nudity and beauty both registered the demands of the context in particular and answered to deeply ingrained attitudes about human existence in general. Perhaps this was why the type became popular as a grave marker as soon as it appeared in Greece.

Here, two specific points are actually at issue: life versus death, and youth versus old age. Achilles put the first to Lykaon on stark terms:

> Do you not see how beautiful and great a man I am
> Born of a great father and an immortal mother?
> Yet one day death and my fate will overtake me
> Some morning or afternoon or noontime
> At the cast of a spear, or with an arrow from a bow.
>
> *Iliad* 21.108-13.

One is reminded of the stark dichotomy between a kouros such as Kroisos (*K* 136), striding forward resplendent in all his youthful beauty and prowess, and the epigram at his feet:

> Stay and mourn at the tomb of dead Kroisos, whom raging Ares

40. Karouzos, *Aristodikos*, 28–30.

Destroyed one day, as he fought in the foremost ranks.

But old age could hold terrors equal to, if not worse than, Hades:

> We are as leaves in jeweled springtime growing
> That open to the sunlight's quickening rays:
> So joy we in our span of youth, unknowing
> If God shall bring us good or evil days.
>
> Two fates beside thee stand; the one hath sorrow,
> Dull age's fruit, that other gives the boon
> Of Death, for youth's fair flower hath no tomorrow,
> And lives but as a sunlit afternoon.
>
> Mimnermos fr. 2 West (tr. J. A. Pott).

Yet if the prospect of death was so unpleasant, why, like the Tenea kouros, do many funerary kouroi smile? Here, once again, we are confronted with a phenomenon that, like the kouros type itself, is apparently polyvalent. For not only can votive statues smile but also figures in narrative friezes and in pediments as well, even when they are fighting and dying.[41] Clearly the smile invites, on the basis of some intrinsic quality or qualities that it directly manifests, the same kind of explanation as did the kouros itself. Here, a most satisfactory suggestion was offered by Kenner over twenty years ago, but it has yet to find a place in English-language scholarship, so far as I am aware. On the basis of a mass of documentation she concludes that "archaic statues are *automatoi*, they can move of their own accord and are filled with a secret life, with 'something godlike,' as Pausanias remarks (2.4.5). The most obvious expression of this magic life-force is, in my opinion, the 'smile.'"[42]

41. Examples: Boardman, *Greek Sculpture*, figs. 187.3 and 5 (Corfu, Zeus, and dying Titan), 193 (Bluebeard), 194 (Introduction pediment), 198 (Olive-tree pediment), 199 (Gigantomachy pediment), 250 (Eretria), 206.4 (dying warrior, Aegina west), 211 (Siphnian treasury pediment, Herakles), 212 (Siphnian treasury gigantomachy), 213 (Athenian treasury metopes), 215.2 (Megarian treasury, falling giant), 232–35, 237 (gravestones).

42. *Weinen und Lachen in der griechischen Kunst* (Vienna, 1960) 66; cf. Boardman, *Greek Sculpture*, 66. It may be relevant here to point to the first-person ad-

Of course, none of this excludes the smile from acquiring a more specific meaning or meanings in particular contexts; in fact, rather the opposite. Thus, if the Tenea kouros smiles, it may be because in death he is now *makarios*, "blessed," alive in a paradise away from the cares of life;[43] it may be because an *agalma* to a dead man should naturally be smiling and lively in order to delight him; or it may be a matter of simple wish-fulfillment on the part of the living, whereby, as celebration of the vivacity and joy of life's "jeweled springtime," it consoles those who remain. These three options are neither exhaustive nor mutually exclusive; as is the case with most other peoples, Greek ways of coming to terms with death were neither consistent nor constant, and it is quite likely that according to local or personal belief, the smile may have appealed to contemporaries on more grounds than one.

For the votive function of the kouroi, one may turn for elucidation to their partners in service, the korai. Here Schneider's recent work, supported by a wealth of texts, is persuasive.[44] As the author of the Homeric *Hymn to Delian Apollo* expressly states, the Ionian men and girls gathered to dance, sing, and sacrifice in his honor are gracefulness incarnate, appearing deathless and unageing, while Apollo in his turn delights in their gathering.[45] As with the grave-markers, precise circumstance is not addressed by such votives; what matters is that the person, as an offering to the God, should be beautiful. The smile is a part of this vivacious beauty and grace, and as such it is a necessary part of an *agalma* to the god.[46]

In this context it has been remarked that the enormous size of some of the votive kouroi "can hardly have been understood as a portrayal of a normal human being even if dedicated to a divinity, but must have suggested the divinity itself." [47] There may be unexpected truth in this. Canonical and belted kouroi of truly colossal size, ranging from eight to twenty feet in height, have been found at Sounion (*K* 2–5), Naxos (*K* 50), Samos (*K* 24, 25, 78, 79, 127a, and others[48]), Megara (*K* 92), and Thera (*K* 18A-D). Yet no such monsters have appeared in Apollo's great sanctuaries at Delphi, the Ptoion, Didyma, and Delos (I exclude the Naxian Apollo, *K* 15, by definition), and none of those listed above can be directly connected

---

dress ("Ich-Rede") popular on statue-inscriptions and elsewhere: "I am Chares, son of Kleisis, ruler of Teichioussa . . ." (Boardman, fig. 95). This likewise suggests a kind of animism, the kind that in other walks of life led the Greeks to see a god in a river, or to animate mirror supports as human figures or table-legs as lions' paws. It also chimes with their idea that craftsmen and their creations were divinely inspired and so somehow numinous, "seeming to be alive" (compare Hephaistos's tripods, *Iliad* 18.368–80, and Pandora, Hesiod, *Erga* 60–82 and *Theogony* 571–84): cf. Philipp, *Daidala*, chs. 1 and 3 with copious references. On the urge to animate in Greek thought see esp. R. Carpenter, *The Esthetic Basis of Greek Art* (Bryn Mawr, 1921), ch. 1; and for different views of the "Ich-Rede," see M. Burzachechi, "Oggetti parlanti nelle epigrafi greche," *Epigraphica* 24 (1962) 3–54 (animistic); A. E. Raubitschek, "Das Denkmal-Epigram," *Fondation Hardt, Entretiens* 14 (Geneva, 1968) 3–36 (dedicator speaks through his dedication); M. L. Lazzarini, "Le formule delle dediche votive nella Grecia arcaica," *Atti della Accademia Nazionale dei Lincei. Memorie. Classe di Scienze morali, storiche e filologiche.* Ser. 8.19.2 (1976) 171 (metrical convenience); Hölscher, *Tierkampfbilder*, p. 100 also stresses the animism of archaic sculptures, this time in the context of lion-groups.

43. See E. Vermeule, *Aspects of Death in Early Greek Art and Poetry* (Berkeley, 1979), 72–73; on the "godlike" nature of the smile, see L. Schneider, *Zur sozialen Bedeutung der archaischen Korenstatuen* (Hamburg, 1975) 27–29, with bibliography. Curiously, Richter, *Kouroi*, does not discuss the smile at all, while Ridgway, *Archaic Styles*, seems to leave her promise to do so (p. 14) unfulfilled.

44. See Schneider, *Bedeutung*.

45. *Hymn to Delian Apollo* 146–55; L. Schneider (see above, note 43) 5–7.

46. Schneider, *Bedeutung* 27–29; cf. the smiling dancers on the Didyma and Ephesos column drums, Boardman, *Greek Sculpture*, figs. 219–20, and note in this context that on the Introduction pediment Herakles smiles—as well he might—but Zeus does not: Boardman, fig. 194.

47. Ridgway, *Archaic Style* 67.

48. Freyer-Schauenburg, *Bildwerke*, nos. 30, 31, 34, 47; the recently discovered kouros dedicated by Ischys (Kyrieleis *Führer* 25 and fig. 32) measures rather over 5 metres in height, and seems to make a pair with the fragments Richter, *Kouroi*, entries 24, 25, and 79 (all from the same kouros: Freyer-Schauenburg, 61–65, no. 29A-C, pls. 16–17).

with Apolline worship: the Sounion kouroi are most probably offerings to Poseidon and the Samian ones (by far the largest) are from the Heraion. Indeed, the complete absence of giant kouroi at the four great Apolline centers, and the fact that the Naxian Apollo's identity was clearly indicated by attributes, might suggest that they were *not* considered appropriate offerings to Apollo, either because they resembled him too much for comfort or because they smacked of *hubris*, or both. Clearly, it would not be sensible both to upstage and to annoy the archer-god right in his own domain.

In fact, I suspect that the dedicant intended such magnification of scale in the first instance simply to seek a proportionate increase in the pleasure experienced by the recipient divinity, by presenting him or her with a truly "godlike" image: *isotheos* is a powerful word of commendation for mortals from Homer onwards,[49] and heroes were regularly imagined as being of gigantic stature. Of course, the dedicant's stock with both the god and his fellow men would also rise in proportion, though murmurings of *hubris* were no doubt heard in some quarters, especially as resentment of aristocratic arrogance and excess intensified. In this context it is worth noting that most of these giants belong to the early years of kouros-making, and none seems later than circa 550 B.C.

In sum, it seems to have been the kouros type's very *lack* of specificity that occasioned its enormous popularity in archaic Greece. For not only could it fulfill, with equal success, two quite different functions (votive and funerary) but it was also easily adaptable to serve as an image of a god. Apollo was a particular favorite here, since he represented quite literally the apotheosis of the physical and moral qualities desired in the perfect man and mirrored in the kouros itself.

Yet this was not all. There were secular satisfactions to be had from the kouros—homosexual titillation apart. As prestige pieces ordered by the upper-class elite, whether lifesize or colossal, they portray its members, by implication, as *isotheoi*—completely autonomous, ageless, beautiful, and happy.[50] As Schneider has argued for the korai, they work to enhance the solidarity of that elite, to stress its unity and uniformity, and to present a united front to lesser mortals, its detractors and enemies included.[51] To this end, the kouroi testify not only to the wealth and the "godlike" physical beauty and power of the upper classes but also quite literally to their closeness to the gods themselves, placed as they are in their sanctuaries.[52] As symbols of a united, ageless, and all-enduring elite of individually brilliant men and women (witness the great diversity in hairstyles, facial types, and—in the korai—dress), these statues both concretized and perpetuated the values of this elite from generation to generation, buttressing it and its members against the world at large.

Yet if the kouros indeed functioned as something of a generalized aristocratic symbol, why is it almost entirely absent from the Peloponnese? The Tenea kouros apart, only Kleobis and Biton (*K* 12A-B), and a few rather miserable torsi and fragments (*K* 41, 73, 91, 163a, and others), survive to show

49. See most convincingly, D. Roloff, *Gottähnlichkeit, Vergottlichung und Erhöhung zu seligem Leben* (Berlin, 1970). For *isotheos* in Homer see, for example, *Iliad* 2.565 (Euryalos), 3.310 (Priam), 4.212 (Machaon), 9.211 (Patroklos), 11.472 (Ajax), 23.569 (Menelaos).

50. On the values of the archaic aristocracy, see esp. C. J. Starr, *The Economic and Social Growth of Early Greece, 800–500 B.C.* (New York, 1977) ch. 6. It was Nancy Tersini who first alerted me to the possibility that the kouroi might have been as much symbols of the aristocratic status of their dedicators as they were dedications and that their very sameness could have been symbolic of class; see also A. M. Snodgrass, *Archaic Greece: The Age of Experiment* (Berkeley, 1980) 178.

51. Schneider, *Bedeutung*, 35; cf. Starr *Early Greece*, 136 and esp. n. 45 on the solidarity of the archaic aristocracy; intermarriage among the various clans was regular.

52. Compare the numerous occasions in Homer when a hero is called "dear" (*philos*) to the immortal gods: *Iliad* 6.318 (Hektor), 10.527 (Odysseus), 17.203 (Achilles), 20.347 (Aeneas); cf. Fränkel, *Poetry and Philosophy*, for the development of such sentiments in archaic lyric.

that the kouros was even known there at all.[53] Lack of marble cannot be the whole answer: if other centers like Athens, Delos, and Samos could import marble by sea, why could not Corinth, entrepot center of the east Mediterranean as it was, or Argos? If Peloponnesians had been interested in kouroi at all, no doubt we would now be finding them.

One possibility that (to my knowledge) has not been canvassed is that this prejudice against the kouros, which seems also to extend to Aegina and Megara,[54] may not be exclusively Peloponnesian but may be more generally Dorian. Not only do the vast majority of kouroi come from non-Dorian areas of Greece (Attica, the Cyclades, Ionia) but also even the Dorian states of the south Aegean (Crete, Melos, Thera, Rhodes, Knidos) are exceedingly poor in kouroi compared with their Ionian neighbors.[55] Possibly, it could be only because some of these states, like Thera, were near dynamic Ionian centers of kouros-production like Naxos or Paros that they have left us any kouroi at all. Boeotia and Phokis are special cases, being only part Dorian at best, but even here very few kouroi have come to light outside the two great sanctuaries of Apollo at the Ptoion (around 120 kouroi) and at Delphi (a mere 7), and, as in the case of the Tenea kouros and the Melian, Theran, and Rhodian kouroi, Cycladic influence is omnipresent.

So, then, Dorian conservatism, a byword in the fifth century, may have deeper roots than has been previously imagined. Maybe their attachment to wood *kolossoi* and the Daedalic style was stronger than elsewhere. At any rate, the vast majority of *xoana* and *sphyrelata* recorded in the sources are located in Dorian areas, and Daedalic seems to have been particularly at home in the Peloponnese, Crete, and at Rhodes.[56] For offer-

ings, the people apparently preferred tripods or smaller objects, and for grave-markers, the occasional simple stone slab.[57]

Historical circumstance introduced the kouros to Greece, historical circumstance allowed it to flourish there, and historical circumstance was to contribute to its demise. This last event is often described in purely formal terms as if, circa 480 B.C., the time had suddenly come for the kouros to "come alive." This is paradoxical to say the least, since to archaic Greek eyes it was alive already, as we have seen. To be sure, the increasing naturalism of Attic kouroi such as Aristodikos (*K 165*: see figure 6) does sit ever more uneasily with their ancient pose; and the dichotomy between such kouroi and, say, the Kerameikos kouros base illustrated in figure 7 does indeed make the former look antediluvian by comparison, although other contributing factors must not be overlooked. One of these factors seems to have been a reaction against aristocratic rule that, apparently for the first time, manifested itself in certain key centers in the form of specific action against images associated with the traditional aristocracy.

The ancient historians relate that Lygdamis of Naxos helped Peisistratos to come to power in Athens, probably in 547/546 B.C., and that Peisistratos soon returned the favor by installing Lygdamis as tyrant of his home island. Lygdamis then aided Polykrates in yet another successful coup d'état on Samos, possibly around 540 B.C.[58] Now Peis-

---

53. List, Ridgway, *Hesperia* 44 (1975) 428, n. 4.

54. Preserved kouroi, *K* 72, 73, 86, 92, 92A.

55. Preserved kouroi (excluding statuettes), *K* 18A-D, 19, 49, 114 (Thera); 86 (Melos); 124-27, 154 (Rhodes); 177 (Crete); 129 (Kalymnos).

56. See the list in J. Papadopoulos, *Xoana e Sphyrelata* (Rome, 1980) 101-13—though the statistics are

skewed somewhat by the fact that much of our information comes from Pausanias, who only describes Southern Greece; see R. J. H. Jenkins, *Dedalica* (Cambridge, 1936), with Boardman, *Greek Sculpture*, 13–15.

57. J. Boardman and D. C. Kurtz, *Greek Burial Customs* (Ithaca, 1971) 180–83.

58. Herodotus 1.61.64; Polyaenus 1.23.2; cf. R. Sealey, *A History of the Greek City States 700–388 B.C.*, 128, 142–43; on the chronology of the Samian tyranny see R. Tölle-Kastenbein, *Herodot und Samos* (Bochum, 1976) 13–20, and esp. P. J. Rhodes, *A Commentary on the Aristoteliem Athenaion Politeia* (Oxford, 1981) 198, 209–10. My thanks to Frank de Rose for this last reference. H. von Steuben, *Kopf eines Kuros* (Frankfurt am M., 1980), reached me after the completion of this section in 1981; though our arguments coincide to great

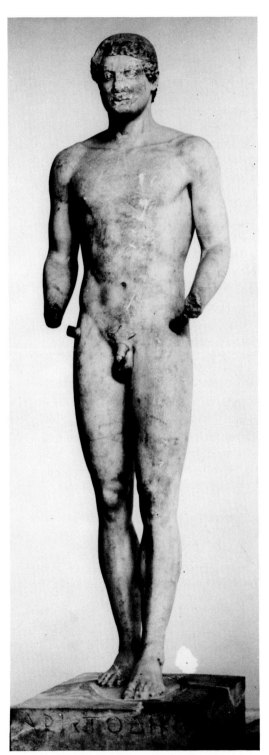

Figure 6. Aristodikos, Athens, National Museum, inv. no. NM 3938.

istratos and his sons seem to have attempted to conciliate their aristocratic rivals, even the Alkmeonidai, who were allowed to hold the archonship under the tyranny.[59] Concomitantly, there is no decrease in expensive dedications and funerary monuments in Peisistratid Athens; indeed, the Akropolis bristles as never before with statuary, funerary kouroi increase in numbers, and grave-reliefs reach unprecedented levels of elaboration.

In the two island states, both prime centers of kouros production for over a century, the situation was very different. It is perhaps no coincidence that on both islands the production of kouroi, hitherto intensive, ends in the same period. Meanwhile massive civic building projects (popular because of the employment opportunities they offered to the demos) get under way.[60] These, together with extensive military expenditures, drove both tyrants deeply into debt, which both tried to assuage by confiscations from their exiled opponents.[61]

Of the two tyrants, Lygdamis was the more inventive:

> having exiled his opponents, he found that no one would give him a fair price for their property, so he sold it back to the exiles. And their dedications, which were lying around the workshops half-finished, he also sold back to the exiles and to anyone else who would buy them, allowing each purchaser to have his name inscribed on the offering.
> (Aristotle, *Oeconomica* 2.1.1346b7–13)

With this and the populist bias of Lygdamis

---

degree, I have decided to retain my text for the convenience of English-speaking readers and those without easy access to his monograph.

59. See Sealey, *Greek City States*, 135–42.

60. The latest comprehensive study of the Naxian kouroi, G. Kokkorou-Alewras, *Archaische Naxische Plastik*, Diss., Munich, 1975, puts the collapse of the school precisely around 540 B.C., but without reference to the text of pseudo-Aristotle quoted below; on the temple of Apollo at Palati, see G. Gruben, W. Koenigs, *AA* (1968) 693–717; (1970) 135–43. On Polykrates' building, see Tölle-Kastenbein, *Herodot und Samos*, 53–82; Walter, *Griechische Heiligtum*, 74–82; Kyrieleis, *Führer* 47–48.

61. For Lygdamis, see below; for Polykrates, see Herodotus 3.44, 57–59, 122–25; Tölle-Kastenbein, *Herodot und Samos*, 23.

Figure 7. Kouros Base from the Kerameikos, Athens, National Museum, inv. no. NM 3476 (photo: Deutsches Archäologisches Institut, Athens).

in mind, it is hardly surprising that the Naxian school of kouros carving came to an abrupt end precisely around 540 B.C., the approximate date of Lygdamis's accession.[62] Polykrates seems to have been less precipitate, though by 525 B.C. large bands of Samian exiles were roving the Aegean, extorting money from Siphnos and elsewhere.[63] Concomitantly, the decline of Samian kouros-production was a little more protracted than was the case on Naxos, but no less final. The last of the half-dozen mostly rather second-rate kouroi made in this period, a potbellied figure of unprepossessing appearance (K 153), dates to circa 520 B.C., when Polykrates' hapless successor Maiandrios was attempting to come to terms with a recalcitrant demos: the mood had changed, the slogan was now *isonomia*, equality of rights, and there was no going back.[64]

In Athens, certain classes of monuments eventually also disappear from the scene, but only after the establishment of the Kleisthenic constitution in 508/507 B.C.: grave-reliefs, funerary kouroi, and votive eques-trian statues seem to be the main casualties. In Jeffery's comprehensive catalog of archaic Athenian funerary monuments, where dates are based on historical, epigraphical, and sculptural considerations independently of politics, nothing is dated after circa 500 B.C. (cf. figures 6 and 7).[65] It is tempting, with Milchhöfer, Friis Johansen, and others,[66] to associate this seemingly abrupt termination of patronage in a hitherto flourishing industry with the funerary legislation discussed by Cicero but only vaguely dated by him to the period between Solon (circa 590 B.C.) and the revival of the grave-reliefs in the late fifth century:

> But somewhat later [than Solon], on account of the enormous size of the tombs which we now see in the Kerameikos, it was required by law "that no-one should make a tomb which required more than three days work for ten men"; nor was it permitted to adorn a tomb with stucco-work nor to place the so-called

62. Latest discussion in Rhodes, *Commentary*.
63. Herodotus 3.44–8, 57–9.
64. Freyer-Schauenburg *Bildwerke*, 4–5 and nos. 52–57; cf. Herodotus 3.142–43.

65. L. H. Jeffery, "The inscribed gravestones of archaic Attica," *BSA* 57 (1962) 115–53.
66. A. Milchhöfer in *AM* 5 (1880) 172; K. Friis Johansen, *The Attic Grave Reliefs of the Classical Period* (Copenhagen, 1951) 120—with bibliography; cf. D. C. Kurtz and J. Boardman, *Greek Burial Customs*, 89–90, 121–22, who remark that plastered earth mounds and built tombs, sometimes with unsculptured stelai, are standard for "rich" graves of the period circa 500–450 B.C.

Herms on it; nor to deliver eulogies of the deceased except at public funerals . . .

Cicero, *de Legibus* 2.64-5.

As for equestrian statues, these were presumably frowned upon by the demos because they quite literally raised the rider above his fellow-men.[67] Almost two hundred years were to pass before the practice was revived, and then the recipients were Macedonians.[68] So, whatever the exact motivation and date of these various disappearances, a strong circumstantial case might be made for associating them with the new drive for *isonomia* in post-Peistratid Athens, a phenomenon already evident a decade earlier in post-Polykratean Samos;[69] in Athens, this manifested itself concretely in the new constitution of 508/507 B.C., and later in the explicitly anti-tyrannical and anti-aristocratic device of ostracism.[70] For its part, the solidarity of the landed elite was weakened by the greater role allotted to city families,[71] the apparent limitation of individual land ownership to within the deme in which one was registered, the consequent appearance of newly landed and enriched men on the scene,[72] and the attempts of the elite's own

Figure 8. Attic Red-figure Cup from Chiusi, Oxford, Mississippi, University Museum (from *Hesperia* 8 [1939] 162, fig. 1).

members like Kleisthenes to cultivate the demos as a political ally.[73]

In a reformist atmosphere of this kind, the elite may well have come to consider the kouros, with all the associations that it evoked, more of a liability than an asset, and because of this they may have simply abandoned it to its fate. If the kouros was indeed banned from Athens (by now almost its only major center of production)[74] around 500 B.C., it would not be the least of the ironies that frequent the history of art if aristocrats themselves had a hand in the affair.

Whatever the truth may be, other modes of sculptural address, powerful in their novelty and untainted by the associations of the

67. On the equestrian monuments see H. Payne and G. M. Young, *Archaic Marble Sculpture from the Akropolis* (London, 1959) 51–52, pls. 11, 16, 134–40; R. A. Stucky, "Überlegungen zum 'Perserreiter,'" *Antike Kunste* 25 (1982) 97–101; cf. Aristotle, Ἀθηναίων πολιτεία 7.4; comprehensive catalog, H. Schrader, *Die archaischen Marmorbildwerke der Akropolis* (Frankfurt, 1939) 212–44, pls. 134–50. Dedication of horses alone seem to continue for a little longer, till circa 480 B.C. (AkrM. 320), and the inscribed bases show that one or two groups of a man *leading* a horse were set up in the later fifth century: cf. A. E. Raubitschek, *Dedications from the Athenian Akropolis* (Cambridge, 1949) nos. 59–177 for inscribed low bases that could have or did carry equestrian monuments, of which nos. 136 and 139 are the only certain post-Persian examples. Chariot groups dedicated after a victory in the games were apparently unaffected: cf. no. 174.

68. The earliest known to me is Asandros of Macedon, *IG* II², 450 (314/313 B.C.).

69. Cf. Sealey, *Greek City States*, 158–59, with Herodotus 3.142–43 (Samos); Tölle-Kastenbein, *Herodot und Samos*, 21, 44, n. 108.

70. Resume, Sealey, *Greek City States*, 164–66.

71. Cf. ibid., 154–55.

72. I owe this and the following suggestion to Prof.

Phillip V. Stanley, who will address the entire issue in a forthcoming book on sources of wealth in archaic and classical Athens, working from statistics culled from J. K. Davies, *Athenian Propertied Families* (Oxford, 1971) and other sources.

73. See, for example, Herodotus 5.66.

74. The Ptoion sanctuary went into swift decline between circa 500 and 480 B.C., and the market for sculpture there evaporated. Theban domination of its affairs may have had something to do with this, but the sources are thin: cf. J. Ducat *Les kouroi*, 448–50.

kouros, were already at hand (figure 8).[75] The Leagros base in the Agora shows that very soon after 500 B.C. this golden boy of the Athenian *jeunesse dorée* had himself portrayed in a new posture, with the right leg

advanced and presumably slightly relaxed.[76] Like his "brothers," the Kritian and Blond boys (*K* 190–191) he was no doubt subtly mobile, pausing as if to think.[77] In these statues the stereotyped, automatonlike stride and blithe optimism of the kouroi have given way to a new individuality and a calculated introspection. Even in Athens, the archaic world and the upper-class solidarity that had sustained it were now finally over.

75. Cup in Oxford, Mississippi (ex-Baltimore, Robinson): *ARV²*, 177 (Kiss ptr. no. 3); A. Raubitschek, *Hesperia* VIII (1939) 155–64, fig. 1. The connection— or not—with the Agora base is highly controversial: see, most recently, E. D. Francis and M. Vickers, "Leagros Kalos," *Proceeding at the Cambridge Philosophical Society* 207 (1981) 97–136, pl. 1. Of course, action statues as such were nothing new: compare, for example, the Ugento Zeus of circa 520 B.C. (N. Degrassi, *Lo Zeus stilita di Ugento* [Rome, 1981]) and its companions on the Foundry Vase and elsewhere. Seen from this perspective, Leagros and his fellows are positively (and deliberately?) conservative. Cf. Snodgrass, *Archaic Greece*, 182–85.

76. Raubitschek (see note 75).
77. Cf. *K* 156, from Eutresis, whose right leg is slightly relaxed and right hip lowered, and whose torso twists slightly to his left. His right arm was raised to shoulder height (holding a spear?) while his left hand rested on his hip. See most recently, K. Demakopoulou and D. Konsola, *Archaeological Museum of Thebes: Guide* (Athens, 1981) 39, no. 7 and color pl. 5.

11. Figural Pillars: From Asia Minor to Corinth to Rome

CORNELIUS C. VERMEULE III

DEPARTMENT OF CLASSICAL ART, MUSEUM OF FINE ARTS, BOSTON

Introduction

The overlifesized men in eastern dress standing against Corinthian pillars have long stood for Antonine to Severan triumphal art at Corinth (figures 1 and 2). They have been reconstructed as forming part of a row of, evidently, six figures from the upper story of an ornamental facade bordering the Agora. That they are captives or client princes is confirmed by the reliefs of two bases.[1] One shows traditional Roman imperial motifs of mourning females, sad little children, a pile of shields and a helmet, and handcuffed males. The second features a captive and Victoria crowning a trophy.

Two ideal heads of females also survive to indicate that the eastern males were complemented or spaced apart by figures that may have been geographical personifications. They have the swept-back hair and open mouths of divinities on the frieze on the Altar of Zeus at Pergamon. One thinks of Armenia and Mesopotamia, or Parthia and Media, or two near-frontier cities, depending on what

area the Romans were defending when the monument was being planned.

Modern writers have mentioned, time and again, that Roman imperial artists could be specific in urban and military landscapes and frustratingly general in the symbolism of conquest. All that can be said of the eastern group on the base with the woman, child, bound male, and arms is that the helmet is unusual, more Roman than foreign. Perhaps the symbolism is that of a client kingdom subdued after a revolt. The cuirass of the trophy on the second base, a Greek field version of Roman armor with the small, semicircular tabs characteristic of the Severan period, also suggests this. Again, the bases alone would date the ensemble without hesitation to the years 195 to 200 A.D., when Severus fought both the refugees from the army of C. Pescennius Niger and the Parthians under Vologases IV, not to mention the wavering cities and the territories along the frontiers.

The Facade at Corinth

The facade that included these standing architectural figures and the subsidiary panels has been studied in depth, from an architectural and an aesthetic point of view.[2] The

1. I am grateful to Henry S. Robinson and Charles K. Williams, who gave me permission to review the captives. Thanks are due to Mary B. Comstock, John J. Herrmann, Jr., Kristin Anderson, Florence Wolsky, Eleanor Bergin, Michael Padgett, and Emily T. Vermeule for various kinds of help; also to Sheldon C. Binder and Norman J. Selverstone for essential work of restoration in Cambridge. Besides general debits of admiration, I owe much to Professor Amyx for extensive help and encouragement when the Vermeules were in Berkeley five years ago for Emily Vermeule's term of Sather Lectures.

2. F. P. Johnson, *Corinth* IX, *Sculpture 1896–1923* (Cambridge, Mass., 1931) 101–7, nos. 217–26. R. Still-

Figure 1. Eastern Captive or Client Prince, Old Corinth, Museum.

Figure 2. Eastern Captive or Client Prince, Old Corinth, Museum.

structure belongs to the second half of the second century A.D., as early as about 155 and possibly as late as the Severan campaigns of the 190s. The carving fulfills all the expectations of the best Antonine-Pergamene baroque, and the later date is suggested by the traditions of careful workmanship persisting in the conservative ateliers of western Asia Minor.

Professor Richard Stillwell has compared the architectural details of the facade with those of Roman Miletus at the height of the Antonine period. What this further look at the Corinthian facade hopes to demonstrate is that the ensemble is a unique manifestation of the art of Roman imperial Asia Minor in the heart of Greece. Figural pillars of the type of the captives at Corinth appear in Rome in the century from Hadrian to Caracalla. Thus, Corinth can be seen as perpetuating its long-standing role as a place where designs and styles passed from Asia Minor to Italy. This is one of many themes around which Professor D. A. Amyx has built a lifetime of creative scholarship.

The Traditional Attic Figures

Figural pillars in Greece and in the Latin west had a long history of influence from Attic workshops. Attic designs were adopted in Asia Minor in the Roman imperial period, just as they had been in all the arts from Hellenistic times onward. Theaters were a favorite place for incorporating such pillars, but other types of architectural decoration in carved marble, including porches and balustrades set against the heavy stonework or masonry of imperial buildings, included these figures. Architecture in late archaic and classical Greece had already shown possibilities for the human figure functioning as a column or as a part of a pillar. Furniture in the Hellenistic period, from Pergamon to

Pompeii, had broadened the repertory of subjects and had made eastern figures popular.[3] Athens had figures of kneeling Persians supporting tripod basins, and the cities around the bay of Naples featured supports for tables and for sideboards in the form of a young easterner, perhaps Attis, standing in pensive pose against a pillar.[4]

Influence of Attic Architectural Supports

The majority of monumental figural supports in the area of Rome are Attic, and Attica supplied inspiration for such subjects and similar supports from Ephesus to the Peloponnesus. This makes the appearance of a large facade with males in the iconography of northwest Asia Minor and females in Pergamene style at Corinth in the most prosperous decades of the Roman Empire a tribute to the initiative of the city's planners and architects.

The so-called Caryatids of the Erechtheum are the best known and most widely diffused examples of Athenian influence on monumental architectural sculpture in the imperial age. Their role is all the more forceful to modern students of ancient art because both the originals and the generations of copies survive; the latter appear in vastly different contexts, from the balconies of the Forum of

well, chapter 2, in *Corinth* I, part 2, *Architecture* (Cambridge, Mass., 1941) 55–88. The various guides and reports also give vital information.

3. A number of these supports, and further bibliography on them, is collected in an article by me, "Hellenistic and Roman Furniture-Supports" in *Essays and Studies Presented to Dows Dunham* (Boston, 1981) 180–92.

4. J. B. Ward-Perkins, A. Claridge, J. J. Herrmann, A. Herrmann, M. Comstock, F. Wolsky, C. Vermeule, *Pompeii A.D. 79* (Boston and New York, 1979) 161, no. 113; V. Tran tam Tinh, "Les problèmes du culte de Cybèle et d'Attis à Pompeï," in *Neue Forschungen in Pompeji* (Recklinghausen, 1975), 283. The kneeling Persians in Pavonazzetto in white marble and in giallo antico are to be found in Copenhagen, Naples, the Vatican, and Madrid. They all seem to date to the second century A.D. and to relate to the Sileni of the balustrade of the Theater of Dionysos in Athens. See F. Poulsen, *Katalog over antike skulpturen*, Ny Carlsberg Glyptotek (Copenhagen, 1951) 381–82, nos. 546–47; A. Blanco, Museo del Prado, *Catalogo de la Escultura* (Madrid, 1957) 108–9, no. 208-E, pl. 83, and bibliography.

Augustus in Rome to a canal-side facade in the Canopus area of Hadrian's Villa at Tivoli.[5] The Maidens of the Erechtheum were reproduced and circulated almost as manifestations of state and municipal artistic policy in the ages of Augustus (27 B.C. to A.D. 14) and Hadrian (117 to 138). Augustus rose to power when Pasiteles and his pupils were mass-producing Attic art for markets all over the Roman west. Hadrian, who made the title Augustus a virtual second name on his classicistic coinage, could hardly ignore the decorative message of the Erechtheum's south porch. The Acropolis Maidens marched majestically into the repertory of Hadrian's aesthetic collectibles, ready to be copied wherever and whenever the emperor's phil-Hellenic tastes and innovative amateur architecturalism passed the word.

After Hadrian's death, the mantle of Hellenic classicism passed to Herodes Atticus, richest citizen of the age and a Greek honored with portraits wherever his pocketbook reached, including Hadrianic and early Antonine Corinth. His temple to the Triopian or Cnidian Demeter and the tomb of his wife Regilla off the Appian Way, about 165, were natural objects for architectural embellishment. Two Athenian artists, Criton and Nicolaos, were commissioned to produce, in a sleek archaistic style, a set of four or more basket-bearing maidens, Canephorae, whose appearance could well be said to have marked the end of over a century and a half of such suave atticism in all sizes and shapes.[6] Here, too, there appears to have been an Augustan connection. A similar Canephora, dated to the early years of the Christian era, was found in the theater at Tralles (Aidin), again evidently one of a set because another such figure found its way into the ill-fated collection of the Evangelical School at Smyrna.[7]

Attica and Asia Minor: Differences in the Supports

In general, the supports copied from Attic models, most notably the Erechtheum Maidens and the basket-bearing females of the Inner Propylaea at Eleusis during the 40s B.C.,

5. T. L. Donaldson, *Architectura Numismatica: Architectural Medals of Classic Antiquity* (London, 1859) 92. C. Vermeule, *Greek Sculpture and Roman Taste, the Purpose and Setting of Graeco-Roman Art in Italy and the Greek Imperial East* (Ann Arbor, 1977) 5, 9, figs. 2–4 (p. 32 contains a word about the commercial motivation for the eastern figures in the "Stoa of the Colossal Figures" at Corinth and their pan-Mediterranean connections).

The Roman Forum or Agora of Corinth had its own structure that featured copies of one or more of the Erechtheum Caryatids. The structure was west of the south stoa and south and southeast of the west shops. C. K. Williams, II, noted "a copy of one of the maidens from the porch of the Erechtheum (S–74–26), probably of the first century after Christ. Fragments of at least one other suggest that some architectural element exists in the area which, as yet, has not been uncovered in the present excavations." In Society for the Promotion of Hellenic Studies, London, *Archaeological Reports for 1974–75*, 7, fig. 7; C. K. Williams, II, J. E. Fisher, I. Sun Martin, "Corinth, 1974: Forum Southwest," *Hesperia* 44 (1975) 22–23, nos. 26–27, pls. 8, 7 (the Caryatid and a fragment of a head). Another structure in the general area, the southwest corner of the Agora, incorporated a support copied from a different Attic original of the Erechtheum period or slightly later: H. S. Robinson, in *Archaeological Reports for 1960–61*, 8–9, fig.6. The basket on the head of this Caryatid has twisted fluting, the preserved parts having a hole for a metal fountain-pipe running through it. The style of the head recalls that of fountain nymphs and similar decorative figures based on the type named "Venus Genetrix" on coins of Hadrian. All this academic architectural art is far less serious in spirit than the mighty eastern "captives" and their related symbolism.

6. A. H. Smith, *A Catalogue of Sculpture in the Department of Greek and Roman Antiquities, British Museum*, part VII, vol. 3 (London, 1904) 99–102, no. 1746; E. Strong, *Art in Ancient Rome*, vol. 2 (New York, 1928) 130–31, fig. 447.

Corinth long ago yielded its famous, complete commemorative herm-shaft of Herodes Atticus, but Isthmia has given evidence that Herodes' circle of pupils was honored, just as on the benefactor's country estates from Kiphissia to Probalinthos. Prof. P. Clement reports a splendid head of Polydeukes from demolition fill in the south firing area of the Roman Bath: *Archaeological Reports for 1978–79*, 12, fig. 12.

7. G. Mendel, *Catalogue des sculptures grecques, romaines et byzantines*, vol. 2 (Constantinople, 1914) 257–60, no. 541. The Tralles-Cherchel supports were created in Athens and have Hadrianic (?) replicas of the head-type there: see B. S. Ridgway, *The Severe Style in Greek Sculpture* (Princeton, 1970) 144, under no. 6.

Figure 3. Supporting Female from the Inner Propylaea at Eleusis, Eleusis, Museum (photo: Archives, Boston, Museum of Fine Arts).

are virtually freestanding.[8] However heavy and solid these females seem to be, they maintain what Attic classicism admired almost to excess, that is, the clarity and the completeness of the human figure (figure 3). Sculptors in Asia Minor, Syria, and the Holy

Land, doubtless influenced by traditional back pillars in Egypt and by contemporary practices in Syria, notably Palmyra, felt completely at ease with human figures growing out of columns, pilasters, and simple, rectangular slabs. The furniture supports with eastern youths standing against rectangular pillars came to the bay of Naples from western Asia Minor, just as the businessmen of Puteoli paid their own artistic, iconographic tribute to the cities shaken up by earthquakes early in the reign of Tiberius (14 to 37).[9]

About a decade before Herodes Atticus commissioned his archaistic maidens for Regilla's temple and tomb or cenotaph, the Athenians ordered the Tritons and Giants, six symmetrically arranged on either side of three doorways, for the rebuilt Odeion of Agrippa in the Athenian Agora.[10] The mythological monsters were not copies but rather imaginative Antonine baroque creations based on the Poseidon and the Hephaistos of the west and east pediments of the Parthenon. Poseidon and Hephaistos were two of the most powerful elder male divinities represented in Attic art during an age when majestic women (Athena, Demeter) alternated with the quiet clarity of maidens and athletes on the Parthenon frieze or in funerary stelai.

About A.D. 66, in the closing days of that misunderstood actor Nero, Attica and Asia

8. Smith, *A Catalogue of Sculpture*, 101; C. Vermeule, *Greek Art: Socrates to Sulla, From the Peloponnesian Wars to the Rise of Julius Caesar, Art of Antiquity*, vol. 2, part 2 (Boston, 1980) 110–11, 314–15, fig. 156. The Caryatid from Corinth (see above, note 5) had a "pick-dressed band" cut into its back from shoulders to base, for some form of jutting attachment, not application directly to a wall. The figure was originally worked out in the round. The accessible Maidens on the Athenian Acropolis, three of them, were copied selectively: G. Lippold, *Handbuch der Archäologie*, vol. 3, no. 1 (Munich, 1950) 192; M. Brouscaris, *Athens Annals of Archaeology* 1 (1968) 61–64. The Caryatid at Corinth copies the eastside, rear figure.

9. C. Vermeule, "Numismatic Sources and Parallels for the Cities on the Puteoli Base in Naples," in *Festschrift for Bluma Trell* (London, 1981); C. T. Seltman, *Cambridge Ancient History*, Volume of Plates IV (Cambridge, 1934) 138–39, pl. [b].

10. I. T. Hill, *The Ancient City of Athens, Its Topography and Monuments* (Cambridge, Mass., 1953) 76–77; H. A. Thompson, *The Athenian Agora, A Guide to the Excavations and Museum* (Athens, Princeton, 1962) 70–74, pl. 5; B. Ashmole, *Architect and Sculptor in Classical Greece* (London, 1972) 125, fig. 140; J. Travlos, *Pictorial Dictionary of Ancient Athens* (New York, 1971) 365–77. The Tritons and Giants, of course, curve their snaky lower limbs up around heavy, rectangular pillars that had capitals above and behind their heads. As remodeled circa 150, the Odeion of Agrippa showed influences from Italy and from the Ionian coast of Asia Minor. The pillars are mythological, not historical, but the physiques of the figures, as stated, were also conditioned by the greatest traditions of Attic art.

Minor met, decoratively speaking, across the *pulpitum* of the Great Theater at Ephesus. The figures in high relief that set off the slabs showing mythological hunters comprised the Ephesian Amazons and satyrs.[11] Athens and the northern Peloponnesus had contributed freestanding models for Amazons back in the days of Kresilas, Polykleitos, and Pheidias. Satyrs and Sileni were a part of the Athenian decorative scene in Hellenistic times and, most notably, in the reign of Hadrian when the standing or crouching Dionysiac males enframed doors and balustrades of the Theater of Dionysos.[12]

Asia Minor in Rome

The biggest, most famous examples of figural pillars of Greek type in Rome are the pair of Pans from the Theater of Pompey in the heart of early, imperial Rome. These tall, basket-bearing figures were carved in two sections with their back-slabs, like the easterners from Corinth. The Pans were carved of Luna marble, so they could not be imports from Ionia, Mysia, or Bithynia.[13] The last

area was remembered for its cults of Pan in the imperial age. Drillwork and shadowed chiseling show that these Pans were added to the theater complex sometime during the Antonine and Severan periods, at the time when the captives and the personifications were being planned and installed.

Asia Minor at Corinth

Exotic figures in high relief were no strangers to Roman imperial art; witness all the unusual provinces of the podium of the Hadrianeum in Rome.[14] Another temple to Hadrian, the largest such structure in the ancient world, located at Cyzicus in northwest Asia Minor, and its subsidiary porticoes seem to have produced a further wealth of iconographic prototypes.[15] Which eastern

---

11. M. C. Sturgeon, "The Reliefs on the Theater of Dionysos," *AJA* 81 (1977) 46; F. Eichler, *JOAI* 43 (1956–1957) figs. 1, 5–6.

12. M. C. Sturgeon, "The Theater of Dionysos," 31–53, and references, especially 48, 49, figs. 6, 7, and p. 50. Hadrian and Herodes Atticus knew of and exploited the Egyptian tradition in the representations of Antinous at Marathon, in Rome, or at Villa Adriana: see G. Lippold, *Die Skulpturen des Vaticanischen Museums*, vol. 3, no. 1 (Berlin, 1936) pls. 49, 50.
A matching pair of Antinous-like Egyptian figures, 2.04 cm high, was included among the decorative statuary at the Egyptian-style gate, pylons, walls, and small temple in the Micron Elos of Marathon. P. M. Fraser, *Archaeological Reports for 1968–69*, 6–7, fig. 6. A. Vavritsas, *Athens Annals of Archaeology* 1 (1968) 230–34, figs. 6–9. There were also Isiac females of Neo-Attic type, in Egyptian pose and with the traditional back pillar. The whole enterprise was, as has long been recognized, another effort by Herodes Atticus to honor and to rival Hadrian at the same time.

13. H. Stuart Jones, *A Catalogue of the Ancient Sculptures Preserved in the Municipal Collections of Rome, the Sculptures of the Museo Capitolino* (Oxford, 1912) 22, no. 5; 25, no. 23, pl. 2; E. S. Strong, *Art in Ancient Rome*, vol. 1 (London, 1929) 86, fig. 80. The

inspiration, probably enlarged, came ultimately from Athens and was employed, at a maximum height of 1.195 m, in the Temple of Aphrodite at Cyrene: Janet Huskinson, *Roman Sculpture from Cyrenaica in the British Museum* (London, 1975) 24–25, no. 47, pl. 20. The Cambridge University statuette came from the garden below the grotto of Pan at the foot of the Athenian Acropolis: L. Budde, R. Nicholls, *A Catalogue of the Greek and Roman Sculpture in the Fitzwilliam Museum* (Cambridge, 1964) 26–27, no. 49, pl. 11.

14. The "provinces" of the podium are almost perfect manifestations of figural sculpture against rectangular slabs, for they are lined up like symbolic protectors of Hadrian's geographical phil-Hellenism, the way statues of that emperor offered by the same regions stood along the precinct-wall of the Olympieion at Athens, also in reality a temple to Hadrian. See J. M. C. Toynbee, *The Hadrianic School, A Chapter in the History of Greek Art* (Cambridge, 1934) 152–59, pls. 34–36; C. Vermeule, *Roman Imperial Art in Greece and Asia Minor* (Cambridge, Mass., 1968) 430.

15. The Hadrianeum at Cyzicus is a partial enigma because much of the building survived until after Cyriac of Ancona's time and the fall of Constantinople in 1453. The sketchbook from E. P. Warren's and Bernard Ashmole's collections in Oxford shows much more, with greater accuracy than the usual Quattrocento notebook, and various key sculptures have turned up from the site, which was much quarried by the Ottoman builders of Istanbul. C. Vermeule, *Roman Imperial Art in Greece and Asia Minor* (Cambridge, Mass., 1968) 454; C. Vermeule, "Dated Monuments of Hellenistic and Graeco-Roman Popular Art in Asia Minor: Pontus through Mysia," in *Studies Presented to George M. A. Hanfmann* (Cambridge, Mass., 1971) 174.

Figure 4. Head from a Smaller Version of a Similar Figure, Kansas City, Nelson-Atkins Museum of Art (photo: Ross E. Taggart).

eastern youths, who may be based on Mên rather than on Attis.[18] These wings may have given this particular facade or tempietto a seasonal connotation, popular for rows of figural supports in northwest Asia Minor in the Antonine period.

All this evidence from Asia Minor to Rome provided a complete iconographic and stylistic background for the facade at Corinth. The large standing figures were set off by the little rectangular bases with reliefs of subjugation in front, leaving no doubt as to the triumphal connections of the facade. There were even smaller copies or prototypes indicating the popularity of such eastern captives or princes, one, a head, being in the collection of the Nelson-Atkins Gallery of Art, Kansas City, Missouri (figure 4).[19] Corinth could, therefore, blossom forth with a strong statement of imperial triumphal art of the northwest Asia Minor type, as a crossroads to Rome, in an era when Athens and Aphrodisias controlled most figural decoration.

war gave impetus for the Corinthian structure depends on the date of the facade, but it was perhaps the war in Judaea at the end of Hadrian's reign, the eastern campaigns of Lucius Verus in the 160s, or the conflict between Septimius Severus and Parthia thirty years later.

Cyzicus had more than its share of eastern figures standing against pillars. Those figures now in Copenhagen feature Attis standing at regular intervals in front of a temple-precinct wall.[16] They appear to have enriched a shrine of Cybele, which is dated in the second century A.D. A pair of pillars with satyrs was also found.[17] There was also a set of winged

The Pillars of the Severan Bouleuterion at Askelon

If anyone were to think the quality of the young easterners at Corinth too fine to date later than the 150s, he has only to examine the delicate carving of the Nikai on orbs sup-

16. F. Poulsen, *Katalog over antike skulpturen, Ny Carlsberg Glyptotek* (Copenhagen, 1940) 104–5, no. 121, English edition: *Catalogue of Ancient Sculpture in the Ny Carlsberg Glyptotek* (Copenhagen, 1951) 105, no. 121. The whole concept is so much more sophisticated than the Italic, "Telamon"-type console supports in tufa from, say, the Odeon at Pompeii: see A. Maiuri, *Pompeii* (Novara, 1951) pl. 41.

17. P. Devambez, "Deux piliers décorés trouvés a Cy-

zique," *RA* (January-June 1937) 176–94: Istanbul Museum, nos. 4506, 4507. A Dionysos against a rectangular slab probably comes from the theater at Cyzicus: G. Mendel, *Catalogue des sculptures*, vol. 2, 384–85, no. 637.

18. Th. Macridy-Bey, Ch. Picard, *BCH* 45 (1921) 436–70. G. Mendel, *BCH* 33 (1909) 259–62, no. 8; S. Reinach, *Répertoire de la statuaire*, vol. 5, no. 1 (Paris, 1924) 221, nos. 2, 3.

19. Nelson Fund. The marble is given as Pentelic, but I wonder about western Asia Minor. H.: 12½ in. = 0.32 m. C. Vermeule, *Apollo*, vol. 99, no. 147 (May 1974) 316–17, figs. 7, 7A. Since a head of about the same size (H.: 11½ in. = 0.293 m) in Parian marble was found in the Tenuta di Palombaro near Rome, figural pillars with eastern males may have been carved for the imperial villas around Rome, like their earlier counterparts as furniture supports. See Smith, *A Catalogue of Sculpture*, vol. 3, 80, no. 1709.

ported by figures of Atlas from the large ad-
ministrative hall at Askelon. There also survives a relief of Isis with Horns from another
such pillar, although this pillar does not quite
measure up to the quality of the Nikai on
orbs.[20] It was clearly the triumphal motive
rather than the Egyptian gods that interested
the Severan carvers at Askelon. The composition of Nike being supported while standing against a support had also been used,
probably in a symmetrical pair, to enrich the
frames of a door in the wall of the proscen-
ium of the theater at Tralles (Aidin).[21]

Late Antique Pillars

In the late Roman period tastes in figural
pillars shifted to the double-sided reliefs in
the upper stories of buildings or porticoes.
The grandest manifestation dated in the Gal-
lic revival of the late third century, the "Pa-
lais de la Tutelle" or "Piliers de Tutelle" at
Bordeaux, was demolished in 1677. Here
there were twenty-two Corinthian columns
topped by pillars with two figures in relief on
each. The figural subjects on either side of
the pillars or together at the corners included
every manner of divinity and bound captive
found up to this time in Greek and Roman
imperial art.[22]

More ideal in subjects than the figures in
Bordeaux, and more modest in what has survived, the so-called Incantada from the area
of the agora at Salonika, long housed in the
Louvre, must have been constructed during

the early Tetrarchic period, between 292 and
303, when Galerius was building public
monuments to justify selection of the city as
an imperial capital.[23] The flat awkwardness
of the minor female divinities looks ahead to
Constantinopolitan architectural carving
after about 325 and, on a smaller scale, to
ivory plaques all over the Empire.[24]

Conclusion

The facade of the captives at Corinth was
built by some official and his architect who
admired the exotic in triumphal iconography. The Forum of Trajan with its numerous
standing Dacians had made such statues and
reliefs common sights in Rome. The Corinthian planners wanted something more than
the maidens and Sileni of Athens or Villa Adriana. They brought the magnificence of civic
Asia Minor to the greatest city of the Peloponnesus. Corinthians could show that, at
the height of the Roman Empire, they could
still exploit the unusual in a tasteful fashion
and, as they had always done, pass on the
results to the cities of Italy.

Asia Minor also went in for the near-
bizarre in architectural decoration, the
temple to Hadrian at Ephesus being a well-
preserved example. At Izmit-Kandira (Kum-
luköy) in Bithynia, a tempietto featured unusual half-figured pillars. Three-quarter figures of seasons on rectangular bases were

20. M. Avi-Yonah, *The Holy Land* (New York,
1972) 96, 100, 101; Avi-Yonah, *Encyclopedia of Archaeological Excavations in the Holy Land*, vol. 1 (London, Jerusalem, New York, 1975) 126–28, 2 illus. Reinach, *Répertoire de la statuaire*, vol. 2, no. 1 (Paris, 1897)
389, no. 4.

21. Mendel, *Catalogue des sculptures*, vol. 2, 51–52,
no. 290. In June 1986, Emily T. Vermeule called my attention to the pillar of Nike holding up a shield with a
boss and a second shield or a tympanum, in the court-
yard of the Konya Museum.

22. Ch. van Essen, *BCH* 50 (1926) 205–12. E. Espér-
andieu, *Recueil des bas-reliefs de la Gaule Romaine*, vol.
2 (Paris, 1908) 142–44, no. 1089.

23. The heights of these pillars were 2.06 m. They
supported the entablature of a gallery forming the upper
story of the monument. See *Encyclopédie photogra-
phique de l'art, Le Musée du Louvre*, vol. 30, no. 10 du
Tome 3 (Paris, 1 June 1938) 312.

24. The surviving marble Victoria from Constantinople's landward gate is an excellent example. The Vic-
toriae on orbs, holding up images in shields, against the
columns of the consular thrones of ivory diptychs pro-
ject the story of the figural pillar into the sixth century
A.D. See C. Vermeule, *Roman Imperial Art in Greece
and Asia Minor*, 63–64, fig. 25. Victoria against columns, a pair in each panel, on the diptych of Anastasius,
A.D. 517, in Paris, Cabinet des Médailles: C. Vermeule,
"A Greek Theme and its Survivals: The Ruler's Shield
(Tondo Image) in Tomb and Temple," *PAPS*, vol. 109,
no. 6 (December 1965) 389, fig. 46.

tied into the architecture at the lower rear area.[25] Facades such as these might have been acceptable in country shrines, like the Attic, Herodes Atticus's contribution of a rare class of Amazon to a building at Louku in the Peloponnesus.[26] Corinth eschewed such facades in its civic center. Instead, the city took the best from public buildings at Cyzicus or Miletus.

The sestertius of Marcus Aurelius struck at Rome between December A.D. 172 and 173 shows that Rome succumbed to the unusual in temple facades during the decades scrutinized here. Above the inscription RELIG(IO) AVG(VSTI), the front view of a temple shows four columns on a podium of four steps. The columns are in the form of half-figures, like herms or terminal figures, appropriate since a statue of Mercury appears inside and since all the emblems of that god fill the semicircular pediment.[27] Other Roman

Figure 5. Minerva-Victoria, Support from the Domitianic "Porta Romana" at Ostia (courtesy of Ostia Excavations).

imperial coins show that bold, baroque architectural experiments originated in the eternal city with the decoration of funerary pyres. Figural pillars cover the pyre of Antoninus Pius dedicated by Marcus Aurelius in the Campus Martius in the year 161.[28]

---

25. N. Fıratlı, in M. J. Mellink, "Archaeology in Asia Minor," *AJA* 70 (1966) 159, pl. 42, figs. 18, 19: brought to the Izmit (Nicomedia) Museum. We first saw them with Nezih Bey in 1961.

26. See Reinach, *Répertoire de la statuaire*, vol. 2, no. 2 (Paris, 1898) 425, no. 4. S. Karouzou, National Archaeological Museum, *Collection of Sculpture, A Catalogue* (Athens, 1968) 66, no. 705: "It was found before 1830 in the Monastery of Loukou in Kynouria (Thyreatis), where Herodes Atticus had a villa. This would have been on the propylon of one of his buildings."

27. H. Mattingly, *Coins of the Roman Empire in the British Museum*, vol. 4 (London, 1940) 628–29, nos. 1441–48, pl. 83, 7; Donaldson, *Architectura Numismatica*, 91–93, no. 25. This type of building must have created a mild stir in Antonine times, for it certainly shocked the early Victorians: "Amid all the caprices of ancient art, and within a few years after the classic temple of Antoninus and Faustina [in the Roman Forum] had been erected, it is impossible for those who have studied the monuments of ancient taste, to suppose that this frontispiece represents the elevation of a temple. It is true that the triple temple of the Athenian Acropolis [the Erechtheum] has its caryatid adjunct, but the details are pure in design, and refined in execution, and redeem the original questionable conception. But there is something so ungraceful and undignified in a terminal figure, and the circular pediment appears so at variance with the canons and all existent examples of sacred art of this period, that we can only satisfactorily account for the irregularity by supposing it a licence allowable in a subordinate detail," Donaldson, *Architectura Numismatica*, 91–93. The facade of the captives at Corinth was neither cute like the tempietto of the sea-

sons near Nicomedia nor bizarre like the temple of Mercury commemorated by Marcus Aurelius in Rome. For a building in Greece, it was grand, noble, and unusual.

28. Donaldson, *Architectura Numismatica*, 176–83, no. 47. From the days of Hephaistion and Alexander the Great, Greek and Roman sculptors used the temporary luxury of funerary carts and pyres for flights of architec-

The monumental architectural pillar fronted by an unusual mythological figure seems to have reached Ostia from Asia Minor on its way to Rome, in the reign of Domitian (81–96). An impressive figure, a triple-crested Athena with huge wings, may have been an early, unorthodox representation of Dea Roma conceived in a manner pleasing to Domitian's cult of Minerva (figure 5). A reconstruction of Ostia's "Porta Romana" shows this pillar in the attic or upper story, on the right-hand side of the broken entablature flanking the inscription and over the

arched gate below. No trace of the complementary or pendant figure has been found.[29]

Corinth, it may be stated again, witnessed the passage of unusual architecture from east to west and chose one of the finest of these facades for the heart of the civic areas in her great crossroads city.[30]

---

tural fancy that otherwise would have had to wait for years to be translated into the architectural enrichment of permanent buildings.

29. E. Strong, *La scultura romana da Augusto a Costantino*, vol. 1 (Florence, 1923) 132; and *Art in Ancient Rome*, vol. 2 (New York, 1928) 67; C. Vermeule, *Studies in Roman Imperial Numismatic Art* (London, 1953) fig. 47; R. Meiggs, *Roman Ostia* (Oxford, 1960) 66–67. For the graphic reconstruction, see G. Calza, G. Becatti, *Ostia* (Rome, 1955) 72, the pillar on p. 73, and the accompanying text, p. 24, where less certainty is voiced about the details of reconstruction.

30. Mixed assessment of Attic and western Asia Minor sources: A. Boëthius and J. B. Ward-Perkins, *Etruscan and Roman Architecture* (Baltimore, 1970) 378.

12. The Corinth Chariot Krater and Some Relatives

EMILY VERMEULE

DEPARTMENT OF THE CLASSICS, HARVARD UNIVERSITY

It is with hesitation that one offers to such a connoisseur of vases as D. A. Amyx a discussion of a connection in an uglier and more bizarre field than his own, especially when the connection was noticed long ago.[1] However, the Mycenaean pictorial krater with chariots and groom, from the Byzantine and Mycenaean pit behind the Julian Basilica at Corinth, is more important than its record of publication might lead a student to suppose, and its odd short-hand devices may deserve another look.

When Professor Weinberg published the big amphoroid krater (figures 1, 2, and 3) in 1949,[2] along with the fragments that assure its early-thirteenth-century B.C. context, he drew attention to the near-singularity of the vase on the Greek mainland and explored its possible relationship with the pictorial painters' workshops at Berbati.[3] The mass of pictorial fragments from the 1913–1914 excavations at Tiryns was still unpublished, the fragmentary chariot krater from Mycenae was still unexcavated, and the examples in Furtwängler and Loeschcke were all sherds, so that the Corinth krater was, at the time of its discovery, practically the only near-complete vase of its kind in a clear stratigraphic context that could be compared to the numbers of chariot kraters known from Cyprus. Professor Weinberg stressed the importance of the find for the continuing discussion of where such kraters were made, and Mrs. Immerwahr argued eloquently for the priority of the Argolid in the manufacture and the development of pictorial styles.[4] Now, with the discovery of a closely related krater in the 1971 excavations by the Evangelistria Church in Nauplion,[5] the authority and the wide circulation of mainland chariot kraters can no longer be doubted, and the Corinth krater emerges as a bold eccentric member of a larger group.

The Corinth vase, with its very tall neck (figure 1), is an almost top-heavy example of the kind of amphoroid krater that went out of fashion in the second quarter of the thirteenth century B.C. and was normally re-

---

1. S. A. Immerwahr, *Archaeology* 13 (1960) 9, figs. 8 and 9, juxtaposed the pictures of the vase from Corinth and a krater from the Metropolitan Museum and remarked on their similarity.

2. S. Weinberg, "Investigations at Corinth, 1947–1948," *Hesperia* 18 (1949) 155–57. The dimensions are max. h. 0.385 m, d. 0.336 m. The vase was republished by Immerwahr, *Archaeology*, note 1; E. Slenczka, *Tiryns* 7 (1974) pl. 44.1; F. Vandenabeele and J.-P. Olivier, *Les Idéogrammes Archéologiques du Linéaire B* (Paris, 1979) 131f., fig. 89a-b.

3. While much of the Berbati pictorial is unpublished, Å. Åkerström has illustrated samples in *Bericht über den VI. Internationalen Kongress für Archäologie* (Berlin, 1939) 296f.; "En Mykensk Krukmakares Verkstad," *Arkeologiska Forskningar och Fynd* 1 (1952) 32–46; *Atti e Memorie del 1° Congresso Internazionale di*

Micenologie 1 (Rome, 1968) 48–53. Three of the published chariot kraters are earlier than the Corinth krater, LH IIIA:2.

4. *Archaeology* 13 (see above, note 1).

5. E. Deïlaki, *Deltion* 28 (1973) Chron. B 1, 90–93, pl. 90 st.; *BCH* 102 (1978) 669, fig. 68; *JHS ArcRep* (1978–1979) 18, fig. 22.

placed by the open bell krater. It stands early in a series of nine mainland Late Helladic IIIB kraters with scenes of chariots or horses and grooms, with more to come from Berbati. Besides Corinth and Nauplion the productive sites are Mycenae and Tiryns, as usual, and there are two unrelated pieces from Kopreza in Attica.[6] The clear, quick, stylish drawing on the Corinth krater is not the work of a novice, and the charge that it is by a painter "unused to such subjects" represents a justified observation on the rendering of the chariots, which is probably to be explained in another way.[7]

On each side the curious chariot moves left, carrying three people; on the fuller side (figures 1 and 2) it is preceded by a groom between two tall, elaborate palm flowers. On both sides there are running broken spirals above the reins; on the more fragmentary side there is an antithetic spiral under the horses' bellies and a row of triangles pendent from the reins. The bodies of the long, weak horses are joined, their heads are separated, and their split legs are sunk deep through the triple ground line so that the chariot wheel moves just above the lowest band. The horse heads are long, thin, and bulbous at the nose, and the manes are dressed in three characteristic plumes. The harness is interesting for the large ladder-patterned rein ring, outlined in dots, displaced from the yoke (since pole and yoke are not rendered) to the backs of the horses' necks; the four reins attach here and then start again from the front of the necks rising at a sharp angle up to the muzzles. This is one of the Mycenaean documents that tend to confirm Mrs. Littauer's suggestion that chariot teams were some-

Figure 1. Mycenaean Chariot Krater, Old Corinth, Museum.

times driven, not with bits, but with dropped nosebands, applying pressure on the nostrils, which might on occasion be slit to compensate for blocked air.[8] The breastband is enriched with white, more conservatively than on the slightly later krater from Mycenae.[9]

The human figures in the chariot are drawn as spotted footless cylinders with a pronounced bulge at the top rear of the torso to represent the shoulder-arm mechanism; they have reserved heads (twice above dark necks) with ruffled dark hair laid flat across the skulls, curved prong noses, dot-circle eyes, and quick bumps for the chins. The groom in front of the team, a figure very popular in the early thirteenth century, is drawn in the new style of the era, with a similar reserved head but solid from eye to foot, the broad shoulder line shrinking to a single thin stroke for the front of the torso so that the action of the arms is visible where the body bulk is reduced; two thirds of the figure is made of long powerful legs with bulging but-

6. These are classified in the Ripe period in E. Vermeule and V. Karageorghis, *Mycenaean Pictorial Vase-Painting* (Cambridge, Mass., 1982), as distinguished from the Transitional period of the later thirteenth century, for which the Mycenae krater is a model (see below, note 15); there are at least twenty-eight Transitional kraters and fragments, and at least forty-one of the Late, LH IIIC period.

7. F. Stubbings, *Mycenaean Pottery from the Levant* (Cambridge, 1951) 33.

8. M. A. Littauer, "Bits and Pieces," *Antiquity* 43 (1969) 291f.

9. See below, note 15.

Figure 2. Detail of Krater in Figure 1.

tocks and sharp knees like horse hocks.[10]

All is normal and practiced here, except for the chariot (figure 3). The traction system is reduced to two arcs, the lower arc being the horses' tails, which connect to the wheel and function as the pole-support, and the upper arc apparently being the pole-brace on which the driver and the first passenger stand. The box of the dual chariot is drawn as two small spotted fan shapes in the V-angle between the pole-brace and the wheel, and the second passenger, in the first of these compartments, is sharply reduced in size to fit under the painted loop around the handle root. It is curious, considering the schematic reduction of the chariot, that the rear projection, which in earlier pictures probably represented the end of the pole running under

Figure 3. Detail of Krater in Figure 1.

the chariot floor, is still maintained as a small square support between box and wheel.

Apart from the chariot, the style of drawing is very close to the work of a vase painter whose recognized work includes three kraters found in Cyprus, the new krater from Nauplion, and, probably, a scrap from Ugarit. The best known of these vases is the Cesnola amphoroid krater in the Metropolitan Museum (figure 4) with a spiral-breasted "goddess" behind the chariot instead of the

10. The most exaggerated form of this style is the dancing (?) man on the jar fragment from the Argive Heraion, C. Waldstein, *The Argive Heraeum* II (Cambridge, Mass., 1905) pl. LV. 47. Static figures make the reverse emphasis, all shoulder and torso, slight leg; see, for example, Slenczka, *Tiryns* 7 (1974) 25, no. 39, fig. 6, pl. 8.1d.

Figure 4. Mycenaean Chariot Krater, New York, Metropolitan Museum of Art, inv. no. 74.51.966.

Figure 5. Mycenaean Chariot Krater, Rochester, Memorial Art Gallery of the University of Rochester, inv. no. 51.204.

usual fronded palm flower.[11] A simpler scene, the near-twin of the Nauplion krater, decorates the fine vase in Rochester (figure 5), which was acquired by Frederick Morgan in Cairo but was photographed earlier in Cyprus, with other pictorial vases, one from Enkomi.[12] It was probably in Cyprus, not on the mainland, that it received matt purple dipinto signs on the lower body. A third, fragmentary krater from Enkomi (figure 6) is probably by the same painter, and the scrap from Ugarit depicting the spiral-breasted

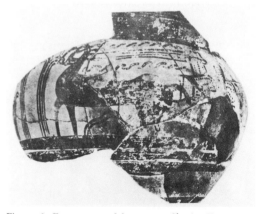

Figure 6. Fragmentary Mycenaean Chariot Krater, Enkomi, inv. no. T.3/1.

"goddess" should be related.[13] These vases share the same stately palm flowers, broken running spirals above (and below) the reins,

11. Metropolitan Museum of Art 74.51.966 (CP 1405), A. Furtwängler, G. Loeschcke, *Mykenische Vasen* (Berlin, 1886) 29, fig. 17 (reversed); D. Fimmen, *Die kretisch-mykenische Kultur* (Berlin/Leipzig, 1924) 97, fig. 82; S. Immerwahr, *AJA* 49 (1945) 545f.; *Archaeology* 13 (1960) 9, fig. 9; A. Furumark, *The Mycenaean Pottery* (Stockholm, 1950) motive 1.10, 1.17 (reversed); G. M. A. Richter, *Handbook of the Greek Collection*[2] (Cambridge, Mass., 1953) pl. 4g; S. Iakovides, *AJA* 70 (1966) 46; Vandenabeele and Olivier, *Idéogrammes* 102, fig. 65. The painter of this and the following vases is listed by Vermeule and Karageorghis (see above, note 6) as Painter 30.

12. Rochester 51.204, V. Karageorghis, *The Memorial Art Gallery of the University of Rochester, Gallery Notes* 17, no. 5 (1952) and *BCH* 93 (1969) 162f.

13. Enkomi krater, Swedish Excavations Tomb 3/I, V. Karageorghis, *Opuscula Atheniensia* 3 (1960) 143, pl. 6.1–2; Slenczka, *Tiryns* 7 (1974) pl. 43.2. Ugarit fragment, C. Schaeffer, *Ugaritica* 2 (1949) fig. 124.4.

Figure 7. Mycenaean Chariot Krater, Nauplion, Museum, inv. no. 1971 T.B.

Figure 8. Mycenaean Chariot Krater from Ugarit, Paris, Musée du Louvre, inv. no. AO 20376

Figure 9. Fragmentary Mycenaean Chariot Krater, Mycenae.

the team's split legs sunk deeply through the framing bands, the low-riding wheel, the spotted bolster bodies with flat ruffled hair and prong noses. The Enkomi krater has the ogival ornament under the bellies; the Rochester and Nauplion (figure 7) vases have circles in the upper quadrants of the wheel. The differences from the Corinth krater appear in the more canonical dual chariots, spotted boxes with a concave front, with driver and passenger in each section from waist or knee level up. The details of hitching are fairly odd but consistent, the pole-brace attached to the horses' rumps with the pole-support dangling loose from it vertically; each team has two tails arching close to the wheel like carpentered elements, an idiosyncracy that might lead to the curious solution on the Corinth krater.

The painter of the Corinth krater is not alone in shrinking the static parts of his chariot, pushing the driver toward the horses, and emphasizing the parts that move and work together, but he is among the first. The famous "chained bird" krater found at Ugarit (figure 8) is another with three people riding, the driver shown from the waist up out on the dangling pole-support; it is contemporary.[14] The slightly later fragmentary krater from Mycenae (figure 9) sets two "chariots" back to back by the handle.[15] On

14. Louvre AO 20376; C. Schaeffer, *BSA* 37 (1936–1937) 212f., figs. 1–3, and *Ugaritica* 2 (1949) pl. 35, figs. 89–90; V. Karageorghis, *AJA* 62 (1958) pl. 101, fig. 10; S. Benton, *JHS* 81 (1961) 48; J. L. Benson, *AJA* 65 (1961) pl. 109, figs. 45–46; P. Demargne, *The Birth of Greek Art* (New York, 1964) 257, fig. 355. Benson attributes the vase to his Bamboula Painter.

15. A. J. B. Wace, *BSA* 48 (1953) 6, pl. 1b; W. Taylour, *BSA* 50 (1955) 266, no. 36; H. Wace and C. Wil-

Figure 10. Fragmentary Mycenaean Chariot Krater from Tiryns, Nauplion, Museum, inv. no. 13 208.

Figure 11. Fragmentary Mycenaean Chariot Krater from Tiryns, Nauplion, Museum inv. no. 13 214.

the left the working parts of the chariot are reduced to a single line projecting from the team's rumps, with driver and passenger balanced on it from the waist up; on the right the "box" is two small spotted ovals on a similar line. Since the box is nearly eliminated, the team's tails can curl around behind the chariot wheel, acting as pole-brace and pole-support.

These new thirteenth-century distortions perhaps spring less from naïveté or a disintegrating tradition than from a new urge for expressiveness. The painters highlight the chariot masters and their horses, cutting out the fussy distraction of the box and traction system, keeping the wheel as an essential moving part; it is the mechanical parallel to the groom figures, whose static torsos are reduced while their long powerful legs are exaggerated. These are the forerunners of the same devices, or desires, in Geometric painting. The merger of men and horses conveys the idea of a dashing operation without the drudgery of full representation. The end of

the process is seen on a pair of Late Helladic IIIC kraters from Tiryns:[16] on the first (figure 10) the chariot box exists, bridging the wheel and the horses whose tails hang down as the pole-support had on the Nauplion group, and the driver holds the reins in his mouth; on the second (figure 11) the chariot is gone, and three human figures perch directly on the team's backs.[17] The Corinth krater seems to represent the beginning of a trend toward the emphatic shorthand formula, successful enough on occasion, although the better later painters take a different, more meticulous path.

The close relationship between the Corinth and Nauplion kraters and the distribution of the latter painter's work in Cyprus and possibly at Ugarit do something to document the spread of merchandise from Argolid pictorial workshops. There is clear evidence for the same pattern in the workshops of a bird painter at Mycenae in the four-

liams, *Mycenae Guide* (1963) pl. 11; C. M. Bowra, *Horizon* (1961) 81; S. Marinatos and M. Hirmer, *Crete and Mycenae* (New York, 1960) pl. 234; M. Davidson and L. Cottrell, *Horizon Book of Lost Worlds* (New York, 1962) 278; H. Catling, *AJA* 72 (1968) pl. 22.12.

16. N. Verdelis, *ArchEph* (1956) par. 6, figs. 10–11; Slenczka, *Tiryns* 7 (1974) nos. 85–86, pl. 3.1, 2, pl. 4.

17. Slenczka, *Tiryns* 7 (1974) 42, argues for riders.

teenth century B.C., a chariot painter at either Berbati or Mycenae, also in the fourteenth century B.C., and in the workshops of two bull painters at Tiryns in the thirteenth century B.C.[18] Since attributions and work-

shop assignments are still relatively rare in the field of Mycenaean pictorial painting, and the mechanisms of the trade in such vases are consequently still largely hidden from us, the Corinth chariot krater assumes a special importance in economical and historical terms, as well as for its curious, experimental formulas.

---

18. In Vermeule and Karageorghis, *Mycenaean Pictorial Vase-Painting* these painters are listed as 4 (bird krater at Mycenae, I. Papademetriou, *Praktika* [1950] 220, fig. 23; from Enkomi, BM C 372, *CVA* British Museum 1, pl. 9.4); 15 (bull krater from Berbati, Nauplion Museum 11 628, H.-G. Buchholz and V. Karageorghis, *Altägäis und Altkypros* [Tübingen, 1971] no. 1024; from Tiryns, N. Verdelis, *ArchEph* [1956] par. 7, fig. 14; jug from Tiryns, Slenczka, *Tiryns* 7 [1974] no. 41; from Enkomi, BM C 416, *Catalogue of Vases* I.2, 86; C 583, *CVA* British Museum 1, pl. 16.3; Pierides Collection 42, *CVA* Cyprus 2, pl. 5, 1–3); 19 (Tiryns krater, Slenczka, *Tiryns* 7 [1974] no. 84; krater from Klavdhia, BM C 399, *CVA* British Museum 1, pl. 6.16, and Pierides Collection 34, *CVA* Cyprus 2, pl. 6, 1–3). Painter 9 is more complicated; his charioteers are found at Berbati and Mycenae; then there are two at Maroni on Cyprus, one at Tel Dan, one at Tell el-Ajjul, and one at Miletos, the widest spread for any identified painter, whose workshop is apparently firmly fixed in the Argolid (Berbati, Å. Åkerström, "Krukmakares Verkstad," 35, fig. 5 [see above, note 3]; Mycenae, J. Crouwel, *BSA* 67 [1972] 99, fig. 1, pl. 30a; Maroni, BM C 358, 359, *Catalogue of Vases* I.2, 71; Tel Dan, A. Biran, *Israel Exploration Journal* 20 [1970] 92; Tell el-Ajjul, Stubbings, *Mycenaean Pottery from the Levant* [1951] 86, fig. 33; Miletos, C. Weickert, *VI. Internationalen Kongress* [see above, note 3] [1939] pl. 24).

13. On the Evidence of Style

PATRICIA LAWRENCE

SCHOOL OF ART, LOUISIANA STATE UNIVERSITY, BATON ROUGE

J. D. Sandys, contributing an article on vases to the English edition of Seyffert's *Dictionary of Classical Antiquities*, availed himself of the evidence of its inscriptions to place the Dodwell pyxis (*Necrocorinthia* NC 861) in the "earlier half of the seventh century B.C."[1] In 1891, the study of vase painting was past its infancy (if only for late archaic and classical styles), but most classicists still took into account but rarely evidence obtained from the laboratory, from the methodology of art history, or even from field archaeology unless to illustrate Pausanias.

Less than a century later, Classics as conceived by our grandparents is by some felt to be endangered by an academic conglomerate of social, computer, and laboratory sciences, but the evidence of style is sometimes no better understood, even among those working with figured pottery, than it was a century ago.

It is reasonable to call "objective" things that anyone possessing the requisite faculties can verify and to call "subjective" that which can be verified only by and in its conscious subject.[2] One's friend is as real as any fossil; he is harder to classify or to tabulate. The style of the Hermes at Olympia is as objectively real as the chisel marks on his back, and if we could fully understand both the style and the technical traits, they would lead inevitably to a single, true conclusion as to the date of the Hermes. The history of Corinthian commerce, the evidence of epigraphy, and the contextual and stylistic study of Corinthian vase painting today are all equally conducive to an early-sixth-century date for the Dodwell pyxis.[3]

The fine dating, however, depends on style. This is because figural style is incomparably more complex and distinctive than letter forms and more abundantly available. Unlike the literary testimonia for early Cor-

---

1. *A Dictionary of Classical Antiquities*, from the German of Dr. Oskar Seyffert, revised and edited, with additions, by Henry Nettleship, M. A. and J. E. Sandys, Litt.D., London, 1891. According to the Preface, p. iv, the article for the entry *vases* was newly written by Sandys. The date and the reasoning are from Dodwell himself, *Tour Through Greece*, vol. 2 (London, 1819) 199.

In 1981, when this essay was written, Payne's *Necrocorinthia* (1931) deserved a jubilee. It appeared only forty years after Sandys's article. It is easy today not to give full credit to Payne's brilliant accomplishment and originality.

Preaching begs an excuse. This essay owes its existence to temporary limitations on time and travel that at the time of writing prevented new research or even an attempt to say the last word on the Chimaera group. What I have written is presumptuous, but it would be unpardonable if it were not offered to D. A. Amyx, to whom it owes whatever is not wrongheaded. It could not have been written without the generosity of the Avery Library, Columbia University, and the Institute of Fine Arts, New York University, the free use of which was granted to me in 1980–1981. Thanks also are due to the Reverend Mother Mary Christabel, C. H. S.

2. In *AJA* 63 (1959) 353, on NC 1048, the writer herself misused "subjective." Despairing of reducing reasons for the attribution to readable prose, she took this refuge, wrongly, since the sources of the "impressions," which she proceeded to list in part, are right there, on the plate. Birgitte Rafn, *Acta Archaeologica* 49 (1978) 154, n. 25, saw the same evidence.

3. NC 861 ("NC" refers to the catalogue of *Necrocorinthia*); the Dodwell Painter has been Amyx's lifelong companion: "Dodwelliana," *CSCA* 4 (1971) 1–48.

inth, figural style is, whatever its shortcomings, primary evidence and, again, much less fragmentary than the historical tradition.[4] Despite imperfect unanimity, it still is more consistent and far more exact in its results than laboratory analyses: "The Dodwell pyxis was made in Corinth at about 600–590 B.C." A laboratory would be content solely to isolate the clay or to pronounce on the antiquity of the glaze-paint.[5]

The excavator with sherds in a foundation trench wants a *terminus post quem*, which he may obtain from an art historian. But is it "objective"? In the first place, how does one know that this scrap of a feline forepart is by the same artist at the same point in his career as the all but complete vase in Munich? If we want confirmation of our dating, we may have profiles drawn. Profile drawings (even of wall sherds from a pyxis) are interesting and helpful, though we do not know whether painters and potters always worked as teams, and even unknowable factors, such as the potter's working at a wheel of a slightly different height or the different texture of two batches of clay, could affect the profile quite meaninglessly with respect to dating. We seek to confirm stylistic evidence with tables of profiles as something that can be controlled and drawn up, but profiles, just because they are less personal, are more subject to chronologically irrelevant accidents than is the artist's style.[6] The

art historian does not neglect tabulated evidence, but he is, perhaps, surprised when a series of Corinthian profiles, by itself, is eloquently unambiguous.

Style is "the man himself."[7] Some personalities are strong and emphatic, so that his admirers recognize a great actor even when he appears in an anonymous bit part. Even a great man is not recognized by those who have not followed his career, but recognized or not, he is, objectively, very much himself. Many more are like minor regional painters of modest but real distinction, the delight of true cognoscenti who hope to collect their work by bidding moderately at auctions. Though the escalation of antiquities prices as much as the desirability of preserving the evidence of grave groups precludes collecting Corinthian vases so pleasurably, most of the better vase painters are of this class. A Macmillan Painter is as rare as a Brygos Painter and as easy to recognize, but Corinthian vase painting in general demands the devoted expertise required for the connoisseurship of good minor landscape paintings. Yet the stylistic personalities are not less objectively real because they are modest. At the bottom, of course, are personalities that only their mothers could discern; the art historian will sort these into groups, if he can.[8]

Implicit in the foregoing statements are requirements that the student of European painting takes for granted: thorough training in method, much practice, and an eye for style to begin with. If you couldn't distinguish typical passages of Schumann and Chopin, you would be ill equipped to go into musicology. If you went ahead and fed their

---

4. Needless to say, we should have no *dates* at all, but only relative chronology, without the foundation dates derived from written history. Probably we shall never be more certain than we are now of the absolute date for the fall of the Kypselids or the foundation of Selinus (see G. M. A. Richter, *Korai* [London, 1968] 25, for a useful summary and bibliography).

5. See D. A. Amyx, "The Case of the Dunedin Painter," *CSCA* 1 (1968) 13–34, especially the last four pages.

6. Even when we have whole series of profiles of complete vases, the evidence of archaeological context and style is still needed to determine whether variant models are successive or concurrent and how long they remained in vogue. Without the corroboration of stratification and animal style, we could have had little confidence in interpreting the kotyle profiles, *Corinth* VII, 2, 76–77, figs. 1–2, or the collection of oinochoai illus-

trated in the same work, pls. 46–56 (not to mention the coarse pitchers on pls. 77–78).

7. J. D. Beazley, *ABV*, Introduction, p. x: "The phrase 'in the style of' is used by some where I would write 'in the manner of': this has warrant, but I was brought up to think of 'style' as a sacred thing, as the man himself."

8. The word *group* is used in all the literature on vase painting in two ways, as here for sorting related substylistic figure work and as below for stylistic associations of recognizable hands.

harmony to a well-programmed computer, after months of work you might confirm what any musician hears. No mystique is invoked; we are variously endowed, though like any infant prodigy, the "born connoisseur" needs to be taught and tested. No one is born with discipline.

Undisciplined writing that claims the evidence of style is gravely offensive to those who lack the special training and the "eye" to control it. Sufficiently irritated, they will pronounce it subjective, wishful thinking, a private game, and reject good and bad together.

It is perfectly true that when an expert in style finds the true place of a work of art, whether on sight or after months or years of puzzling, he sees the solution all at once, entire. He nonetheless is obliged to retrace his steps deliberately and to isolate the component traits and qualities productive of the coherent stylistic impression that his memory matched correctly from its ordered store of images.[9] Further, he must go to all lengths to help the reader to verify his insight, setting forth the isolated elements in the clearest, plainest way possible. If he cannot do so, rigorous reexamination is in order. If he suspects special pleading in his own arguments, he should doubt their validity. The study of style is perfectly objective, but its practitioners are as prone to human weaknesses as any other scholars.[10]

If the writer has any authority in presenting these principles, she owes it all to D. A. Amyx and learned it first on a group of especially handsome Corinthian vases—the Chimaera group, which continues to attract scholarly attention. In fact, the principles enunciated ex cathedra can be illustrated from the literature on the Chimaera Painter and the styles related to his own, for several questions remain open.[11]

* * *

First, there is the specialist's uncanny seeming knack of attributing tiny fragments. He cannot, in fact, do so unless the preserved part reveals something decisive. *Corinth* VII, 2, An 95 is betrayed by its line quality, and its fabric and its syntax match others of the Chimaera Painter's plates; the Ny Carlsberg plate[12] is also decorated on both faces. With these two in the list, we no longer shall suppose that the combination of a vertical composition on the face with a tondo on the bottom is evidence of lateness. Corinth KN–55, a tiny bit of a votive plaque, preserves so telling a part of the Chimaera Painter's feline jaw that its highly plausible reconstruction was made without the slightest difficulty.[13] A

---

9. See below, following the discussion of generic and personal style. If the certainty given by insight is absent, no amount of checking will bring conviction, but if the experience of insight cannot be confirmed methodically, it may well have been illusory.

10. A treatise on method cannot be put in a footnote. Here are some favorite working rules: (1) Show, don't tell; if they don't look right together, no quantity of argument will help. (2) Use "foils"; that is, to learn which similarities are significant, bring into comparison some roughly contemporary work, not specially related. This is a good way to get started on the right track, one that H. R. W. Smith taught in his pots courses at Berkeley. (3) Do a lot of drawing; your camera is not really an extension of yourself and will not help you to get inside of or memorize the style. Think while your draw; try to make the same number of strokes, drawn in the same direction as the vase painter did; such work is more val-

uable than a more plausible facsimile drawn otherwise (it is *not* for publication), because you want to learn the artist's physical hand itself. (4) Observe characteristic contours and the shape of negative spaces; learn the hand's "rubricas"—in drapery, on haunches, in rosettes, wherever he casually leaves squiggles and hooks in configurations that amount to confessions. (5) Do not ignore the subsidiary ornament; of course, it may have been done by assistants, but even if it was, it is bound to mean something.

11. This essay did not aim to bring the Chimaera Painter up-to-date. The limitations alluded to at the end of note 1 were only one deterrent. A complete review of the whole group by the writer is now (1986) completed. There is unpublished material from the Demeter Sanctuary on Acrocorinth. Several unpublished pieces brought to my attention since 1981 may be representative of a host. I took this occasion to devote a paper to principles, none of them new or esoteric yet sometimes ignored.

12. Amyx, *Corinthian Vase-Painting of the Archaic Period* (Berkeley, in press, 1986) 168, no. A–10, pl. 64, 2a-b.

13. *Corinth* XV, 3, no. 1322, pl. 55 and (reconstructed) pl. 112.

good test of connoisseurship is the power to predict. If the reconstruction of KN–55 had caused perplexity, the attribution would be less certain.[14]

The pot man's ability to produce dates ("perhaps about 585 B.C.") also rests on discipline that the nonspecialist relying on him will do well to demand. It is not enough, desiring a synchronism, to go searching through collections of pictures for things that seem similar and to be satisfied when some have been found. The Painter of Palermo 489 really *is* like the Painter of Louvre E 574, and even the Chimaera Painter, in many typical traits. Such similarity needs to be explained. The real reasons were already indicated in 1959,[15] besides being implicit in *Necrocorinthia*,[16] but Birgitte Rafn had to spell them out again in 1978.[17]

It is, indeed, in working out general chronology and in making basic distinctions that the study of pot profiles can be decisive. Their profiles prove conclusively, as Callipolitis-Feytmans demonstrated and Rafn emphasized, that the plates of the Chimaera group are Middle Corinthian (MC).[18] Within

the career of a single artist, however, excessive reliance on the profile (in principle, on any single, isolated criterion) overlooks uncertainties stemming from accidents of preservation or discovery and from our almost total ignorance of the practical organization of the Corinthian industry.[19] We do not know how many potters, how many painters, would constitute a typical workshop, or even if there was a typical arrangement. We do not know whether associations were usually stable. We do not know how often painters did their own potting. We do not know whether owners were other men than the craftsmen, and, if there was a foreman or entrepreneur-owner, we do not know whether shop uniformity was always, or ever, imposed on normally competent craftsmen. Furthermore, we cannot determine, unless the black-figure style can tell us, whether, for example, two varieties of MC plate that were decorated by the same artist, or by related hands in one group, are successive, chronologically overlapping, or concurrent. In no case is the quantity preserved anywhere near an amount sufficient to allow statistical techniques to be brought to bear. In the case of the Chimaera group, the profiles reassure us that the Carrousel Painter is as early as the decoration suggests and that the Copenhagen sphinx and pantheress plates (NC 1054–55) are as late as their style; so too is NC 1047.[20] Within the career of the Chimaera Painter, profiles are helpful only in a rough way. Though the profile helps me profitably to reconsider the relative date of NC 1044,[21] it fails to distinguish NC 1040 devel-

14. Similarly, working in Greece, we became convinced that a pattern of broad, evenly spaced bands (see D. A. Amyx and P. Lawrence, *Corinth* VII, 2 (Princeton, 1975) 85, last paragraph) was significant evidence for the coherence of the Lowie group. If, on returning to Berkeley, we had failed to find this pattern on the bottom of the Lowie Museum oinochoe, our faith in the value of the pattern as a criterion would have been shaken.

15. Lawrence, *AJA* 63 (1959) 362–63.

16. In the basic chapters, pp. 43–66.

17. Rafn, *Acta Archaeologica* 49 (1978) 166–70. Rafn's exhaustive review of the difficulties in I. Strøm's article could not be more patient or thorough. Her conclusion, p. 179, seems perfectly acceptable; some further refinement may be possible. (The idea, p. 178, that the Columbus Painter was in the same workshop, seems less certain.)

18. It is high time that we admit that the plates *Necrocorinthia* nos. 1054–55, and no. 1047 as well, have all the stylistic characteristics of Late Corinthian (LC) I and ought to be so classified. As Mme. Callipolis says in "Evolution du plat corinthien," *BCH* 86 (1962) 134, nos. 63, 64, "peuvent être placés à l'aube du CR I." And NC 1047, no. 68, has "tous les charactères des plats du Corinthian récent I." However, the writer cannot invoke this authority to confirm her placement of these three plates while she overrides the dating by profile for NC

1048 and Berkeley 8/104, "Evolution du plat corinthien," nos. 62 and 67, respectively, which Mme. Callipolis groups with them.

19. Amyx and Lawrence, *Corinth* VII, 2 (Princeton, 1975) 83.

20. D. Callipolitis-Feytmans, "Evolution du plat corinthien," *BCH* 86 (1962) 134 and 154, no. 68.

21. In 1959, *AJA* 63 (1959) 352, I felt that the Boread had a complexity that allied it to NC 1042, considerably later than the namepiece. But the Boreads on the Rodin pyxis lid and on the Hermitage pyxis, and the Potnia Theron on NCG 3289 (Rafn, *Acta Archaeologica*

opmentally from NC 1041 or from New York MMA 41.11.1, or NC 1048, which is early,[22] from NC 1047, which is very late.

Such pronouncements must not be, however, a merely arrogant pitting of one kind of evidence against another. If I am justified in insisting that NC 1048 is much earlier than NC 1047 (as much as two decades earlier), my assertion must rest ultimately on study of the entirety of Corinthian pottery (shapes, figurework, floral ornament—all) parallel to the entirety of contemporary Attic pottery, and both parallel to the development of contemporary sculpture. The field archaeologist or historian relying on us should require such a foundation; it can be self-taught. There are mistakes that cannot be made by someone who has traced or drawn, for example, several hundred Attic and Corinthian palmette-and-lotus ornaments. If we would override a date based on the profile alone, it must not be for failure to understand shape development or to give it due weight in assessing the body of evidence; only, we may not draw conclusions from one criterion that the other germane criteria do not confirm. Similarly, we ought never to isolate an artist's work on one vase shape from his whole output, and we ought never to date, even sequentially, the

works of one hand in a group without cross-checking to the sequential development both of his companions and of artists working concurrently who are not so closely related. For example, in Corinthian, palmette-and-lotus ornaments alone will place the Chimaera Painter between (later than) the Eurytios krater, NC 780, and the Samos Painter's kotylai in *Necrocorinthia*, NC 950–52. In Attic, by the same criteria, he will be placed from the Gorgon Painter to the KX Painter. But this conclusion is proved by the history of the plate shape, by the development of animal and figure style, by filling ornament, by the shape history of the Chimaera Painter's pyxides and flat-bottomed aryballoi,[23] and by the female heads on two of the pyxides.[24] It is well to remember that this network of confirmation is now so firm and so closely woven that whoever proposes to alter any part of it must be prepared to cope with all the ramifications in other centers and in other media. The historical evidence for the dates of Corinthian pottery leaves much to be desired, but the dating of

49 (1978) 154, no. 8; Amyx, *Corinthian Vase-Painting of the Archaic Period*, 168, A 10) suggest that it is not so late; I had thought, in my youth, too abstractly. On the other hand, Rafn, *Acta Archaeologica*, 173, n. 147, astutely remarks that it cannot be especially early.

22. In 1963, photographs of the plate that is now NCG 3289 inspired a complete review of the Chimaera Painter, which has remained unpublished. There I compared the goat protome on the bottom of NCG 3289, and several other traits in the Potnia, with NC 1048, concluding that both are quite early (the Ny Carlsberg plate has contour incision on the Potnia), though perhaps not quite so early as New York, MMA 41.11.1. Rafn independently in 1978 made similar comparisons, confirming the attribution, *Acta Archaeologica* 49 (1978) 154, n. 25, at end, and by implication the date. The protomai on NC 1048 were already compared, Lawrence, *AJA* 63 (1959) 363, n. 70, with those in one of the Attic Panther Painter's lekanides (*ABV* 18, no. 1); the Attic relationship has now (1986) been studied more exhaustively (see abstract, Lawrence, *AJA* 88 [1984] 250).

23. The Chimaera Painter's Gela aryballos, NC 835, is fairly early; early also the Riehen Painter's Berlin F 1089: Lawrence, *AJA* 63 (1959) 352, no. 9, and 358, no. 6, correctly attributed in Lawrence, *AJA* 66 (1962). Gela, Navarra G. 10, *CVA* 1, pl. 41, is very late. It is already LC I and may be later even than NC 1054–55, by the same hand. The very broad-based shape and the proportions of the single figure, combined with broad expanses of white ground quite devoid of anything that might compensate for absence of filling ornaments, are in stark contrast to the MC shape and aesthetic of Florence 79246 and NC 853 (though they also have no filling ornament).

24. As Rafn, *Acta Archaeologica* 49 (1978) 176, observes, Klaus Wallenstein's dates (*Korinthische Plastik des 7. und 6. Jahrhunderts vor Christus* [Bonn, 1971]) are "perhaps too exact" (or a little too mechanical), but I was wrong, *AJA* 63 (1959) 362, when I spoke of all three pyxides as representing "a very early phase" of MC, and from Wallenstein's dates Rafn drew the profitable conclusion that it is useful to know that the Chimaera Painter did *not* abandon pyxides after the beginning of his career. Now I should range the pyxides at about ten-year intervals: Rodin TC 607, ca. 600, or a little later; Hermitage 5551, ca. 590; Bonn 666 (Wallenstein's correction of the inventory number at NC 892 is right; so also Amyx) at ca. 580, or not much later. This date is Payne's, at NC 892.

practically all seventh- and early-sixth-century art is referred to it.[25]

Next we must illustrate the difficulty that prompted the quotation from Beazley.[26] The word *style* is indeed an ordinary, nontechnical term that can be used in a wide range of senses. It is that which makes a work recognizable as what it is: Asian or European style, Flemish or Italian, Florentine or Milanese, Attic or Corinthian; ancient or modern style, early Christian or Gothic, Quattrocento or Cinquecento, circa 1475 or circa 1485; but also Braque or Picasso, Giorgione or Titian, Kresilas or Alkamenes, Painter of Louvre E 574 or Riehen Painter. It is obvious that as we shift from culture to period to person the criteria change from generic to developmental to personal. If we are talking about "the Chimaera Painter's style" (and personal style is the hardest thing in the world, next to describing a friend or a lover, to talk about), generic, abstract terminology will not help much to define it. In fact, writing on the Chimaera group from end to end (the author herself is guilty) has been vitiated by generic epithets: heraldic (Payne), majestic, monumental (Lawrence), precise, and the like.[27] Such qualities are those appealed to (by Strøm) and in reaction abjured (by

Rafn)[28] as "stylistic." Especially with reference to personal style, they are *not* stylistic. They are vague, and they have proved more misleading than one could have imagined. It is as if, guided by adjectives alone, one attributed a Boucher to Fra Filippo Lippi. The writer did spell out the components of the Chimaera Painter's idiosyncrasy, but it is "monumentality" that has been quoted. The personal idiosyncrasy is the style; mastery of the personal idiosyncrasy is the basis for further attributions; the significant stylistic traits are the ones that can be singled out[29] and objectively controlled to prevent all-too-human wishful thinking from sullying the stringently objective study that reveals "a sacred thing, the man himself."

When an art historian sees something all at once, entire, as we said above, it is not his subjectivity that produces the insight. The resolution of all the visual evidence comes when his assimilation of the works themselves and all their possible comparanda effects a certain critical saturation. He cannot resolve difficulties by some sort of aesthetical alchemy. He cannot distill what is not there. If the plates with floral crosses, NC 1049–51, lack sufficiently decisive traits, we may see that nothing *prevents* their being by the Chimaera Painter, but to give them to him

---

25. For groundwork in the chronology of early Attic black-figure, one may still consult *Necrocorinthia*, 190–202; the dating of all "Daedalic" sculpture, however defined, hinges on the little aryballos, *Necrocorinthia*, pl. 1, 8–11; Richter, *Korai*, pl. 5 (other seventh-century sculpture derives dates from those for "Daedalic"); for the dating of early korai, *Korai*, pp. 25–26.

26. See above, note 7.

27. The "characteristics of the artist's style" given by E. Bell in describing the Cincinnati plate for an exhibition catalogue, W. Moon and L. Berge, eds., *Greek Vase-Painting in Midwestern Collections* (Chicago, 1980) 37, no. 22, "monumentality, precise drawing, rich dichromy, and his treatment of the tondo of the plate," are not, except for the last, *stylistic* traits in Beazley's sense and may mislead persons untrained in style, though they are innocently used to help the visitor to appreciate the plate. For the Columbus Painter is as monumental, the Griffin group has as rich dichromy, and the Perachora Painter is at least as precise. Such verbal tags, appropriate only to a guide or catalog, were what confused Strøm. The whole cluster of phrases could apply to some other hand, not connected with the Chimaera Painter

and even from a remote period; tondo apart, they apply perfectly well to the MPC Hound Painter. Style, by contrast, is seen in the confrontation of lions by the Riehen Painter and the Painter of Louvre E 574, in Lawrence, *AJA* 66 (1962) pl. 55, figs. 5–6; these two lions could bear exactly the same verbal tags; they share such traits as Strøm and Rafn cite as "style." But look at them! They are no more by the same hand than the two little boys by the Brygos Painter and the Foundry Painter juxtaposed by Beazley almost seventy years ago (*Attic Red-Figured Vases in American Museums* [Cambridge, Mass., 1918] 93, figs. 61, 62). Even by the lowest conceivable chronology, the Cincinnati plate is dated, in the *Midwestern Collections* catalogue, at least a decade too late.

28. Rafn, *Acta Archaeologica* 49 (1978) 174, col. 2; 176, col. 1.

29. As Beazley did in presenting the Achilles Painter, for example; *JHS* 34 (1914) 179–226. In the discussion supporting the attribution of Hermitage 5551, Lawrence, *AJA* 63 (1959) 354–55, the writer tried to follow her mentors.

we should want some new piece whose decoration was such as to show that they *must* be either his or else not his but from a distinct hand.[30] Again we have Sir John Beazley's example. Sometimes decisive evidence simply is not forthcoming. We usually suspect where the truth should lie. We surely are tempted to say that, after all, it "must" be so. But Beazley waited till near the end of his life before pronouncing on the identity of the Panaitios Painter and Onesimos. We are wrong when we show less restraint.

In the case of the Painter of Louvre E 574 and the Painter of the Copenhagen Sphinxes we have just such a classic problem of connoisseurship, requiring new scrutiny and exposition beyond the scope of this essay. At the center of the problem is an aryballos, NC 853, mature MC, perhaps as late as circa 580 B.C. Its original publication, cited by Payne, showed the siren and one panther's face, which is exactly like those of the panthers on NC 1054–55, and he attributed the aryballos to that hand. Obtaining new photographs of both its panthers complete, the writer saw that their bodies were altogether unlike those on NC 1055 but exactly like those on NC 801 (Louvre E 574): she removed NC 853 from the Copenhagen plates, NC 1054–55, and attributed it to the hand of NC 801 and Florence, Museo Etrusco 79246. Since then, no one has questioned that these three are by one hand. Because the heads of the panthers on NC 853 certainly seem to indicate one attribution and their bodies another, why not solve everything by identifying the two hands and calling NC 853 a "link"? The answer is

that, with so few pieces even in the combined lists, there was much too much that would not match, that made no sense. True, the forelegs of the Florence lions showed that the Painter of Louvre E 574 was closer to NC 1054–55 than the Chimaera Painter ever was. True, as J. L. Benson also observed, the siren on NC 853 is developing toward the formal elegance of the sphinxes on NC 1054 (though she still has some way to go). True, a fondness for fussy detail was observable throughout the career of the Painter of Louvre E 574. But for many years evidence was lacking to account for the incongruities.[31] The aryballos G.10 from the Navarra collection in Gela[32] was rightly attributed to the hand of NC 1054–55 and shows their style modified for a bulging shape, but it is at least as late as the pair of plates and its attribution did nothing to reconcile NC 853, an earlier and far more refined aryballos, with them. J. L. Benson showed me photographs and drawings of two new flat-bottomed aryballoi in Palermo which he attributed to the Painter of Louvre E 574 (Amyx independently also lists one of them).[33] In fact, the second of these is by the Chimaera Painter, and their close relationship to each other is evidence of unexpected stylistic intimacy, for a brief period, between the Chimaera Painter and the Painter of Louvre E 574. Both of these aryballoi are too early to help resolve the problematic affinities of NC 853.

Special pleading may not always be evi-

---

30. Some floral crosses, especially those with lotuses, are stylistically distinctive. For example, the Catania palmette-lotus cross (*Bollettino d'Arte* 45 [1960] 250, fig. 5, 2), though the photograph is small, is very close to Berkeley 8/104, which, with Corinth KP–1773 (Corinth XV, 3, no. 750, pls. 36, 116), I have attributed to the Chimaera Painter (in a forthcoming article, "The Chimaera Group at Corinth"). The style of the Berkeley plate, studied firsthand, is certainly the Chimaera Painter's; see above, n. 10, (4). But *Perachora* 2 (1970) pl. 80 (for the man's head) and pl. 82 (for the floral cross) is by the same hand as the Copenhagen plates, NC 1054–55.

31. As Lawrence, *AJA* 66 (1962) 185: "In our present state of knowledge, we gain more by admitting its insolubility." Benson, *Antike Kunst* 7 (1964) 80, endorsed Strøm's identification of these two hands but (in an article on another painter) did not discuss it beyond observing percipiently a "desiccation" in NC 853 as "a plausible prelude to the precise and practised draughtmanship and the austerely formal conception of the Copenhagen plates." See above, note 27.

32. Rafn, *Acta Archaeologica* 49 (1978) fig. 9; for the whole vase, CVA 1, pl. 41. See also n. 23.

33. Palermo, Fondazione Mormino (Bank of Sicily), nos. 319 and 621; cf. AA (1969) 338, sub no. 19. Amyx, *Corinthian Vase-Painting of the Archaic Period*, 172, no. A 5.

dent to the reader; the author may have had to convince himself, especially if frustrated by limitations beyond his control. In such a case, he will remain uneasy about his judgments, however many times afterward he has checked and examined from every angle the available evidence. The writer remains uneasy about what she has not been able to see of the pyxides in the Chimaera group.[34] There is no problem with the Hermitage pyxis, perfectly preserved, clean, and beautifully photographed. So much as is visible in available pictures of the Bonn and Musée Rodin pyxides suffices to show that they are by the Chimaera Painter but not to interpret their significance in his oeuvre. The inadequate photographs of the badly damaged Bonn pyxis only suggest (in the incipient attenuation of the animals and the chimaera's "tall," vertical haunches) the late place in the career of the Chimaera Painter that its female heads require.[35] One can see, too, that the Rodin kotyle-pyxis is early: the proportions, the filling ornament, the half-jelled animal types all are MC, but just barely. It is only a little later than NC 669 (see below, note 37), which is still Early Corinthian (EC). Musée Rodin TC 607 must be contemporary with some of the Carrousel Painter's work, and the relationship of the Carrousel Painter to the Chimaera Painter is more important than ever, now that we see that none of the work of the Painter of Louvre E 574 known to us, or even Bloesch's Zürich aryballos by the Riehen Painter, is as early as already well-formed early work by the Chimaera Painter

himself:[36] he did not learn from them. For this reason, the direct influence of late EC work such as the Columbus Painter was producing at that time seems likelier to have contributed to his formation. Take the Carrousel plates; take a very creative young decorator; allow him to be impressed also by the Columbus Painter's alabastra—you need no more, taking stock of his originality, to produce the Chimaera Painter. I take for granted a rich artistic environment in which, for example, the sophisticated chimaera formula would be available, in some medium or another, to any emulative youngster. We delude ourselves if we hope to reconstruct everything. The place of the Rodin pyxis, however, among the Chimaera Painter's early works and its chronological relationship to the Carrousel Painter's plates might be better defined, and such definition will require firsthand study. Where stylistic decisions are difficult, the exact character of the incised line becomes all-important.[37]

The word *style* has caused mischief in yet another application. Payne himself spoke of

34. Lawrence, *AJA* 63 (1959) 354, nos. 12, 13, 14; Rafn, *Acta Archaeologica* 49 (1978) 154–55, nos. 13, 14, 15.

35. Compare the derivative Attic chimaera on the lip cup signed by Eucheiros (*ABV* 162, no. 2, btm.), cited and illustrated by Rafn, *Acta Archaeologica* 49 (1978) 185, fig. 18. The Bonn Chimaera already shows some development in that direction. Wallenstein's date (n. 24, above) is Payne's at NC 892 (pl. 48, 5), with which I agree, but Hermitage 5551 is probably a little later than his "600–595", that is, not at the very beginning of MC as the kotyle-pyxis in the Musée Rodin is. A pyxis *can* be later than the mold used for its heads, though not earlier.

36. The Cincinnati plate, Moon and Berge, *Greek Vase-Painting in Midwestern Collections*, 37, no. 22, is considerably earlier than any known work of theirs. A relative chronology of the Chimaera group is proposed in my forthcoming "The Chimaera Group at Corinth."

37. In 1962, I overlooked the Perachora fragment, which seems to be the Carrousel Painter's very earliest work (*Perachora* 2, no. 1943, pl. 72). It's "carrousel" is of little harnessed pegasoi. On the face of the plate, the filling ornament, the lotus, and the animals are still typically EC; so too Hopper, *Perachora* 2, p. 193, no. 1943. When "Notes . . . " went to press, *Perachora* 2 had not yet appeared. The attribution seems certain; for example, compare the hatching on the horses' tails. It is listed by Amyx, *Corinthian Vase-Painting of the Archaic Period*, 166, A4. On the other hand, without having seen it, I reported that NC 669 (Berlin head-pyxis) seemed to be his. Though Rafn did not reject this attribution ("has been added"; *Acta Archaeologica* 49 [1978] 176), now that the vase is well published (Richter, *Korai*, pl. 7), I more than doubt it; Amyx also has withdrawn the attribution: *Corinthian Vase-Painting of the Archaic Period* 166, B1. Its relevance as an antecedent to the Chimaera Painter's head-pyxides is undiminished; the style is related and antecedent to that of the Rodin kotyle-pyxis. My firsthand study of these pyxides is now (1986) included in the forthcoming "The Chimaera Group at Corinth."

a "white-dot style."[38] Again, the usage is "not without warrant,"[39] but it is not to be confused with personal style. The addition of white dots[40] seems to have been an option so widespread in Middle Corinthian workshops that, though some artists eschewed them, their presence may signify nothing at all. They remain more common on alabastra and aryballoi than on other shapes; they are absent from almost all the plates. White dots alone should not be taken for evidence of influence or used as grounds for grouping. If at the outset (NC 380ff.) the embellishment was confined to a certain stylistic group whose decoration was designed for it, a generation later white dots entail no such relationship; they don't affect the design or the style of Florence, Museo Etrusco 79246 at all.

The requirement of a sound basis for forming a Group can also be illustrated from the bibliography on the Chimaera Painter and that on the other hands stylistically associated with him.[41] To bring order out of chaos, we try to establish relationships among known painters and so arrange them with reference to an outstanding, dominant talent. It should be realized that the demonstration of a Group is much more difficult than proving attributions to individual hands. Multiple, diverse bonds are wanted. As Birgitte Rafn saw, such Groups, to be useful or meaningful, should reflect actual working associations, and these are hard to prove. Signs of some influence or similar aesthetic qualities do not suffice.[42] Besides, it is too seldom remembered that an artist's relationship to a group may pertain to only part of his career. At the date of Athens NM 971 (NC 841),[43] the Otterlo Painter's animals ally him closely to the Chimaera group; later he seems to go his own way. For the Erlenmeyer Painter, I still doubt whether so much can be claimed; *if* he began with work like the Yale, Stoddard, alabastron,[44] he might be said to have issued from a member of the Chimaera group, the Painter of Louvre E 574. He followed his own bent (a strong one) and absorbed other influences thereafter.[45]

This essay will have served its purpose amply if it clears the ground for new substantive work on a basis of shared understanding. If besides it is of interest to students or to scholars who only occasionally use the results of studies in vase painting, the writer hopes to have shown the importance of a tradition of personal teaching and scholarly apprenticeship in these studies.

---

38. *Necrocorinthia*, 234, D, NC 380, ff.

39. See above, note 7.

40. Payne's essay on the white-dot style, as seen on NC 380, is one of his finest and most characteristic. The comparanda in metalwork (fig. 122) and embroidery, or some other kind of figured textiles, could not have been more perceptive and instructive.

41. See above, note 8.

42. Rafn, *Acta Archaeologica* 49 (1978) 173; there is not sufficient or unambiguous evidence for her attractive hypothesis of "five painters and several potters." The Chimaera Painter seems to have worked in the Potters' Quarter neighborhood (see *Corinth* XV, 3, p. 10), a crowded warren, to judge from our evidence, in which stylistic independence would be harder to maintain than

incessant interchange. We must remember, too, that it was a commercial industry; whatever was selling well would be influential. Such circumstances allow for manifold and shifting influences without, in general, requiring actual working associations.

43. Rafn, *Acta Archaeologica* 49 (1978) 162, no. 2 (a partial list drawn for discussion from Benson's article, *Antike Kunst* 14 (1971) 13–24, nos. 1–40, pls. 1–5), but in the style of the later aryballoi, such as we found near the top of the Anaploga Well, Amyx and Lawrence, *Corinth* VII, 2 (Princeton, 1975) An 29 and An 30, pls. 74, 105, nothing specific to the Chimaera group is to be seen. Perhaps also, at a certain date, the Chimaera group itself was dissolved. Note that late flat-bottomed aryballoi by the Otterlo Painter are tall and globular, while a late one by the artist of the Copenhagen plates, NC 1054–55 (Gela, Navarra G. 10; see note 23, above) diverged from the shape of NC 835, NC 853, Florence 79246, *et al.*, differently, becoming broad at the base. Perhaps by this date it is unrealistic to speak of a "Chimaera group." The pyxis in Bonn and NC 1042 seem to be the latest things that we have by the Chimaera Painter himself.

44. Rafn, *Acta Archaeologica* 49 (1978) 160, no. 1 (Benson's no. 1, *Antike Kunst* 7 [1964] pl. 22, 2).

45. Among those illustrated by Benson, *Antike Kunst* (1964) pl. 24, figs. 1–2, 5, 6 surely suggest that the Chimaera aesthetic has been forgotten and had never made a deep impression. Indeed, if any later artist can be said to keep alive the colorful *horror vacui*, without the precision, of the original "white-dot style" (NC 380), surely it is the Erlenmeyer Painter when most himself, at his least inhibited.

14. Middle Protocorinthian Periodization

J. L. BENSON

DEPARTMENT OF ART HISTORY, UNIVERSITY OF MASSACHUSETTS, AMHERST

It is a pleasure to offer a contribution to a volume that recognizes the many years of arduous and fruitful labor of D. A. Amyx in the vineyards of connoisseurship. His acumen in sorting the painters of multitudinous groups of Corinthian vases has helped to illumine an important stage of ancient Greek art. I shall take this opportunity to discuss a theoretical but, I trust, nonetheless vital aspect of connoisseur-oriented studies.

In my publication of the Potters' Quarter finds,[1] I introduced a modification of the usual periodization of Protocorinthian pottery. Early Protocorinthian (EPC) remains the same, as does also Late Protocorinthian (LPC). Moreover, I also use the current terms Middle Protocorinthian I and II (MPC I-II). The modification lies in defining the subphases I and II differently than usual. Whereas MPC I is usually equivalent to the First Black-figure Style and MPC II is usually equivalent to the Second Black-figure Style, my MPC I is subdivided into two phases: A and B, which between them include all the First Black-figure and part of the Second Black-figure Styles. My MPC II denotes only the mature part of the Second Style, including the polychromatic vases. Rather than take space to justify this departure in the Corinth volume itself, I promised there to do so elsewhere. In the following short essay I

present my conception of the problem in large terms and in the realization that only a full publication of workshop lists will give readers the final basis for judging the validity of my views.

Readers familiar with my dissertation[2] will know that my interest in the development of Protocorinthian style goes back that far. I was impressed with the fact that Humfry Payne had not only discovered the integrality of the Protocorinthian period of pottery painting at Corinth—thus modifying the views of his immediate predecessor, K. F. Johansen[3]—but also that he had further conceived of this period in terms of a triadic progression (EPC-MPC-LPC), thus again modifying the purely descriptive terminology of Johansen (for example, *Époque des aryballes pansus*). Nevertheless, in setting bounds to the middle period, Payne followed Johansen's lead in spirit by speaking of a First and Second Orientalizing Style (more or less equivalent to Style Archaïque, Classes A and B) in *Necrocorinthia*.[4] He altered these to First and Second Black-figure Styles in *Protokorinthische Vasenmalerei*.[5] It must be stressed that neither Johansen nor Payne had

1. *Corinth* XV, 3, The Potters' Quarter, The Pottery, by Agnes Newhall Stillwell and J. L. Benson (Princeton, 1984) 9–10.

2. J. L. Benson, *Die Geschichte der korinthischen Vasen* (Basel, 1953) 65–71.

3. K. F. Johansen, *Les vases sicyoniens* (Paris, 1923).

4. *Necrocorinthia* 7–15. This comes under the chapter entitled "Early Protocorinthian Vase-Painting." In the plates vases of this category are labeled MPC.

5. H. Payne, *Protokorinthische Vasenmalerei* (Berlin, 1933) 21–23.

been able to concern himself much with connoisseurship or with the more theoretical principles of style periodicity: their results appeared to be more pragmatically based.

It was at this point that my dissertation, proceeding along both of the lines just mentioned, set in. It so happened that my venture into the very complex sphere of Protocorinthian connoisseurship was taking place at precisely the same time as Thomas Dunbabin and Martin Robertson[6] were attempting the same thing. Despite many satisfying agreements our work showed differences at least partly owing to the fact that in my studies of workshops, I was simultaneously taking into account theoretical considerations of stylistic development derived from, or at least inspired by, the writings of Wölfflin, Buschor, and Schefold. In the Oxford tradition they were—as they pointed out in their postscript—concerned to relate groups to one another. A judicious synthesis of these two approaches may prove better than either one in isolation.

For my part I thought, for example, that I could discern a certain—one might well say ideal—periodical development, provided that one focused on particular relationships such as that between figure and (filling) ornaments: at first these elements tend to be equally balanced in size and in importance, a phase that could be called EPC I. Whereas at first the figures were virtually limited to plants and to animals, in a second stage these appear in greater variety, and human beings are also shown—all of this in a much more defined significance wherein ornaments tend to support and to enhance the mood of the figure, for example, in reflecting the explosive energy of a hero's struggle. If this can be called EPC II, then in a third stage the ornaments tend to become smaller and rather cunningly subordinate in a decorative sense to the figures (EPC III).[7] The figures have, in their turn, advanced from somewhat ungainly to smoothly integrated, almost flowing, forms that, however, still recall the expressivity of the original impulse that turned Corinthian artists away from the world of Geometric forms. In this way there is an early period with three phases that lead up to a striking new impulse occurring near the middle of the seventh century B.C., whereby artists seemed inspired to attempt more sculpturesque effects in the figures and even in the vase forms, which, on occasion, recall Daedalic statue features.[8] Not so much excitement as dignity and calm radiate from the figures. Filling ornaments are often abolished or, if retained, tend to be used in small format as a rhythmic background.[9] This has more the character of a period than a subphase and should logically be called MPC. Following this, the newly created forms submitted either to continuing refinement or else to dissolution into looser, rougher elements (LPC). At this point—in the system of both Johansen and Payne—the style of Corinthian pottery changes in such a way that the term Protocorinthian is no longer applicable (despite considerable overlapping of substance), so that we are no longer concerned with it here.

The approach that I have sketched out above in the broadest terms drew, of course, on the relative chronology of Payne but sought a rationale for that order stronger than any hitherto presented. It was in principle approved by Dunbabin,[10] who, nevertheless, pointed out that Payne's system was more convenient and that no help for absolute chronology could be won from my system. With both of these comments I can concur. And yet convenience in itself must surely

6. "Some Protocorinthian Vase-Painters," *BSA* 48 (1953) 172–81.

7. Examples: EPC I: Payne, *Protokorinthische Vasenmalerei*, pl. 5, 2 EPC II: Payne, *Protokorinthische Vasenmalerei*, pl. 11, 1–5; EPC III: Payne, *Protokorinthische Vasenmalerei*, pl. 14, 2–4; (here figure 5).

8. Payne, *Protokorinthische Vasenmalerei*, pl. 22, 3–4.

9. Payne, *Protokorinthische Vasenmalerei*, pls. 17–18; pl. 22, 2.

10. T. Dunbabin, "The Chronology of Protocorinthian Vases," *ArchEph* (1953–1954) part 2, 251, esp. n. 1.

be a secondary, not a primary, quality in scholarship. Moreover, in re-studying this period and particularly the existing painter lists (still only those of Dunbabin-Robertson and my own) in connection with publishing the Protocorinthian finds from the Potters' Quarter, I became aware that the universal attempt to adhere to Payne's conception of MPC—as this can be gleaned from the specific dating of vases given in the key to the plates of *Protokorinthische Vasenmalerei*—has, since I wrote on the period, resulted in inconsistencies that seem not to have been noticed, or at least, not to have been commented upon. If taken seriously, these inconsistencies reflect a problem in achieving a rational relative chronology.

In particular I was struck by the fact that the well-known Toulouse oinochoe, which has somehow become a key piece in the thinking about MPC style development, really belongs with the First Black-figure Style rather than with the second, where Payne placed it. Dunbabin and Robertson made it the name-piece of their Toulouse Painter, whom they derived directly from the Cumae group and dated EPC-MPC.[11] As there is universal agreement that the Cumae group is EPC, there can be little doubt that the Toulouse Painter belongs to MPC I or First Black-figure Style, if this placement is correct. I must confess that I did not see this when I was writing *Die Geschichte der korinthischen Vasen*, partly perhaps because I could find nothing else to attribute to the master of the oinochoe, and hence left it at Payne's date.[12] But now, although I am still somewhat dubious about actual attributions, I am fully prepared to accept the earlier placement. In order to be doubly sure about it, I took the trouble to study the Toulouse piece first hand and also obtained some additional photographs (figures 1, 2, and 3) that are very much needed to complement

the views shown in *Protokorinthische Vasenmalerei*, pl. 12. I believe that these photographs demonstrate the tremendous dramatic expressivity of the plant ornament. Its still coordinate relationship to the animal—although by position the plant seems to assume dominance here—recalls the criterion I proposed for EPC I in my system, but it does so in a heightened dramatic form that corresponds with the sense of the filling ornaments in the Ajax Painter's scenes; ornaments that appear like so many exploding firecrackers underlining the unbridled energy of the human figures: *Protokorinthische Vasenmalerei*, pls. 10–11. Thus, the Toulouse oinochoe should logically be, like the Ajax pieces, my EPC II or, in my present terminology, MPC IA.

The implications of this must be further discussed, for they are far-reaching. On the one hand, of course, I must admire the astuteness of Dunbabin-Robertson in grasping an important relationship that I overlooked—and that, incidentally, helps to corroborate my interpretation of period style. On the other hand, those scholars have failed to see, or at least advertise, the consequences of this for Payne's conception of the Black-figure Style. Indeed, Dunbabin, as Payne's literary executor, specifically codified Payne's system in two places[13]—with no comment on its internal validity—and it still stands with little modification as canonical among large numbers of scholars. The part in question is:

First Black-figure Style = MPC I (700–675 B.C.)
Second Black-figure Style = MPC II (675–650 B.C.)

We may elucidate the problematical situation that has resulted by comparing the rather similar, if rough, floral decoration of the kotyle, Aigina number 189 (figure 4), which W. Kraiker[14] characterized quite appropriately

11. Dunbabin and Robertson, "Some Protocorinthian Vase-Painters," 175.

12. Benson, *Die Geschichte der korinthischen Vasen*, 125, no. 863.

13. Dunbabin, "Chronology of Protocorinthian Vases," *ArchEph* (1953–1954) part 2, 247; Dunbabin in *Perachora*, 2 (Oxford, 1962) 6.

14. W. Kraiker, *Aigina* (Berlin, 1951) 41.

Figure 1. Protocorinthian Oinochoe, Toulouse, Musée Saint-Raymond, inv. no. 26.106.

Figure 2. Second View of Oinochoe in Figure 1.

as not much earlier than the Toulouse oino-choe and then dated EPC. But how can this be if the Toulouse piece is (Dunbabin's) MPC II rather than MPC I? The visual comparison suggests that Aigina number 189 must be lat-est EPC if not, perhaps, already early MPC I, while the oinochoe should be some way into MPC I. The shape of Aigina number 189 appears virtually identical to that of Aigina number 197 in the drawing on Kraiker's pl. D (but these do not look like true profiles). In any case, Kraiker's placement of Aigina number 197 as contemporary with the Cu-mae oinochoe (*Protokorinthische Vasenmal-erei*, pl. 7, 1–2) cannot be objected to. Never-theless, K. Kübler,[15] apparently in order to uphold Payne's dating of the Toulouse jug to the Second Black-figure Style, placed ap-

15. K. Kübler, *Kerameikos* 6, 1 (Berlin, 1959) 128.

Figure 3. Third View of Oinochoe in Figure 1.

Figure 4. Protocorinthian Kotyle, Aigina, Museum (after W. Kraiker, *Aigina*, no. 189, pls. 14 and D).

MIDDLE PROTOCORINTHIAN
Syracuse (from a drawing by R. Carta)

Figure 5. Protocorinthian Oinochoe, Syracuse, National Museum, 42648 (after H. Payne, *Necrocorinthia*, pl. 7).

proximately fifteen years between the Cumae oinochoe just mentioned and the Ithaca oinochoe number 138, which Robertson[16] more reasonably characterized as "particularly close to an example from Cumae (the same one)." Kübler then allows ten more years for the emergence of his number 1267 plus a further ten years for the creation of the Toulouse oinochoe, thus reaching a grand total of thirty-five years between the first and last links of his chain! Surely, the chain is inappropriately lengthy.

In the light of this problem, some further comment on oinochoe shapes is necessary. The publisher of the splendid oinochoe from Tauros, D. Skilardi,[17] after carefully considering this factor, places his piece at about 660 B.C. (the very beginning of my MPC II) and the well-known Megara Hyblaea oinochoe (figure 5) before that. There are good reasons to accept that relative order, as I shall show shortly. In any case, the Megara Hyblaea piece may stand as the representative of the earlier aspect of the Second Black-figure Style, which is my MPC IB. Further, one may leave Kübler's number 1267 as characteristic of the earliest First Black-

figure Style,[18] along with, perhaps, the Ithaca oinochoe number 142—placed in the same position by Robertson. Both display the rugged energy of the MPC IA period (my term), which finds both its fullest expression in the Toulouse oinochoe and, at the same time, a limitation, as in the monumental figure of the goat, which more than hints at a crisis in the relation of figure and ornament.

* * *

In my necessarily brief discussion of the MPC period in *Corinth* XV, 3, pp. 9–10, I spoke of an articulation based on the succession of three artist generations represented by the Toulouse Painter, the Hound Painter, and the Aigina Bellerophon Painter. In *Die Geschichte der korinthischen Vasen*, I had already discerned the chronological succession of the latter two. But again it fell to Dunbabin and Robertson to recognize that the Hound Painter belongs to the generation *following* the Toulouse Painter. Their terse comment on the Hound Painter is "Pupil of the Toulouse Painter" and they date the former M-LPC in contrast to their dating of the lat-

16. M. Robertson, "Excavations in Ithaca, V," *BSA* 43 (1948) 36.

17. D. Skilardi, "Ἀνασκαφὴ παρὰ τὰ Μακρὰ Τείχη καὶ ἡ οἰνοχόη τοῦ Ταύρου," *ArchEph* (1975) 66–149.

18. Kübler's suggested absolute date for the Toulouse oinochoe: circa 690–685 B.C., is not unreasonable but it must be noted that he used a different time scale (*Kerameikos* 6, 1, p. 120) than Dunbabin and, of course, than mine.

ter as E-MPC.[19] While Dunbabin and Robertson claim more knowledge (in their list) about the works of the two names than I would, their emphatic temporal separation of the two artists seems to me indisputable. Yet it can hardly be understood except on the basis of such a stylistic progression as I am proposing—whereas Payne's assigning of the two both to the beginning of the Second Black-figure Style creates only confusion.

Therefore, before discussing the Hound Painter phase of MPC (my IB, equivalent to the earlier part of Dunbabin's II), I must now propose something not articulated in *Die Geschichte der korinthischen Vasen* but something that has grown out of its method, namely, that the torsional and curvilinear plant ornament of the Cumae and Toulouse groups constitutes more than a particular theme (though it is one): it was the fundamental deeply felt experience through which Corinthian artists liberated themselves from Geometric habitude. By this I mean the change from a mentality engrossed in rectilinear abstract ornaments to the same mentality caught up in substantive[20] curvilinear ornamentation. I see the first stirrings of this already in the running spiral of the Thapsos Class vases, and then its implementation in EPC Egyptian-derived plant and animal forms[21] leading directly into the Cumae-Toulouse aesthetic in question. It is true that other impulses from other sources were also introduced in the late eighth and early seventh centuries B.C. in Corinth. Nevertheless, it was not until the process I have referred to went from strength to refinement that a completely new stage began, namely, the statuesque style of MPC II (my terminology). Nor can the process be appreciated without reference to the fact that in carrying it out, Corinthian artists made two compromises: first, they retained rectilinear ornamentation to a considerable extent in subordinate positions; and second, they largely retained silhouette figures but gradually articulated them with incisions. It should be needless to point out that I am referring here only to the main line of development, as it can be discerned from our distant vantage point. This then allows us to recognize retardataire or avant-garde features. Thus, the Megara Hyblaea oinochoe (figure 5) has a conspicuously placed serpentine line on the shoulder, as if to induce enough sinuosity in the animals below that they cannot quite reach the truly statuesque stage. Hence, a date of MPC IB is probably appropriate.[22]

It is, however, the works of the Hound Painter that show animal representations whose sinuous gracefulness of contour is smoothly combined with similar plant motifs, complementary but subordinate. The hounds crouch convincingly (figure 6) in contrast to the half crouching, half walking position of the Toulouse goat (figures 1 and 2). Both of these animals are probably derived from Near Eastern prototypes.[23] But

19. Dunbabin and Robertson, "Some Protocorinthian Vase-Painters," 177 (see note 6, above). While no attempt to date closely is made by the authors here, one can still be surprised that they did not point out their differences with Payne's system.

20. In the unpublished dissertation of S. McNally, Payne is said to have used this adjective.

21. This will be discussed in a forthcoming article on the Reserved Cocks workshop.

22. Payne's dating in *Necrocorinthia* (p. 121) is rather vague. I must admit that the date I gave in *Die Geschichte der korinthischen Vasen* (133, no. 1209) is too late; evidently I did not compare it closely enough with workshops. Dunbabin and Robertson, "Some Protocorinthian Vase-Painters," 177, call it an early work of the Aigina Bellerophon Painter. Although I can only regard this as speculation at present, I am pleased that it puts the piece exactly where I believe it to belong in the MPC relative sequence. It is appropriate to mention here also the oinochoe fragment An 257 published by D. A. Amyx and P. Lawrence in *Corinth* VII, 2 (Princeton 1975) 149. It is unfortunate that the representations were not better preserved. The long, sharp nose of the male head has a certain similarity with some of the Ajax Painter's heads, but the conception in general looks more Attic; for example, the charioteers of the lid, K. Kübler, *Altattische Malerei* (Tübingen, 1950) 53. The double curve of the foreshoulder line of the uppermost quadruped of *Corinth* VII, 2, pl. 101 as well as the animal's contour presuppose the Hound Painter's work. Although the shape of the neck of the vessel could fit an earlier date, we do not have a dense enough series to date shape closely. I would suggest tentatively MPC IB.

23. The explanation for the goat's position might be that several Near Eastern types have been conflated.

Figure 6. Detail of Protocorinthian Kotyle, London, British Museum, inv. no. 1860.4-4.18 (A1530) (after H. Payne, *Protokorinthische Vasenmalerei*, pl. 14, 2-4).

the Toulouse master has adjusted the front part of his animal to flatter the plant volute at the expense of logical coordination with the rear part. The Hound Painter has not only avoided the awkward pose and situation but also has succeeded in adapting (foreign) feline claw formations in the service of a truly native theme, the hound. This is not a judgment but a fact intelligible only in a periodical context that allows quality to be judged by criteria suitable to the times of each work.

When I originally proposed to designate the sequence from the Cumae group to the

Representations of lions with closed forelegs and walking back legs occur three-dimensionally in North Syrian sites: E. Akurgal, *Orient und Okzident* (Baden-Baden, 1966) 56–57. But the bent legs of our goat recall more strongly an Assyrian wall painting from Tell Barsip (A. Parrot, *Arts of Assyria* [New York, 1961] 262, fig. 336): a running goat with single horn and one leg bent down, the other bent back. If the Toulouse master suppressed the latter leg, he had his scheme. At any rate, since the goat was an animal the painter could have studied from nature, had he desired, we have an indication of how dependent artists of the time were on artistic prototypes. The Hound Painter seems to have added—perhaps from nature—the deep frontal crouch to his animal—an altered version, possibly, of a Near Eastern lion type (cf. Akurgal, *Orient und Okzident*, 196, fig. 127). In any case, the influence of Near Eastern prototypes is unmistakable in the treatment of the hound's claws, adapted from lions, of course (Akurgal, *Orient und Okzident*, 104, fig. 70; 108, fig. 78).

Hound Painter as EPC I-III, the purpose was to provide a means of grasping how the Geometric mind-set was modified through the exploration of a new leading idea (torsionality) by successive generations. In setting out to relate groups, Dunbabin and Robertson were actually doing the same thing and with the same results. But since Dunbabin did not reflect this when he canonized Payne's roughly set divisions (for Payne surely had no intention of their becoming dogma), my feeling is that it is too late to do more than to make the *minimal* changes in the now customary terminology that will correct the confusion harbored in it.

* * *

In setting a division *after* the Hound Painter and related groups as well as before them, I have in mind not only my conception of MPC I as a whole but also remarks made by Payne himself that show a seminal realization of problems which could arise from his concept of a First and Second Black-figure Style; it seems to me unlikely that he would have allowed his thinking on the matter to be arrested in a rigid system that revealed defects. In *Necrocorinthia* he states that the "kotyle at Aegina with Bellerophon and the Chimaera, pl. 4, 1–2 . . . is evidently *rather later* than the kotyle with coursing hounds, one of which is illustrated on pl. 5" (p. 11; italics mine). So far, so good; what follows is more problematic: "the drawing is suppler and less angular, but the connexion is obviously very close." If the adjectives refer to the Aigina kotyle, it is difficult to justify the comparative form of supple: both kotylai have figures that could perhaps be described as supple as a secondary quality; but surely the Hound Painter's animals and plants (figure 6) flow more quickly in contour than those of the Aigina Bellerophon Painter (figures 7 and 8). The only angularity in the former is in the leg joints where it is justified on a naturalistic basis (figure 6), whereas the animals of the later painter tend to be blockish (figure 8), and the subsidiary ornament as-

Figure 7. Fragment of Protocorinthian Kotyle, Aigina, Museum (after W. Kraiker, *Aigina*, no. 253, pl. 18, top).

Figure 8. Fragment of Protocorinthian Oinochoe, Aigina, Museum (after H. Payne, *Protokorinthische Vasenmalerei*, pl. 19, 3).

sociated with them is outspokenly angular (figure 7).

The significant quality of the later painter's animals is the implication of dignity and statuesque calm they bring with them—undoubtedly from a new interpretation of sources[24]—and these are terms not really applicable to the figures of the Hound Painter with their strong recollections of torsional excitement. Furthermore, Payne quite rightly associated the Aigina pyxis lid fragment (*Protokorinthische Vasenmalerei*, pl. 4, fig. 3) with the Hound Painter's period. And yet the visual contrast of this piece alone with the Aigina kotyle fragments makes it clear that they are too different to belong to the same subperiod, unless, that is, one tried to make a case for two quite different streams

24. While previous to this time Protocorinthian artists seem to have drawn certain aspects, perhaps only details, from Near Eastern animals and worked them into conceptions with a quite different spirit (as my analysis of MPC I animals shows), the Aigina Bellerophon Painter seems to have been the first to grasp both the corporeality and the ritualistic dignity of the beasts that guarded Near East palace entrances and that walked in stately fashion in processions on orthostats and on ivory artifacts from the North Syrian and Assyrian regions, to mention some possible sources. I take this to be a parallel to the more conspicuous turning to Egyptian inspiration in the sculpting of the human figure.

of style existing side by side—which is, of course, exactly what Payne does *not* do. Nor would a study of workshops permit it.

With this final clarification, which necessarily strengthens Payne's tentative caesura between the Hound Painter and the Aigina Bellerophon Painter into the more substantial cut between MPC I and MPC II, it will be possible to take up again the theme that I originally broached in *Die Geschichte der korinthischen Vasen* concerning a short but brilliant culmination of Protocorinthian style just before and after the mid seventh century B.C. (by current archaeological dead reckoning). This is, of course, too large an undertaking to attempt here, especially since it must depend on presentation of the evidence of connoisseurship. As a token for this I append a list of names of the workshops and painters I am at this stage of my studies assigning to the subdivisions of MPC. Meanwhile, a few remarks may suffice to sketch out some important aspects of MPC research.

* * *

It will be evident that this essay is rather consciously concerned with methods. The categories of artistic biography of personal and suprapersonal intentions of artists have arisen, leading to considerations of periodicity and of generation spans. While this is not the right place for drawing conclusions, some explanation of standpoint is in order.

The stylistic groups, workshops, and actual painter lists here discussed must be understood as the best available—but yet because of insufficient data tenuous—evidence for the relative chronology of our period. But it should remembered that in this sphere more is not automatically better. The accumulation of data per se can even make the problem of recognizing the truly consequential bewilderingly difficult, as D. A. Amyx and others are well aware from the study of mature Corinthian pottery. The glue that holds data together has to be hypotheses that yield a presumed relative order of works in a suprapersonal and, if possible, a personal series. While Johansen dealt with Geometric and Protocorinthian and Payne dealt with Protocorinthian and Corinthian as extensively as possible on the basis of grave groups, literary references,[25] and so forth, ultimately each had to depend greatly on a sense of style in broad terms and, it might seem, in a rather intuitive sense. The addition of research based on lists of artists' works in a more individual sense can be a means of refining the conclusions previously reached. In my opinion, the opportunity should be taken at this point to penetrate, with discussably organized intellectual hypotheses, into the sphere of the more intuitive systems proposed by the predecessors. In this way an interaction of two approaches can take place.

As the Appendix shows, we are on extremely unstable ground in regard to artistic biography in the early part of MPC, with mostly rather loose groups. In the later part defensible, though rather short, lists of works attributable to individual hands become slightly more numerous. In the light of all this it is perhaps something of an act of faith to speak of artistic generations. If so, nevertheless, given the span of years that are to be covered in the absolute chronology, the assumptions I have made from the internal evidence, namely, fifteen years for the Toulouse Group, fifteen years for the Hound Painter, and ten years for the Aigina Bellerophon Painter correspond precisely with the "indiction" of fifteen years worked out for an artistic generation by George Kübler[26] on evidence drawn from many sources. In fact, he cites in a footnote a literary variant of the problem that "proves the rule" much as does our series:

> H. Peyre observed that occasional short generations of ten years occurred when the work demanded: in other words, that the independent variable is not the generation but the work it has to do.

Theoretically, the ten-year span I reckon with could be interchanged with either of the fifteen year periods. However, the continuation of the Chigi Painter (who plays Ghiberti to the Aigina Bellerophon Painter's Donatello) into the LPC period with relatively little change in style suggests a short duration for (my) MPC II. And it is hardly necessary to say that the indictions personalized here with names for convenience could still be valid even if, for example, the Toulouse master should turn out to be an early phase of, rather than the teacher of (as Dunbabin and Robertson), the Hound Painter and so forth.

As for artistic intention, discussion of this on the personal level has to await presentation of the lists (although I have anticipated it in some cases above). On the suprapersonal level Kübler's reference to the work a generation has to do can be taken as a point of departure for my assumption that the work of several generations (indictions) may *collectively* amount to an overriding theme

---

25. Payne, of course, pioneered in the field of (mature) Corinthian connoisseurship. He did not live long enough to organize and reap the benefits from this approach.

26. Kübler, *The Shape of Time* (New Haven, 1962) 105. The footnote cited below is on the same page. It should be noted that there are no deterministic overtones in Kübler's approach to periodicity.

that constitutes the work a whole subperiod or period has to do. I believe this to be a quite practical assumption. It brings under scrutiny the otherwise very little examined or discussed reasoning which has set the greater and smaller divisions of Greek art we call Geometric, Archaic, Protocorinthian, Early Classical, etc. These names, far from being purely conventional, as might at first be thought, are vital reference points in the phenomenon of periodicity, which it is now time to take seriously.

Appendix:
Summary of Workshop Dating

Much has been written about the absolute dating of Protocorinthian pottery, owing to the critical position it holds in the history of Greek colonization. The theories of various scholars have been summarized in chart form by L. Banti in *Enciclopedia dell'Arte Antica* 6, 507. To this can be added the chronology proposed by J. N. Coldstream, *Geometric Greece* (New York, 1977) 385. While I accept Coldstream's starting date of 690 B.C. for MPC (cf. *AJA* 74 [1970] 305), my conception of the nature of MPC development as indicated above allows at most fifteen years for the extent of MPC IA, so the MPC IB begins at 675 B.C. In the circumstances this is also convenient in falling on a quarter century mark. As I have no reason to disagree with Dunbabin's date of 650 B.C. for the end of MPC II, I place the beginning of that period at 660 B.C. Another addition to the chart would be Paolino Mingazzini: "La Datazione della Ceramica Protocorinzia e di altre Ceramiche Archaiche," *Memorie dell'Accademia dei Lincei Classe di Scienze Morali*, serie 8, vol. 19 (1976) 491–531.

Although absolute dates vary according to the interpretation of historical and stylistic data by various scholars, I do not know of any internal criticism of Payne's First and Second Black-figure Styles other than that implicit in the lists of Dunbabin and Robertson and what I offer here. This statement excludes the recent attempt by Mingazzini to downdate the Chigi olpe to circa 570 B.C. By inference he rejects Payne's system and all the workshop analysis that has been built on it concerning the seventh and sixth centuries B.C.: see, for example, his comments on the Toulouse oinochoe and the Hound Painter's kotylai ("La Datazione della Ceramica Protocorinzia," p. 478) and on the Bellerophon kotyle from Aigina (pp. 474–76), which he dates 570–60 B.C., or later than the Chigi olpe.

In the following lists I do not include silhouette and pattern workshops which will be dealt with separately.

MPC IA 690–675 B.C.
Hopping Birds Workshop (straddles EPC and MPC IA)
Toulouse Group
Ajax Painter
Ithaca Hare Group

MPC IB 675–660 B.C.
Corneto Painter
Hound Painter
Nola Workshop
Aetos Group
Aigina 263 Workshop
Pyxis Lid Painter
Ithaca Kyathos Group

MPC II 660–650 B.C.
Chaironeia Workshop (straddles MPC IB-MPC II)
Berlin Centauromachy Group
Aigina Bellerophon Painter
Fighting Rams Workshop
Columbia Workshop
Race Group
Corinth CP 2295 Group
Chigi Painter
Painter of Perachora 438

15. Observations on Proto-Volute Kraters

DIETRICH VON BOTHMER

DEPARTMENT OF GREEK AND ROMAN ART, THE METROPOLITAN MUSEUM OF ART,
NEW YORK

In 1925 Andreas Rumpf put together six late Corinthian kraters of an exceptional shape that he linked with the only form of krater known in Chalcidian and also common in Laconian.[1] Two years later he added a seventh Corinthian vase and underlined the alien character of these vases in a Corinthian morphological development.[2] He assumed that the special shape of Corinthian kraters had been borrowed from Chalcis. Humfry Payne, in *Necrocorinthia*, brought the number of Corinthian examples up to nine and stressed that the Chalcidian vases of this shape were *later* than the Corinthian examples.[3] Since the Laconian kraters associated with the Corinthian and Chalcidian parallels are usually without figured decoration, they have not been studied afresh in the most recent monograph on Laconian.[4] Rumpf also noted two Attic examples, one a late black-figured krater once in the Munich market,[5] the other an early fifth-century red-figured vase in Agrigento: I have never seen the publication of the former and am unable to identify the latter.

Though many more Chalcidian vases have come to light since Rumpf's publication, Chalcidian kraters remain as rare as ever. The only addition I can make to the four already put together by Rumpf in 1925 is a small vase exhibited at the Basle antiquities fair in 1978,[6] attributed by Dr. H. A. Cahn to Rumpf's stylistic group of the Leipzig amphora. Nor has the list of Corinthian kraters of this shape grown appreciably and proportionally in the last fifty years,[7] and numerically both the Corinthian and the Chalcidian kraters are outnumbered by the scores of Laconian kraters.[8] Quantity does not, of course, always imply seniority, but Lane has argued that the Laconian products go back to the second quarter of the sixth century, and he also observed that the inspiration did not come from Corinth but from Laconian bronze vases,[9] and Rumpf went so far as to identify the volute krater with the one called Laconian in antiquity.[10]

1. *AA* 1923–1924 (published in 1925), col. 78.
2. A. Rumpf, *Chalkidische Vasen* (Berlin/Leipzig, 1927) 122–23.
3. H. Payne, *Necrocorinthia* (Oxford, 1931) 330, nos. 1477–85.
4. C. M. Stibbe, *Lakonische Vasenmaler* (Amsterdam, 1972) 11, note 2.
5. Auction Sale Cat. Weitzinger no. 5 (Munich, 1918) pl. 51, no. 1515.

6. Stand 34 (Münzen und Medaillen A. G.), manuscript catalogue no. 101. Height, 12.05 cm; width, 19.4 cm; diameter of mouth, 14.9 cm; diameter of foot, 7.6 cm.
7. For a remarkable newcomer see figures 12–15 and note 52.
8. An up-to-date list does not exist, but already in 1930 Paolino Mingazzini counted 64 examples in *Vasi della Collezione Castellani*, vol. 1 (Rome, 1930) 186–87, to which E. A. Lane made many additions (*BSA* 34 [1933–1934] 149ff.).
9. *Collezione Castellani*, 149.
10. In *Charites* (1954) 127–35.

Figure 1. Obverse, Attic Black-figure Krater by Sophilos, New York, The Metropolitan Museum of Art, acc. no. 1977.11.2.

In 1961, however, Paola Pelagatti claimed that the Laconian terracotta kraters are "di derivazione probabilmente calcidesi,"[11] and Claude Rolley refuted most of Rumpf's arguments for a Laconian origin of the Vix krater and related bronze vases.[12]

Archaeological literature, of course, abounds in conflicting theories always most attractively presented and cleverly reasoned, but those of us who follow the treacherous movements of the tides with the caution of a mariner are seldom left high and dry on a beach. We are helped in steering a clear course by the knowledge that even the most beautiful classifications are often menaced by new evidence, and the constant need to readjust our ideas in the light provided by these newcomers, while vexing at times, keeps us in trim.

When asked by the editor of this volume in honor of D. A. Amyx to write on a Corinthian subject, I was at first somewhat embarrassed since I felt that anything purely Corinthian must surely be known to the man who has spent close to forty years of his life bringing Payne up to date and has applied a rigorous system of attributions to a fabric of painted vases that is as plentiful as it is at times discouraging. Moreover, I can truthfully say that ever since I became aware of Dick Amyx's preoccupation with Corinth, I have always shared with him anything Corinthian that I encountered in my traveling or through my work in a museum. What I can now offer to my esteemed friend and colleague is therefore not new to him, and while it touches on the problem sketched above only tangentially, it may serve as proof that there are no impassable frontiers in our chosen fields.

In December 1976 I was offered in Beverly Hills sixty-odd black-figured fragments of an Attic krater that combined all the features of a desirable purchase: rarity, good style, and an attractively low price. Thanks to the generosity of Mr. and Mrs. Martin Fried of New York, the vase was bought on January 28, 1977. It was put together by Shinichi Doi of the Museum's Department of Objects Con-

11. *Enciclopedia dell'Arte Antica* 4 (1961) 446.
12. *BCH* 82 (1958) 168ff.

Figure 2. Reverse of Krater in Figure 1.

servation, but even before the purchase, on a singularly rainy New Year's Day in Berkeley, I discussed it with Dick Amyx.

Though the vase is fragmentary[13] (figures 1–5), the shape could be reconstructed with certainty, and the attribution to Sophilos was beyond question. Moreover, the krater is of imposing dimensions, with a (restored) height of 49.15 cm, a width of 55.4 cm, and a diameter of 48.1 cm. It was briefly described in the Metropolitan Museum's *107th Annual Report*[14] and published two years later.[15] The top of the rim (figure 4) is decorated with upright ivy leaves on straight stems, their tips pointed inward, and with dot-circles suspended in the field near the in-

ner edge of the mouth. The side of the mouth is black. The upper part of the neck, below it, is decorated with an ivy wreath. The individual leaves are equipped with straight stems, but their numbers are not the same: thirty-three above, and only thirty-one below; hence the stems meet each other only once.[16]

The pictures on the two sides are set in panels framed above by black and red tongues. The better preserved panel, here called the obverse (figure 1), shows two "snarling" boars confronting each other that in the *oeuvre* of Sophilos find their nearest parallels in the pairs on a lebes gamikos in Smyrna,[17] two dinoi in the Louvre and Lon-

13. 1977.11.2. Missing are the foot, most of the reverse, much of one handle, and more than half of the rim and neck.

14. 1976–1977 (published 31 October 1977) 52–53.

15. *Notable Acquisitions* (1975–1979) 13–14. It is not mentioned by Güven Bakır in *Sophilos, ein Beitrag zu seinem Stil* (Mainz, 1981) perhaps merely because the publication of the New York krater escaped his attention (cf. Ann Blair Brownlee in *AJA* 86 [1982] 601). Bakır's book, *Sophilos*, is referred to by title only in notes 17–26.

16. Straight-stemmed ivy leaves, with dot-circles or dot-rosettes, later become the favorite lateral frames of Attic black-figured hydriai (see, for example, *ABV* 85, no. 2; *Paralipomena* 45 [Ceramicus Museum, Lydos]; Oxford, Ohio, Miami University, P. 78 C 2.124 [Lydos]; Boston 89.561 [*CVA* 2, pl. 71]; Munich 8561 [fr.]; Louvre F 8 [*CVA* 3 He pl. 60]; *ABV* 174 no. 7).

17. *ABV* 40 no. 20; *Sophilos*, 35, fig. 21 and pl. 41 (A. 21).

Figure 3. Side A/B of Krater in Figure 1.

don,[18] a louterion in Athens,[19] a loutropho-ros-amphora in Athens[20] and another in Warsaw,[21] a tripod-kothon in Boston,[22] or, less fierce and singly, on another long-necked neck-amphora in Athens,[23] the dinoi in London and Herakleion,[24] a louterion in Ankara,[25] and three lekanides in Athens.[26] Two star-rosettes are placed in the background between the two boars, a filling ornament that I cannot match in the vases by Sophilos known to me.[27]

The more fragmentary side, here called the

Figure 4. Top of Rim and Handle of Krater in Figure 1.

reverse (figure 2), also has two animals set in a panel. The beast on the left must be a bull, as is shown by the straight tail, the straight back, and the beginning of a horn. Below the neck are uncertain remains—perhaps part of an elaborate filling ornament. The bull is rather unexpected as an animal given prominence by Sophilos. Lions or panthers normally attack bulls, boars, and deer,[28] but Sophilos has here paired two of their traditional victims in a setting that cannot be called heraldic.

So far I have avoided giving this krater by Sophilos a specific determining name, be-

18. *ABV* 39 nos. 12–13; *Sophilos*, 65 (A. 4), pls. 46–48; 72 (B. 1), pls. 66–70.

19. *ABV* 40 no. 19; *Sophilos* 76 (C. 1), pls. 85–86.

20. *ABV* 38, no. 2; *Sophilos* 67 (A. 12).

21. *Paralipomena* 18, no. 1 bis; *Sophilos* 72–73 (B. 4) pl. 71.

22. *ABV* 41, no. 27; *Sophilos* 69 (A. 22) pl. 29.

23. *ABV* 38, no. 1; *Sophilos* 67 (A. 14) pls. 49–54.

24. *Paralipomena* 19, no. 16 bis.; 18, no. 14 bis; *Sophilos* 64 (A. 1) pls. 1–2; 72 (B. 2) pl. 80, fig. 159.

25. *Sophilos* 68 (A. 19) 17, fig. 9, pls. 15–17.

26. *ABV* 41, nos. 28–30; *Sophilos* 70 (A. 26–28) pls. 58–61.

27. Star-rosettes occur, however, as filling ornaments on the neck-amphora London B 25 (*ABV* 106, no. 1) and on amphorae B: e.g., Halle 52 (E. Bielefeld, *Die Antikensammlung in Halle-Wittenberg* pls. 8–9, no. 52), Louvre E 813, and Conservatori (ex Museo Artistico Industriale; A and B, each, rider).

28. As on the François vase, *ABV* 76, no. 1.

Figure 6. Bronze Krater from San Mauro, Syracuse, Sicily, Museo Nazionale.

Figure 5. Profile Drawing of Handle of Krater in Figure 1.

yond associating it with the variant of the column-krater that since Rumpf and Payne is called Chalcidian. The Sophilos krater in New York, however, is not only the earliest but also so different as to exclude the possibility that it was potted under the influence of Laconian or Corinthian terracotta vases. It is, in fact, remarkably metallic, and it invites comparison with a well-known, though poorly preserved, bronze krater (figures 6 and 7) found in a necropolis on the hills of San Mauro near Caltagirone and acquired in

1903 by the museum in Syracuse.[29] Dated at first by Paolo Orsi in the second quarter of the fifth century B.C., contemporary with the latest Attic black-figured volute-kraters,[30] and attributed by him to an Ionian workshop,[31] the engraved designs on the neck—flute-players and dancing youths on one side, Centaurs on the other—prompted Payne to reconsider both the date and the attribution. He described the San Mauro bronze as "a volute-crater of a primitive kind" and took the dancers on the neck to be of "distinctly Corinthian style,"[32] and Mogens Gjødesen aptly compared the Centaurs with those on a column-krater in Corinth.[33] Lastly, Ioulia Kouleïmani-Vokotopoulou accepted the San Mauro vase as Corinthian and dated it circa 590–570 B.C.[34]

Since the San Mauro krater is poorly (and wrongly) restored, the present reported height of 52 cm is less significant than the more certain inner diameter of the mouth of

29. P. Orsi in *Monumenti Antichi* 20 (1910), cols. 809–15, pl. 8.

30. Ibid., cols. 812–13.

31. Ibid., col. 814.

32. *Necrocorinthia*, 218.

33. *AJA* 67 (1963) 344.

34. *Chalkai Korinthiourgeis prochoi* (1975).

Figure 7. Handle Zone of Krater in Figure 6.

33.7 cm,[35] and its original shape must have been closer to that of the New York krater by Sophilos.

Its closest link with the Sophilos krater is furnished by the strap that connects the lower arch on the shoulder of the vase with the rim. This strap is flanged and after rising steeply curves gracefully above the level of the mouth and on its return splits into two pronounced hooks or curls. The rise above the level of the mouth is avoided by the potters of the earliest Corinthian kraters of the so-called Chalcidian variety[36] and is also absent in the Chalcidian kraters.[37] The angularity of the strap above the arch, so disturbing aesthetically on the Corinthian krater in Dresden,[38] is in Corinthian not mitigated until the phase represented by the late Corin-

thian krater in the Niarchos collection in Paris (figures 8, 9, and 10)[39] and in Chalcidian not until the small krater recently on the Basle market.[40] Laconian kraters of the Chalcidian variety (figure 11)[41] do not differ much in this respect from their Corinthian counterparts. The earliest Laconian true volute kraters, Louvre E 661 and Villa Giulia 50401,[42] are both surely later than the Sophilos vase in New York.

35. Orsi in *Monumenti*, col. 811.

36. Cf. *Necrocorinthia*, 330, fig. 174.

37. A. Rumpf, *Chalkidische Vasen*, nos. 13–14 (pls. 27–33); nos. 113–14 (pls. 126–30).

38. *Necrocorinthia*, 330, no. 1477.

39. *Münzen und Medaillen Auktion XVIII* (29 November 1958) 25, no. 80, pl. 20.

40. See above, note 6.

41. See above, note 8. Interesting additions to the large body of all-black or mostly black kraters are Leningrad, 1911.6 from Kerch; London Market, *Cat. Sotheby 1 July 1969*, no. 231; Rouen, Campana 25, *Hommes, Dieux et Héros de la Grèce* (Rouen 28 October 1982–31 January 1983) 52, no. 5; Besançon; Troyes; New York 66.11.16, here figure 11, height 28 cm.

42. On Louvre E 661 see also C. M. Stibbe *op. cit.*, 78–79; Villa Giulia 50401 (ibid. 275, no. 105) was dated "not later than 570" by Lane (*BSA* 35 [1933–1934] 148).

Figure 8. Late Corinthian Krater, Paris, Niarchos Collection.

Figure 9. Obverse of Krater in Figure 8.

Figure 10. Side B/A of Krater in Figure 8.

Figure 11. Laconian Krater, New York, The Metropolitan Museum of Art, acc. no. 66.11.16.

The flanged handle strap of the San Mauro krater has two central narrow ridges that are perhaps more decorative than functional, but it is worth pointing out that later Etruscan bronze volute-krater handles of this type, with two horsemen in lieu of the arch,[43] emphasize this meridian, while other handles of later bronze volute-kraters are content without this central ridge. The arch of the San Mauro bronze krater is formed by a two-headed snake firmly grasped in the middle by four fingers of a hand. Snakes become a regular feature of the arch and can be thought of as a functional extension, for greater security, of the plain loop that forms the arch on terracotta kraters.[44] The fingers are unusual but not unique, for they recur on an

43. E.g., Louvre 2635 (A. de Ridder, *Les bronzes antiques du Louvre* 2 [1915] 105, no. 2635, pl. 96; Ferrara inv. 2315 (T 128) from Spina (S. Aurigemma, *Il R. Museo di Spina* [Bologna, 1935] p. 190 and pl. 150); New York 61.11.4 (*BMMA* n.s. 20 [1961–1962] 52, above); Lucerne Auktion, 7 December 1957 (Dr. Jacob Hirsch) 22–23, no. 51, pl. 24; Dallas, private (ex-Paris market).

44. Cf. the snake-legged gorgons on such bronze volute-kraters as Louvre 2636 (A. de Ridder, *Les bronzes antiques du Louvre* 105–106, pl. 95) and its companion in Nîmes; Chatillon-sur-Seine (R. Joffroy in *MonPiot* 48 [1954] pl. 8, 1–2); Munich 4262 (Joffroy, ibid., pl. 22, 1); London 583 (Joffroy, ibid., pl. 23, 1).

Figure 12. Obverse, Corinthian Krater, New York, Metropolitan Museum of Art, acc. no. 1979.11.7.

unpublished bronze handle in Berlin[45] and on the volute-krater from Capua in Naples.[46] Interestingly enough, the Capua krater, which is less provincial and later than the one from San Mauro, shares with the latter the central ridge on the handle strap, which may be considered an Italic (or at least western) feature: on the Berlin handle, said to be from Didyma according to the label (room 6, vitrine 1), the strap is not divided.

Fingers, or entire hands, are relatively rare on bronze vases and utensils. A closer parallel for the *grasping* hands is furnished by a bronze neck-amphora from Paestum,[47] on which two pairs of closed hands at the upper junction of the handles once held the swinging bails that are now lost. As on the three

volute-krater handles, these hands in Paestum are truly helping hands, while the *flattened-out* hands that occur first on the lateral handles of a hydria in Paestum[48] and its mate in Belgrade (from Trebenishte)[49] look less useful. This type survives on Italian soil in an Etruscan workshop of bronze stamnoi, of which the best published examples are in the Rhode Island School of Design.[50]

If we compare the bronze handles of the San Mauro krater, the Capua krater, and one from Didyma, we might be tempted to see in the series a gradual evolution of the volutes—from the early curls of San Mauro to the more advanced though still open contin-

48. Sestieri, *Bolletino*, 62, fig. 22 and 63, fig. 25.
49. L. Popović, *Catalogue des objets découverts près de Trebeništé* (1956) pls. 31–31a.
50. 35.791. David G. Mitten *Classical Bronzes, Catalogue, Museum of Art, Rhode Island School of Design* (Providence, 1975) 147–50, no. 30. (The Sofia hydria from Trebenishte there cited in note 4 does not, however, have hands but protomai of horses.) For handles with flattened-out hands see especially B. A. Raeve in *Sovetskaya Archeologia* 1974, 181–89.

45. M 149 b. Height 16.1 cm; width, with snakes 21.5 cm; width of volute 7.4 cm; depth of volute 6.9 cm.
46. W. Johannowsky in *RendNap* n.s. 49 (1974) 3–19, pls. 2, 2a and 4–5.
47. P. C. Sestieri in *Bolletino d'Arte*, ser. 4, 40 (1955) 62, fig. 21.

Figure 13. Reverse of Krater in Figure 12.

uation of the loops of Capua, and finally to the completed tightened spiral of the Didyma handle. We might also be persuaded that the same progression holds true for pottery, and we would feel justified in equating the stage of the Sophilos krater with that of the bronze vessel from San Mauro. Two questions, however, remain: is the Sophilos krater necessarily later than the San Mauro vessel, and is the potted handle necessarily a deliberate imitation of one in metal? I am not convinced that the volutes, nascent or fully coiled, have to be considered as metallic in origin, for clay can be shaped in almost any manner more easily than metal, and even the flanges are no criterion when we remember the Attic amphorae of type A, for which to date we have not found a single bronze counterpart. Nor do I maintain that the Sophilos krater in New York has to be the first proto volute-krater ever made: it just happens to be the earliest now known to us. Furthermore, Mrs. Karouzou's attempts to identify the shape of

Acropolis 391[51] as that of a volute-krater may well be vindicated one day.

But the story does not quite end here, for another vase acquired by the Metropolitan Museum of Art (figures 12–15)[52] seven years ago, a Corinthian krater of Chalcidian form, has the unique distinction of being the earliest Corinthian krater of that shape. Though fragmentary (and unrestored), the body is almost complete, lacking only the lower part and the foot, as well as most of one handle. On the obverse (figure 1) a swan is shown between two griffin birds, while the reverse (figure 2) is given over to a panther and a wild goat. An owl appears under the handle A/B: the corresponding creature under the handle B/A is lost. The side of the rim is decorated with wriggly lines; the top of the mouth and the handles are black.

51. *ABV* 5, no. 10; S. Karouzou in *BCH* 79 (1955) 195–96.
52. Acc. no. 1979.11.7. Anonymous Gift Fund, 1979. Preserved height, 25.0 cm; diameter 25.7 cm.

Figure 14. Side A/B of Krater in Figure 12.

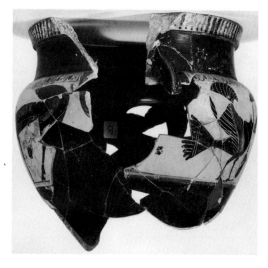

Figure 15. Side B/A of Krater in Figure 12.

Now, all the other Corinthian kraters of "Chalcidian shape" are red-ground and Late Corinthian I, but this newcomer is clearly earlier, Middle Corinthian. Even the subjects, swan between griffin birds and panther facing goat, are early and recall, as Amyx reminds me, vases of his "Hochschule Group"[53]—late Early Corinthian or early Middle Corinthian. There is, therefore, even a question whether the Sophilos krater discussed above is going to keep its seniority for very long, but the questions posed by these two newcomers to our known body of vases are salutary and should encourage us to keep an open mind both in Attic and in Corinthian.

53. D. A. Amyx, *Corinthian Vase-painting of the Archaic Period* (forthcoming) vol. 1, 147–48.

Postscript (27 May 1983)

Konrad Hitzl, *Die Entstehung und Entwicklung des Volutenkraters von den frühesten Anfängen bis zur Ausprägung des kanonischen Stils in der attisch schwarzfigurigen Vasenmalerei* (*Archäologische Studien* 6, Verlag Peter Lang, Frankfurt am Main/Bern 1982), reached me after I had submitted my contribution to *Corinthiaca: Studies in Honor of Darrell A. Amyx.* Hitzl analyzes many of the vases that also appear in my article, and he publishes for the first time in his work (pl. 13a) the bronze handle in Berlin (see note 45).

[For my detailed review of Hitzl see *Gnomon* 57 (1985), 66–71.]

16. Four Corinthian Panthers from Sardis

JUDITH SCHAEFFER

DEPARTMENT OF ART HISTORY, UNIVERSITY OF CALIFORNIA, RIVERSIDE

Four panthers on Corinthian pottery fragments found at Sardis reflect the economic realities of trade between Corinth and the inland kingdoms of Anatolia in the seventh and early sixth centuries B.C.[1] The increased demand for Corinthian ware in the Early and Middle Corinthian periods, and the subsequent rush to fill orders, resulted in a deterioration of workmanship that is remarkably evident in even so brief a series as the four panthers from Sardis. The change, evident especially in the disregard for traditional renderings of animal anatomy, resulted ultimately in the capture of the Corinthian market at Sardis by Attic merchants, who could offer a far more attractive product.

Corinth carried on an active trade with Sardis from the eighth to the mid-sixth century B.C.[2] Corinthian kotylai, alabastra, aryballoi, and even kraters[3] were found at Sardis, proving that the taste for Corinth's colorful, delicately wrought, and patterned ware was not limited to the Hellenic *poleis*

on the coast of Anatolia but rather reached inland at an early date.

Corinthian trade with Sardis—either directly or through trade with the Eastern Greek *poleis*—began under the Heraklids,[4] reached its height during the reigns of the Mermnad kings, Ardys and Alyattes (circa 645–561 B.C.),[5] and ended just before the defeat of King Croesus by Cyrus of Persia in 545 B.C. The earliest Corinthian import found at Sardis dates to the middle of the eighth century.[6] Corinthian ware continued to reach Lydia with no perceptible break from the Geometric through the Late Corinthian periods.

The panther fragments at Sardis were found in two areas: Pactolus North (PN), an industrial area[7] immediately adjacent to the Pactolus River and only a short distance downstream from the Artemis Temple; and

---

1. This article is dedicated to my teacher, D. A. Amyx, in admiration of his exceptional connoisseurship, and in remembrance of many hours pleasantly spent studying both Corinthian and Etruscan panthers at Berkeley.

2. The entire body of Corinthian material from Sardis will be published by the author in the Sardis Monograph series, Harvard University Press.

3. Portions of at least three Corinthian kraters were found at Sardis. One of them, a handle-plate with a fine crouching dog (inv. P.61.339, from PN), dates to the early years of Early Corinthian. Rim fragments from a Middle Corinthian krater (inv. P.60.599A and P.61.256, from HOB) bear a lotus-palmette design.

4. Herodotus, 1.7. For the dating see G. M. A. Hanfmann and others, *A Survey and Sector Index of Sardis* (Cambridge, Mass., 1975) 6.

5. Hanfmann, *Index of Sardis*.

6. A trefoil mouthed oinochoe (Manisa Museum no. 4951) found in a destruction level at HOB. The level is usually associated with the Kimmerian invasion of Sardis. Both the Corinthian and other imported wares found in context suggest an earlier date, no later than the third quarter of the eighth century. I follow J. N. Coldstream for dating the Corinthian Geometric pottery (*Greek Geometric Pottery*, London, 1968), and D. A. Amyx for Corinthian proper (*Corinthian Vase-Painting*, forthcoming): Transitional, circa 630–620/615; Early Corinthian, circa 620/615–595/590; Middle Corinthian, circa 595/590–570 B.C.

7. The area produced clear evidence of gold cupellation, see *BASOR* 199 (1970) 16–26.

the House of Bronzes area (HOB), located downstream from PN and slightly further from the river. Although the House of Bronzes itself dates from the Early Christian period, levels below the house and its surrounding area were rich in imported archaic pottery.[8]

Both PN and HOB suffered from flooding in antiquity. The Pactolus River inundated these areas, depositing beds of loose gravel. Only a few Corinthian vases have survived intact. Some sherds have suffered considerable wear, others have tumbled out of their original context. Nevertheless, the Corinthian sherds were numerous enough to produce a fairly dependable stratigraphy at HOB, though less precise at PN.[9]

Many of the Corinthian sherds found at Sardis belong to the Early and Middle Corinthian periods. The earliest clear example of a panther dates from the Early Corinthian period and is the only panther fragment found at PN:[10]

Inv. P.62.339   (figure 1)
Wall fragment, vessel shape uncertain.
Panther to left, facing outward, preserved from ears to shoulder. Grazing animal in profile to right, nose preserved. A large, incised rosette in the field.
Glaze black, glossy, crackled and worn in places.
Incision sure and firm, but quick and occasionally careless.
Red overpaint on forehead, nose, and neck of panther.
Munsell Nos.: wall: 7.5YR 6/4; slip: 10YR 7/4 (light pinkish brown; very pale brown)
MPH: 0.047; MPW: 0.041; Th. of wall: 0.006
Findspot: PN, Lydian Basement *87.20

The facial type used for the Early Corinthian panther from Sardis can be traced all the way from Transitional[11] to the early years

Figure 1. Corinthian Fragment, Sardis, inv. no. P.62.339.

of Middle Corinthian. It is shared by at least one sculptured example, the panther with a mane of a lion and spots of a leopard in the pediment of the temple of Artemis at Corcyra.[12] The temple at Corcyra, a Corinthian *apoikia* with strong connections to its mother polis, dates to the early sixth century, close in time to the Sardis sherd.

The type is characterized by rounded ears, a strong "Y"-shaped pattern forming the forehead-nose area, eyes with round irises and almond-shaped lids, and a muzzle marked by horizontal arcs. Patterns used to represent facial anatomy in panthers found in Corinthian vase-painting seem arbitrary, but they can be easily understood when compared with their three-dimensional form on the sculpture. It is possible that the sculptural representations, therefore, served as the origin of the painted pattern. For example, the

---

8. See *BASOR* 162 (1961) 12–16; and 166 (1962) 14–15.

9. The stratigraphic evidence will be published in the forthcoming Sardis Monograph on imported wares.

10. All measurements are given in centimeters. Abbreviations used: MPH = maximum preserved height; MPW = maximum preserved width; Th. = thickness.

11. For Transitional, see H. Payne, *Necrocorinthia* (Oxford, 1931), no. 168, pl. 14; and W. Kraiker, *Aigina*

(Berlin, 1951) no. 461, pl. 35. For a Middle Corinthian example see *AJA* 73 (1969) pl. 37, fig. 16, attributed by Amyx to the Detroit Painter.

12. R. Lullies and M. Hirmer, *Greek Sculpture* (New York, 1960) 56–57 and pls. 16–17. This unique combination of panther-lion-leopard may have some special significance for Corcyra, but it also appears in Corinthian vase-painting.

origin of the "Y"-shaped pattern of the forehead-nose area found not only on this sherd from Sardis but also on numerous other representations in vase-painting can be easily traced to the anatomical "wrinkles" of the feline's brow in sculptural works such as the Corcyra pediment. Similarly, the horizontal and vertical divisions of the muzzle on the sculptured felines appear in a simplified form in vase-painting, limited as it is to simple incisions. The downward-pointing eyes with their painted irises and almond-shaped lids found on the panther-beast in the Corcyra pediment make the eye incisions found on many panthers in Corinthian vase-painting understandable. Even the lion's mane of the Corcyra panther-beast is apparently rendered in some painted panthers by short parallel strokes placed along the top of the head and near the cheek (see figure 6). Rib cage, haunch, and shoulder markings are shared by both sculpted and painted examples.[13]

Clearly, both sculptor and painter shared a common repertoire of shapes and markings that were considered appropriate to representations of panthers and panther-lions. This common understanding of appropriate form remains fundamentally the same throughout the Early Corinthian period.

This Sardis panther shares many similarities of design with a panther on an Early Corinthian oinochoe in Leipzig.[14] Particularly revealing are the break in the forehead marking near the left ear in both animals and the position of the panther's eyes: the left eye in both cases slants toward the nose, while the right eye points toward the muzzle. Also similar is the use of a nearly circular arc above the "Y" of the forehead/nose area, as well as the general conformation of the "Y" itself.

Differences, however, do exist. For example, though both panthers have rounded ears, those of the Sardis feline are formed by a continuous incised line, while the ears of the Leipzig panther are created by two broken incisions. More importantly, the outside cheek of the Sardis panther has a strong reverse curve, while that of the Leipzig panther is a simple curve. The Leipzig panther also sports a mane.

It would be unwise to attempt to assign both of these pieces to a single hand on the evidence of the faces alone.[15] Nevertheless, the similarities and peculiarities of incision, especially in the forehead and eye areas, go far to place these two pieces at least in the same workshop, if not to the same hand.

The earliest of the Middle Corinthian panthers from Sardis comes from one of the few nearly complete Corinthian vases found at the site:

Inv. P.62.98 (figures 2, 3, and 4)
Kotyle, joined from twenty-nine pieces.
Two parallel lines of glaze near the rim. Single animal frieze on the body: panther to left, facing forward; bull to right in profile, lion to left in profile, portion of a bird (?) behind the lion. Blob rosettes in the field, some incised.
Glaze almost entirely lost. Remainder is black, dull, and crackled. Fired brown on interior, changing to dark orange near center.
Incision quick, sloppy. Fundamentals of anatomy retained, but careless in details.
Munsell Nos.: wall: between 10YR 7/3 and 7.5YR 7/4; slip: 10YR 8/4 (visible beneath worn glaze). (Very pale brown to pink)
MPH: 0.07; Th. of wall: 0.003; Diam. of rim: 0.11
Findspot: HOB W14/S90 *99.80

The bodies of all the animals on this vase are elongated and heavy, with short, thick legs. The exaggerated length of the lion and the panther is due in part to an effort to fit them beneath the handles of the kotyle. The face of the panther already reflects the degree of deterioration in anatomical pat-

13. The looped shoulder appears regularly in Early Corinthian, cf. Payne, *Necrocorinthia*, pl. 24, fig. 5.
14. *CVA* Leipzig 1 (Germany 14) pl. 53.4, and Payne, *Necrocorinthia*, no. 729, pl. 23, fig. 4. D. A. Amyx suggests that the Sardis shard is "in the tradition of the Sphinx Painter, leaning toward the Chimaera Group, but less fancy."

15. For the problem of identical faces produced by different hands see P. Lawrence in *AJA* 63 (1959) 356–57.

Figure 2. Fragmentary Corinthian Kotyle, Sardis, inv. no. P.62.98.

Figure 3. Second View of Kotyle in Figure 2.

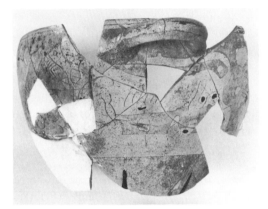

Figure 4. Third View of Kotyle in Figure 2.

terning that has occurred in Middle Corinthian.[16] The ears, small and heart-shaped, are drawn with a single, quick incision and tucked down into the head, as if they had been cut out and pasted on. The forehead area is executed rapidly. It is created by a single line drawn across the head between the ears, then angled down to form one side of the nose. The eyes have become simple circles, with no effort to represent the almond-shaped lid, and they are placed irregularly in the head. Two parallel lines, placed askew on the face, indicate the muzzle. Like the incision of the forehead and the nose, these lines are worked carelessly and are not limited to the glazed area of the muzzle.

The shoulder of each animal on the kotyle

differs: a scroll shape for the shoulder of the panther, a tight curve for that of the bull, and an open curve for the lion. These differences could act as a hallmark for the artist, and they certainly attest to his liking for a variety of patterns. All three animals, however, share the same pattern for the muscles of the foreleg, which is formed by a curve ending in a reverse hook. Although the hindquarters of the panther are missing, the haunch may have had the same peculiar, concave curve that is used for the haunch of both lion and bull.

Examples of Middle Corinthian animals with stocky bodies and short legs appear on a kotyle from Perachora, and on another in Baltimore.[17] However, the long heavy bodies, the general type of panther head, and the lack of a belly stripe relate this work more specifically to the atelier of the much finer Carousel Painter.[18] This painter works early in Middle Corinthian and influences the Chimaera Painter.[19]

In spite of the careless rendering of anatomical form that has occurred in the work of this Middle Corinthian artist, the animals still retain their vigor. The bull shares a heaviness of body with his Early Corinthian ancestors, and the lion stalks at a roar with full chest and powerful limbs.

16. Careless rendering also occurs in Early Corinthian, but more rarely. For an example see Payne, *Necrocorinthia*, no. 669, pl. 26, fig. 2. Overall, the anatomy is much more convincing in Early Corinthian works.

17. T. J. Dunbabin and others, *Perachora* 2 (Oxford, 1962) 254, no. 2472, pl. 100, dated early in Middle Corinthian; Baltimore, Walters Art Gallery, no. 48.2028. The styles are not otherwise similar.

18. Brought to my attention by D. A. Amyx.

19. For the Chimaera Painter see P. Lawrence in *AJA* 63 (1959) 349–63 and *AJA* 66 (1962) 185–87.

Figure 5. Corinthian Fragments (Kotyle?), Sardis, inv. nos. P.61.534 and P.61.133.

A more striking disregard for anatomical clarity occurs on the second Middle Corinthian vase from Sardis, again found at HOB:

Inv. P.61.534 and P.65.133   (figure 5)
Two wall fragments, perhaps from a kotyle.
Goat head to right, in profile; panther to left, facing forward, a portion of the head and body preserved. Blob rosettes and amorphous, incised rosettes in the field.
Glaze applied unevenly, medium brown to black. Interior glaze similar to exterior.
Incision careless and quick. Anatomy misunderstood.
Red overpaint above and below the shoulder incision of the panther, curving down into the first rib interstice; in the second and last rib interstices; on the neck and behind the ear of the goat; a blob dropped just above the goat's beard.
Munsell No.: 10YR 7/3–7/4 (very pale brown)
P.61.534: MPH: 0.047; MPW: 0.045; Th. of wall: 0.005
    Findspot: HOB W10/S100 *99.80–99.60
P.65.113: MPH: 0.065; MPW: 0.045; Th. of wall: 0.005
    Findspot: HOB W10/15/S101–108 *98.40 (intrusive)

The forms of both animals are bulky. The two horns of the goat are a single mass, curving high over the head. His ear is large and thick, his wrinkled forehead massive.

The patterns of the face and the body of the panther show a marked decline in anatomical understanding. For example, only the bottom incision of the ear is represented, and no effort is made to differentiate the interior of the ear from the exterior. A simple incision creates the forehead, curving down from the ear and angling sharply into the nose. Two large arcs, starting just below the ear, mark the cheeks with a design that seems to have no anatomical meaning. The eye is oval in shape, with elongations scratched into the corners, thereby giving the impression of an almond shape, although there is no real understanding of the anatomical differentiation between iris and lid.

A long, unwieldy hump, again with no anatomical basis, runs along the panther's back and is accentuated by the curve of the shoulder incision. The ribs are quickly indicated by a series of incisions that are nearly vertical, vary in length, and have uneven interstices. Moreover, these lines run all the way from the shoulder to the haunch.[20] The bony joints and the ligaments of the legs are marked by curved and straight lines that have only the vaguest reference to the pat-

20. In Early Corinthian works the ribcage is usually confined to the center of the animal. See Payne, *Necrocorinthia*, pls. 14–20.

terns used by Early Corinthian artists. It is as
though this artist were in too much of a
hurry to bother with more than a general
impression of feline anatomy. Even the incised rosette beneath the panther's belly has
lost all resemblance to its floral form. The
incisions are careless, having fallen so far off
to one side (not visible in the photograph)
that they are no longer related to the shape
at all.

Although this panther cannot be assigned
to a particular hand or to a workshop, it does
share some similarities with a Middle Corinthian panther on a kotyle from Perachora,[21] another on a vase in Vienna,[22] and a
third on an aryballos in Taranto.[23]

The last of the four panthers from Sardis
is the lone survivor of his pot. His comic face
looks out at us with a kind of wistfulness, as
though he knew his species would soon become extinct. Like the other Middle Corinthian panthers from Sardis, this panther was
found at HOB:

> Inv. P.61.145   (figure 6)
> Wall fragment, probably from a kotyle.
> Ends of two vertical glaze-lines visible near the
> rim; two horizontal lines below. Panther to
> right, facing outward, only the head pre-
> served. Elongated, blob filler above the pan-
> ther's head.
> Glaze glossy, black and smooth.
> Incision quick and careless with little or no re-
> gard for anatomy.
> Red overpaint on shoulder; a bit dropped ac-
> cidentally on the upper neck.
> Munsell No.: 10YR 8/3 (very pale brown)
> MPH: 0.047; MPW: 0.046; Th. of wall: 0.004
> Findspot: HOB W10/S95 *99.80

The head of this little beast is simply an
extension of his neck, curved around and
kept very low. There is hardly enough space
for the features of the face, and the muzzle
has disappeared altogether. The double arc

Figure 6. Corinthian Fragment (Kotyle?), Sardis, inv.
no. P.61.145.

of the shoulder presses so closely toward the
line of the cheek that the neck is drastically
reduced. The ears are hastily executed. They
are created by four quick strokes that give an
impression of outer and inner ear but have
no real integrity of form. The area between
the ears is marked by two quickly drawn
lines instead of the usual arc. The same kind
of cavalier treatment is afforded the "Y" of
the forehead/nose area. The two vertical incisions of the nose differ in length, and one
actually extends over into the area of the
neck.

A series of parallel incisions are meant to
represent the mane, but these marks have slid
out of their usual position and lie carelessly
on the surface of the face, their original purpose long forgotten. The round eyes are rendered so quickly that their form is angular
rather than circular. They are placed low in
the head, giving the panther a timid appearance. There are no close companions for this
little panther, although something similar exists on a Middle Corinthian work in Montpellier[24] and on several vases from Tocra.[25]

Though retaining some similarity to the

---

21. *Perachora* 2, no. 2472.
22. Vienna, Kunsthistorisches Museen, inv. no.
4.1830, see G. Nicole, *La peinture des vases grecs* (Paris,
1926) pl. 8e.
23. Taranto, National Museum, inv. no. 4850 (Amyx
photographic collection). For the material from Taranto
see *Annuario Scuola Atene* 21–22 (1959–1960) and
Bollettino d'Arte 47 (1962) 153–70.

24. A. F. Laurens, *Céramique corinthienne et etrusco-
corinthienne* (Societe Archeologique de Montpellier)
Catalog, vol. 1, 64–65, pl. 19 (oinochoe inv.
116,SA215), dated end of Middle Corinthian.
25. J. Boardman and J. Hayes, *Excavations at Tocra
1963–1965, The Archaic Deposits*, vol. 1. *BSA* supplement 4 (1966) pl. 23, nos. 314, 315, and 325.

forms familiar from Early Corinthian panthers, this last panther of the group found at Sardis is executed so quickly and with such lack of concern for either form or detail of anatomy that it has turned into a mere impression of a panther. There is a great stylistic distance between this work and the explicit articulation shared by both vase-painting and sculpture in the earlier periods.

By the end of Middle Corinthian, the desire to create dignified animals rendered in anatomically convincing terms has completely given way to the rush to produce for an expanding Corinthian market. The demand for speed produced a generation of craftsmen no longer able or willing to understand the purpose of the forms they used. The balance between form and decoration familiar in earlier periods gives way to decoration alone, decoration that covers the surface of the pot in a sloppy profusion. It is no wonder that the more carefully wrought Attic works began to capture Corinth's numerous markets, not only in the West but as far east as Sardis.

By circa 570 B.C. the Corinthian imports at Sardis had dwindled to a mere trickle and by circa 550 B.C., just prior to the capture of the Lydian kingdom by Cyrus the Great, the Corinthian imports had been completely replaced by Attic wares.[26]

26. The Attic material at Sardis will be published by Nancy Ramage in the forthcoming monograph on imported wares.

17. Little Brown Jug

CEDRIC G. BOULTER

CLASSICS DEPARTMENT, UNIVERSITY OF CINCINNATI

Professor Amyx has written about the Shoe Lane Painter, someone who practiced Corinthian art in recent years.[1] He may welcome a brief note on the work of another neo-Corinthian artist, possibly an older contemporary of the Shoe Lane Painter. An example is to be found on a Doulton jug in a private collection in Cincinnati (figures 1–4).

The jug is a broad-bottomed oinochoe made for John Dewar and Sons. The shape follows rather faithfully the ancient model, with a flange around the middle of the neck.[2] There is a single frieze of animals on the body, with a band of lines and a band of triangles beneath, and a scored line above. There are tongues on the shoulder, three black alternating with one reserved. The body is light brown, and the handle, neck, and lip are dark brown; the lip and the neck are glazed inside. Impressed on the underside of the base are a Doulton emblem, the number 5168, and the word *silicon*.

On each side a lion and a bird face the inscribed panel; below the handle a bird and a goat face each other across a floral ornament. The ornament, palmettes with elongated tendrils ending in scrolls, is a simplified version of an ornament often found on Corinthian vases.[3] In elongated form it serves also to frame the inscription. The animals and the birds may reflect the influence of

Middle Corinthian, though again the drawing has been simplified and the details omitted. Compare the front of the head of the right-hand lion with the head of a lion on a broad-bottomed oinochoe in the British Museum, inv. no. 51.5.7.9.[4] They are somewhat alike, the basic schemes for the head being the same. But on the Doulton jug the ears are not outlined, and they may be represented by the ends of a crescent that crowns the forehead. The same is true also of the lion on the left. The tails are shorter and the stance is less commanding. The goat is bobtailed, and his horn is more modest than those of his ancient Corinthian kin.

The Doulton artist scores points for the filling ornament, which is remarkable for its variety and its neatness. There are a few dot rosettes, carefully executed, and many innovations, each drawn within a circular black field: stars, asterisks, buds, trefoil and quatrefoil ornaments, all done with obvious care. One may wonder about the band of lines below the picture. Here the designer has followed a Protocorinthian fashion rather than the solid band or dot-and-band one might expect in this position on Middle Corinthian. If the designer did see Middle Corinthian in the British Museum, he could have seen Protocorinthian as well.

From the 1880s onwards Doulton made a wide range of flasks and bottles for a number of distillers and spirit manufacturers. A large number of these were for John Dewar. Unfortunately it is hard to give a precise date of man-

1. *Brooklyn Museum Bulletin* XXI, 2 (Spring, 1960) 9ff.
2. *Necrocorinthia* (Oxford, 1931) 277, 199, 315 and 325; R. Hopper in *BSA* 44 (1949) 237–39. Height of the Doulton jug, 135 cm; diameter of base, 12.5 cm.
3. Cf. *Necrocorinthia*, 151, fig. 57 and 152, fig. 59.

4. Ibid., 135, no. 1113 and pl. 28, 4.

Figure 1. Doulton Jug, Cincinnati, Ohio, Private Collection.

Figure 2. Second View of Jug in Figure 1.

Figure 3. Third View of Jug in Figure 1.

Figure 4. Fourth View of Jug in Figure 1.

ufacture as the relevant factory records have rarely survived. This particular model was made at Doulton's Lambeth factory in London, between 1902 and 1910. The material is stoneware, and the word Silicon impressed on the base was a term in use at the factory to describe a particular type of unglazed stoneware characteristic of the factory. . . . There is no record of the identity of the designer. . . . The decoration is printed on the surface before the firing by a transfer process, a familiar technique for wares designed to be made in large quantities. The number 5168 impressed is a shape number.[5]

5. I am much indebted for this information to Paul Atterbury, former editor, *The Connoisseur*. See also Paul Atterbury and Louise Irvine, *The Doulton Story* (Stoke on Trent, 1979) 45–58, and, for bibliography, 104.

A forger seeks to deceive and so works under certain constraints. An avowed imitator may allow play for his own tastes and may introduce adaptations or novelties. In ancient literature plagiarism was accepted as a normal, indeed civilized, practice, a tribute or a compliment to distinguished predecessors. What would an ancient Corinthian potter or pot painter have thought of the Doulton jug? He would surely have admired the sturdy fabric, been amused by the rendering of the creatures in the frieze, and looked with pleasure and approval at the richness and variety of the filling ornament.

18. Corinthianizing Art of the Boeotian Horse-bird Painter

KARL KILINSKI II

DEPARTMENT OF ART HISTORY, SOUTHERN METHODIST UNIVERSITY

Distinguishing among Corinthian, Attic, and Boeotian black-figure vases was a matter of course for Humfry Payne (*Necrocorinthia* 199–206), and so it has been ever since for scholars pursuing the study of these wares. One of the most eclectic groups of vases embodying stylistic features of each of these schools of vase painting is that known as the Boeotian Horse-bird group. This group was so named by Beazley,[1] however, the uniformity of style within the group now permits the more precise designation *Horse-bird Painter*. This artist originally worked in Athens decorating typical Attic vase shapes. What remains of his oeuvre from there is collectively known as the group of the Dresden Lekanis (figures 1, 2, 3), which Beazley, among others, believed to be the work of a single artist.[2] Again, according to Beazley, the painter of the Dresden Lekanis emigrated to Boeotia, where his Corinthianizing traits became stronger. Here, as the Horse-bird Painter, his choice of vase shapes is predominantly Corinthian, when not Boeotian, including the alabastron (figures 4–9), aryballos (figures 10 and 11), and the olpe.[3] Because of the decoration of such vase shapes with subjects and subsidiary ornament derived from typically Corinthian sources, many of the Horse-bird Painter's vases have, in publications and mu-

seum records, been mistakenly ascribed to Corinth. The wanderings of this artist through Attic, Boeotian, and Corinthian styles is matched by a maze of confusions and entanglements in the scholarship. The task of unraveling these accounts will be undertaken elsewhere.

Vases by the Horse-bird Painter were first grouped by Payne as imitations of the Corinthian style.[4] Payne's list of attributed vases has been expanded by many scholars and includes four alabastra in Berkeley added by H. R. W. Smith[5] and several more added by his student—the honoree—D. A. Amyx (who also has been drawn to the works of the painter of the Dresden Lekanis),[6] until at present the known vases by the Horse-bird Painter total over sixty.

One of the previously unpublished attributions to the Horse-bird Painter is an alabastron in Baltimore (figure 4), which was brought to my attention by Amyx several years ago in Athens. Two heraldically set lions constitute the figure scene. Their heads are turned backward, their cavernous jaws are stretched to reveal long protruding tongues. Corinthianizing ornamental elements on the vase are plentiful. Solid black petals ring the mouth, neck, and bottom of the stout alabastron. Black dots decorate the

---

1. *ABV* 22.
2. Ibid.; cf. *Necrocorinthia*, 201f.
3. Hamburg, Museum für Kunst und Gewerbe 1962.130. *CVA* 1, pl. 3, 1–4.

4. *Necrocorinthia* 202–3, 341.
5. *CVA* 1, 21–22, pl. 11, 2–5.
6. D. A. Amyx and P. Lawrence, *Corinth* VII, 2: *Archaic Corinthian Pottery and the Anaploga Well* (Princeton, 1975) 59–60 and the bibliography there cited.

Figure 1. Fragment of Attic Black-figure, Athens, Agora Museum, inv. no. P 210.

Figure 3. Fragment of Attic Black-figure, Athens, Agora Museum, inv. no. P 5468.

Figure 2. Fragment of Attic Black-figure, Athens, Agora Museum, inv. no. P 7036.

Figure 4. Boeotian Alabastron, Baltimore, Walters Art Gallery, inv. no. 48.216.

Figure 5. Boeotian Alabastron, Leningrad, Hermitage Museum, inv. no. 2120.

Figure 6. Second View of Alabastron in Figure 5.

rim of the lip, while a dicing motif frames the top and the bottom of the figure scene, which carries incised rosettes clustered about the crouching lions. Two other alabastra, in Leningrad (figures 5 and 6) and Bremen (figures 7 and 8), attributed to the Horse-bird Painter by S. P. Boriskovskaya and Amyx respectively, bear similar subsidiary decoration in a Corinthianizing manner. They differ from the Baltimore example, however, in that cross-hatching has replaced the typical Corinthian device of simple dots on the lip rims. The figure scenes on these two alabastra also deviate from the Baltimore vase in that they introduce a human element into the array of subjects selected by the painter. On the Bre-

men alabastron a male rider keeps a tight rein on his mount as it gallops to right around the slender alabastron. The rider is nude except for a double-crossed strap on his chest and a band in his hair. The Horse-bird Painter has bestowed on him the distinction of having two left hands. The would-be right hand carries a whip across the horse's mane while the left hand holds the reins, which are shown awkwardly arranged with both strands on the right side of the horse's neck. The alabastron in Leningrad illustrates a subject to which the Horse-bird Painter returned time and time again. Here we see a file of women clad from neck to toe and holding boughs. The women can number

Figure 7. Boeotian Alabastron, Bremen, Focke-Museum, inv. no. 8217.

Figure 8. Second View of Alabastron in Figure 7.

two, as on this vase, three, or, as on one example, four, and except for in this last instance they are depicted sharing a single cloak. This enigmatic procession is confronted by a roaring lion, whose head is turned backward like those on the Baltimore vase. Both the Bremen and Leningrad alabastra have a large lotus ornament positioned vertically in the field opposite the figural subjects. Two other alabastra in Frankfurt am Main and Munich, with similar floral ornaments as the sole decoration, are here cred-

ited to Amyx as attributions to the Horse-bird Painter.[7]

To these five additions I wish to contribute three of my own. The first is an alabastron in Vienna (figure 9) with a raised-winged swan to left. Like the alabastra (figures 5–8),

7. Frankfurt am Main, Liebieghaus Museum, Unpublished; Munich, Antikensammlungen 6433 (290a). Badly worn. J. Sieveking and R. Hackl, *Die königliche Vasensammlung zu München*, vol. 1 (Munich, 1912) 21, no. 290a (A 879).

Figure 9. Boeotian Alabastron, Vienna, Kunsthistorisches Museum, inv. no. 1844.

this vase displays subsidiary ornament identical in design and in placement, including the cross-hatching motif on the lip rim. The second alabastron is in Amsterdam and is decorated with facing sirens.[8] The third ex-

ample is a recently excavated, yet still unpublished, alabastron from Acraephia, now in Thebes. The figural subject of this vase is a raised-winged siren to right. In lieu of illustrating either of these last two alabastra with similar subjects, a photograph of the aryballos in Kassel (figure 10) showing one of its two sirens is offered in their place. This vase, which was attributed by Beazley to the Horse-bird Painter,[9] is pertinent to the subject of this article in many respects, not the least of which is its Corinthianizing vase shape.

The stylistic elements that support the attributions of these new additions are numerous and can be judged against the Horse-bird Painter's work in general. The human-headed figures are rendered with long, dangling hair, a prominent nose, a Y-shaped mouth, and an incised chin that, when viewed with the incised mouth, at first appears to be a double chin. This is the same formula for facial features that the painter used on his Attic figures (figures 1, 2, and 3), although their facial profiles taper more abruptly toward the chin. The pose and drapery renderings of the women in a single cloak on the Leningrad alabastron can be compared with a number of other alabastra by the painter, of which conveniently illustrated examples are in Berkeley and Heidelberg.[10] The lions are short-legged and reveal a long, licking tongue that hangs off the lower jaw. The lion's tail is tipped with a feather-like tuft and its ribs are indicated by several incised sigmas. The lions on the alabastra in Baltimore and Leningrad are readily compared with the lion on an alabastron in Munich by the Horse-bird Painter.[11] The horse is given either a bristle-like or flame mane. Its bridle is rendered in the form of a single incised T, which bisects the length of the head and is anchored in the circular bit

8. Amsterdam, Allard Pierson Museum 700. *CVA* Scheurleer 1, IIIc, p. 6, pl. 4, 4, "Corinthian."

9. *ABV* 23 and *CVA* Kassel 1, pl. 13, 1–3.
10. Berkeley, UCMA 8/352. *CVA* 1, pl. 11, 2a-b; Heidelberg, University 160. *CVA* 1, pl. 21, 6–8.
11. Munich, Antikensammlungen 291b. J. Sieveking and R. Hackl, *Vasensammlung*, 21, pl. 9, 291b.

Figure 10. Boeotian Aryballos, Kassel, Staatliche Kunstsammlungen, inv. no. T449.

Figure 11. Boeotian Aryballos, New York, Metropolitan Museum of Art, inv. no. 06.1021.22.

at the mouth. A double incised strap near the snout holds the bit in place. The horse and rider on the Bremen alabastron can be compared with those on the New York aryballos (figure 11) by the Horse-bird Painter or with horses with bristle-like manes on vases in East Berlin and Geneva.[12] The swan and the siren are endowed with flat feet. The sirens' wings are rendered with spiraling feathers, those of the swan are simply banded, when folded, and its gracefully twisting neck is overlapped by its bill. The sirens on those alabastra in Amsterdam and Thebes can be compared with that on the aryballos (figure 10) while the swan on the alabastron in Vienna is readily associated with those on the aryballos in Geneva and on the tripod kothon in Bonn, both illustrated by Payne.[13]

Of all Boeotian black-figure vase painters, the Horse-bird Painter shows by far the greatest debt to Corinth. Besides decorating typically Corinthian vase shapes, for which he may well have been personally responsible as the potter, his selection of subjects and subsidiary ornament, and their arrangement on the vase surface are largely derived from Corinthian vases of corresponding shapes. The deployment of solid black petals on the bottoms of aryballoi and alabastra, as well as around their necks and radiating from their mouths, are traditional Corinthian decorative formulas. The flanking of the figure scenes with dicing between thin lines, as well as the extensive use of incised rosettes in the field, are also Corinthian in origin. The application of small white dots in rows between incised lines on the animals and the humans alike (figures 10 and 11) is typical of the White Dot Style of Corinthian alabastra.[14] The setting of black dots on the lip rims of alabastra and aryballoi is a Corinthian motif

12. Berlin (DDR), Staatliche Museen 3370. To my knowledge an illustration of this vase is yet unpublished. Geneva, Musée d'Art et d'Histoire H 172. *CVA* 2, pl. 85, 1–5.

13. Musée d'Art et d'Histoire H 136; Bonn, Akademisches Kunstmuseum 550. *Necrocorinthia*, pl. 53, 2 and 1. *AA* (1933) 18, fig. 12 (lions).

14. *Necrocorinthia*, 284–85, 303C.

that the Horse-bird Painter ultimately replaced with cross-hatching and finally with a zigzag line. Another Corinthianizing trait employed by this artist is what might be termed an "echo ornament." Field devices act as fillers for space adjacent to and corresponding to the shape of wings on sirens and sphinxes.[15] Finally, a number of subjects chosen by the painter for his wares are native to Corinthian black figure alabastra. Such examples as the flying eagle, the lion, the siren, florals, Artemis with swans, and even combinations of creatures, as witnessed by the horse-bird itself on the painter's name vase, can all be found on the class of Middle Corinthian alabastra in the White Dot Style, which best correlate in shape and in subsidiary decoration to the Horse-bird Painter's works.

Before dismissing the alabastra attributed here to the Horse-bird Painter, it is worth noting certain transitional aspects of these vases that appear to lend themselves in support of a relative chronology. Within the Corinthian White Dot Style is one class of Middle Corinthian alabastra distinguished by its bulging upper body, which begins to swell almost immediately below the neck.[16] Among the Boeotian alabastra, those in Baltimore (figure 4) and Amsterdam resemble this particular shape more closely than the others, while the Leningrad vase (figures 5 and 6) is not far from this form. The other alabastra become more slender in outline until a shape represented by the alabastra in Bremen and Vienna (figures 7, 8, and 9) is obtained. These vases are, therefore, further removed in shape from the original Corinthian model of inspiration. Furthermore, the Baltimore and Amsterdam alabastra display black dots on the lip rims in the traditional Corinthian manner. The other alabastra

carry cross-hatching in this area, which on the Bremen vase fades into a zigzag, as it is the total pattern on the Munich example. This transition from precise to degenerate forms of ornament follows the change in vase shape. The Leningrad alabastron is not far from the Baltimore example in this transition of vase shape yet a change has occurred in the choice of lip decoration. That the former is later in date than the latter is further substantiated by a comparison of the lions on these two vessels. Those on the Baltimore vase are more powerful, more ferocious, and they are rendered with a double incised shoulder line in the typical Corinthian manner. The lion on the Leningrad alabastron seems tamer, less robust, and it has been given a flame mane in the growing Attic fashion in Boeotia, with which the Horse-bird Painter was thoroughly familiar. The savage impression given by the lions on the Baltimore alabastron has escaped that of the lion on the Leningrad vase in the intervening span of time that undoubtedly separates the two vessels. The results of this brief analysis appear to place the Baltimore and Amsterdam vases early in the career of the Horse-bird Painter. The Leningrad alabastron would be somewhat later in date with the Bremen and Vienna alabastra later still.

The art of the Horse-bird Painter can be seen to embrace several aspects of Corinthian vase painting over a span of years in the early sixth century B.C. That the degree of this Corinthian influence should be so extensive, far beyond that on other contemporary Boeotian vase painters who were generally receptive to external ideas, is surprising for an artist who was originally an Attic vase painter. However, this was no ordinary artist who, for reasons beyond our knowledge, abandoned Attica for Boeotia at a time when Athens, under the guidance of Solon, was encouraging craftsmen to do just the contrary.

15. Cf. Berkeley, UCMA 8/3301. *CVA* 1, pl. 11, 3a-b.

16. *Necrocorinthia* 303C, fig. 138.

19. Etrusco-Corinthian Bilingualism

JÁNOS G. SZILÁGYI

MUSEUM OF FINE ARTS, BUDAPEST

D. A. Amyx's role in the intensive study of Etrusco-Corinthian vase painting that was initiated some forty years ago has been outstanding, not in the least because he always considered the production principally from the point of view of Corinth.[1] That he always bore in mind the precepts of more universal art history in his judgment of the Etruscan material is as important as the basic research he has accomplished to illuminate specific painters.

His theoretical remarks regarding Etrusco-Corinthian vases decorated in the polychrome technique precisely outlined the tasks of future research and produced important guidelines for later scholarship. In further developing Llewelyn Brown's view,[2] Amyx pointed out that "the common feature amongst these works is . . . not stylistic but technical." It thereby follows that polychrome vases need not be necessarily classified as belonging to a single period of Etrusco-Corinthian vase-painting. Amyx also drew attention to the fact that in this case there are two possible hypotheses concerning the entire history of Etrusco-Corinthian figural pottery; that the use of the polychrome technique possibly "covers a considerable chronological range" and that "the painters of these vases were not exclusively 'specialists' in the black-polychrome technique, but artists who worked also in ordinary black-figure." Nor did he neglect to stress that these are mere possibilities that must be decided primarily by "exhaustive stylistic analysis."[3] Fifteen years after the publication of his article, scholarship has proceeded in the direction indicated by Amyx, but now with greater access to additional material; for example, we know today of more than one hundred figural polychrome vases. Hence, indeed, I do not propose to do more here than attempt to take a further step in the direction indicated by Amyx.

Regarding chronology, there now appears to be every justification to presume that the polychrome technique—more precisely, the use of incision for the representation of figures on painted vases—was present throughout the history of Etrusco-Corinthian vase-painting.[4] However, it seems that its *floruit* barely survived the earliest period—the polychrome technique was widespread in the animal friezes of the last quarter of the seventh century, occasionally alternating, even on the same vase, with the black-figure technique. During the middle and late periods, however, it appeared to be limited to occa-

---

1. D. A. Amyx, "Some Etrusco-Corinthian Vase-Painters," *Studi in onore di L. Banti* (Rome, 1965) 1–14; "The Mingor Painter and Others," *Studi Etruschi* 35 (1967) 87–111; "Two Etrusco-Corinthian Vases," *Studies in Honour of A. D. Trendall* (Sydney, 1979) 13–19.
2. W. L. Brown, *The Etruscan Lion* (Oxford, 1960) 58.

3. Amyx, "Vase-Painters," 7–9.
4. For an example, see the alabastron in the Hermitage apparently made in the later period of Etrusco-Corinthian vase-painting; Cf. J. G. Szilágyi, *Wiss. Zeitschrift der Univ. Rostock* 16 (1967) 552, no. 57 and pl. 114, 1.

Figure 1. Detail of Etrusco-Corinthian Olpe, England, Private Collection (photos 1–2: Charles Ede).

Figure 2. Detail of Olpe in Figure 1.

sional improvisations, and the incised drawing was generally not embellished with added colors.

This relative chronological concentration of polychrome vases does not in any way, however, contradict Amyx's suggestion that "the isolation of the black-polychrome vases as a 'Group' seems arbitrary."[5] With the exception of pieces that for the present must be considered more or less isolated examples, it appears that at least two independent branches of the polychrome production must be distinguished.[6] The first branch consists of painters of the Monte Abatone Group who, working in Caere, chiefly decorated large amphorae. Their workshop or workshops tended to follow local traditions in the shape and the decoration of the vases rather than Corinthian models, and hence their products can be called "Etrusco-Corinthian" only in the broadest sense of the term. The second branch is represented by a group of painters working predominantly, if not exclusively, in Vulci and who display a style far

from homogeneous. The shape of the vases and the animal friezes were undoubtedly inspired by Corinthian prototypes. Neither of the two branches can be shown to be earlier than the first Etrusco-Corinthian black-figure vases. In other respects, however, their historical position differs essentially. On one hand, the masters of the vases of the Monte Abatone Group developed their polychrome technique following local *impasto* and *bucchero* vases rather than Greek models. On the other hand, their production comes to an end around 600 B.C., after which time there is no trace of their continuation or their influence. The painters of the other branch obviously borrowed their polychrome technique from Corinth—most likely in imitation of imported Corinthian vases[7]—and their conventions of draftsmanship were continued, at least at Vulci, in local black-figure vase-painting after the polychrome fashion had faded.[8] It is therefore not by

5. Amyx, "Vase-Painters," 8.

6. For the following, see Szilágyi, *Zeitschrift Rostock*, 543–52 and Szilágyi, *La civiltà arcaica di Vulci e la sua espansione* (Firenze, 1977) 50 and 56.

7. W. L. Brown, *Lion*, 58; Amyx, "Vase-Painters," 7–8 and n. 5 (for a dating of the prototypes to the Protocorinthian period). For a new LPC-TR bilingual olpe found at Knossos, see *Archaeological Reports* for 1978–1979, 53, fig. 35.

8. Szilágyi *Civiltà arcaica*, 54–56.

Figure 3. Etrusco-Corinthian Olpe. Swiss Market, 1974 (photos 3–7: Archäologisches Institut der Universität, Zürich).

Figure 4. Detail of Olpe in Figure 3.

Figure 5. Detail of Olpe in Figure 3.

Figure 6. Detail of Olpe in Figure 3.

Figure 7. Detail of Olpe in Figure 3.

chance that Amyx's presumption of "bilingual" vase-painters is borne out by the work of masters who, it would appear, worked in Vulci.

A master who deserves closer attention might well be called the Painter of Polychrome Arcs because of the characteristic decorative pattern on his vases.[9] His first published work is one of two presently known for him, which discloses a polychrome technique (numbers 1 and 2). All of his other known works—all olpai—are executed in the black-figure. The following list comprises works by his hand that are presently known to me.

1. Rome, Museo di Villa Giulia 29300 (figure 8). From Vulci; ht., 25.6 cm; 27.5 cm with rotelle. G. Colonna, *Archeologia Classica* 13 (1961) 11, note 3 and pl. 3, 1; *Civiltà arcaica* no. 40; M. T. Falconi Amorelli, *Vulci, Scavi Bendinelli* (Rome, 1983) 129–31, no. 130, figs. 56–57.

2. London Market in 1981. Ht., 28 cm. *Christie's* 8 July 1981, no. 197 (ill.).

3. Vulci, Museo Etrusco. Unpublished. Scavi Hercle, tomb 13. Ht. 28.2 cm; 28.9 cm with rotelle.

4. Rome, Museo di Villa Giulia 74945. Ex coll. Cima-Pesciotti. Ht., 29.2 cm; 30.8 cm with rotelle. *Finarte, Asta di oggetti archeologici* (Milano, 1970) catalog 11–12, no. 21, pl. 6; G. Bartoloni, *Nuove scoperte e acquisizioni nell'Etruria Meridionale* (Rome, 1975) catalog 203, no. 12.

5. Great Britain, Private Collection (Miss J. O'Connor) (figures 1–2) Ht., 28.5 cm. C. Ede, *Collecting Antiquities* (London, 1976) 31, no. 81 (ill.), and vii.

6. Swiss Market in 1974. Unpublished. (figures 3–7) Ht., 28–30 cm.

7. Italy, Private Collection. Unpublished.[10] From Poggio Buco.

Five of the seven vases are decorated with

Figure 8. Detail, Etrusco-Corinthian Olpe, Rome, Museo di Villa Giulia, inv. no. 29300 (photo: Soprintendenza).

a single animal frieze; only number 6 possesses three friezes and number 7 two. There is nothing iconographically extraordinary about the friezes, of which the most frequent animal types follow Corinthian repertory: primarily the standing or walking lion and panther (both winged on number 1); more rarely a sphinx (numbers 3 and 4); a griffin (numbers 3, 4, and 7); a siren (number 7); a grazing stag (numbers 3, 4, and 7); and a bird (numbers 5, 6, and 7). Without exception, carefully painted dot-rosettes are used as filling ornaments and, in one case only (number 6), these coalesce into a circle. Other decorative elements are executed with equal care: white dot-rosettes on the rotelles, the neck (generally four in number), on the sides of the handles (at times at the top and below), and on the body. Rays with arched sides describing semicircles appear at the bottom of every olpe. On the shoulder of all

9. For a short preliminary notice on the painter, see ibid., 55.

10. Thanks are due Enrico Pellegrini for making photographs available for study.

but vase number 6, there are long tongues that are sometimes polychrome, sometimes merely incised (number 3), or painted in black-figure technique (numbers 4 and 5). The eponymous double braided arcs, the spaces filled with alternate red and white colors, are standard decoration but for two vases (numbers 6 and 7). On the other vases, the arcs appear either below the frieze (numbers 1, 2, and 5) or above (numbers 3 and 4). The zones are separated by red and white lines, but the animal figures are rarely colored—with the exception of those on vases numbers 1 and 2.

Consideration of the shape of the vases, the color and decorative patterns, the filling ornaments, and peculiar features of the incised drawings all serve to link this painter to the vases of the Corinthian Transitional period. The draftsmanship of the characteristic frontal panther heads (figures 2 and 6), however, suggests that this may be regarded as a *terminus post quem* since short lines to indicate the mane at each side of the face—although not entirely unknown in the Transitional period[11]—are more characteristic of Early Corinthian vases.[12] The tails of the walking lions and panthers on numbers 1, 2, and 4 are S-shaped—a feature that became common in Corinth only from the Early Corinthian period[13] and that contrasts markedly with the much more frequent sinuous or circular, turned-back tail that continued Protocorinthian conventions. These and similar traits on the friezes known at present to be by his hand suggest that the painter worked around the years 610–590 B.C.

Known provenances unambiguously point to Vulci as the center of this painter's activity—apparently confirmed by the presence of similar polychrome braided arcs on unfigured olpai from Vulci.[14] In other instances, the field within the semicircles of this exceptionally common decorative pattern are generally occupied at most by a single painted dot. It may very well be that the majority of the olpai with this polychrome variant of the pattern are products of the same workshop.[15]

The eponymous pattern in itself draws attention to the fact that Corinthian vasepainting, though of crucial importance here, was not the sole source on which the painter drew. This may prove outright that he was *not* an immigrant Greek but a native who carried on local traditions on the one hand and, on the other, freely and independently interpreted and reformulated what he observed on Corinthian vases. For the latter, it will suffice to refer to the incisions that systematically appear on the front of the bodies and on the front legs of the lions and panthers. These details are obviously characteristic Etruscan reinterpretation of Greek models and, in this form, mark a personal creation of the painter. Such details appear in their clearest form on the animals of olpe number 6 (figures 3–7).[16]

11. For example, H. Payne, *Necrocorinthia* pl. 13, 1; *CVA*, Louvre 13, pl. 50, 1; *Perachora* 2, pl. 64, 1676 and pl. 68, 2126; etc. According to A. Fermum, *Der Panther in der frühgriechischen Vasenmalerei* (Diss., Freiburg, 1977) 155, such a detail in rendering was an Early Corinthian invention, a statement that is, however, sound only with this proviso.

12. Some EC examples: *Necrocorinthia*, pls. 23, 2,4; 24, 3,5; *Perachora* 1, pl. 27,5; *Perachora* 2, pls. 63, 1608, 1613; 70, 2211, b, etc.; D. A. Amyx-P. Lawrence, *Corinth* VII, part 2, pls. 6,41; 9,58; 101–7, passim; *CVA* Gela 2, p. 6; etc. This rendering is usual also in the MC period; see, for example, *Necrocorinthia*, fig. 140bis; pl. 30,5; *Perachora* 2, pl. 63, 1626; *CVA* Gela 2, pl. 18; *CVA* Hague 1, pl. 6,2; *CVA* New Zealand 1, pl. 44,4; *CVA* Stuttgart 1, pl. 14,5; *CVA* Taranto 3, pl. 4,2; etc.

13. Earlier, it was common only for seated animals. Some EC examples: *Perachora* 2, pls. 60, 1518; 64, 1812; *Corinth* VII, part 2, pl. 50, An 171; *CVA* New Zealand 1, pl. 39,13; etc.

14. Some examples: *Archeologia Classica* 13 (1961) pl. 5,2; *Vulci, Zona dell'Osteria, Scavi della Hercle* (Rome, 1964) 99, fig. 36 (two pieces). An olpe found at Narce was probably imported from Vulci; see I. Edlund, *The Iron Age and Etruscan Vases in the Olcott Collection at Columbia University, New York, Transactions of the American Philosophical Society*, vol. 70, part 1 (1980) 36–37, no. 48, pls. 36,a; 37,b.

15. Polychrome braided arcs of this type on vases from other workshops provide rare exceptions; for example, on an amphora at Tarquinia, Museo Nazionale, RC 2209 (the shape is usual for vases attributed to the workshop of the Monte Abatone Group).

16. Some examples: amphora, Thera, Museum, see *Greek Art of the Aegean Islands* (New York, Metropol-

Two noticeable examples of the assertion of local conventions are the braided arcs and the drawing of the manes that cover the full extent of the backs of the lions and, at times, the panthers as well. The braided arc pattern, which is obviously of Near Eastern origin, appears here and there on Greek—chiefly Cycladic—vases from as early as the beginning of the seventh century B.C. It was not used, however, in Corinth or elsewhere on the Greek mainland or in East Greek areas. Significantly, in Etruria it had been commonly employed for at least a century in various artistic genres before its appearance on vases by the Painter of Polychrome Arcs.[17] There can be little doubt, therefore, that local decorative conventions were its immediate source. The same may apply to the lions' manes. Such manes that covered the full extent of the lions' backs were extraordinarily rare in Corinth, even though they cannot be said to have been confined to the Chigi vase

as generally believed.[18] Since the feature appeared much earlier in central Italy—for which references need be made only to the silver cist from the "Castellani Tomb" at Praeneste or to the gold-plate fibula of the Bernardini tomb—the Chigi vase could not have served as the model for the Etruscan representations, nor could it be used as a *terminus post quem* for the appearance of the motif in Etruria. Furthermore, it does not support the supposition that the motif spread from Caere throughout Etruria.[19] It seems far more likely, however, that, like the braided arc pattern, the motif reached Italy directly from the Near East via Syro-Phoenician transmission.[20] The vases attributed to the Painter of Polychrome Arcs also show that the two chief types of the back-mane rendering—one flame-like, the other as a row of short lines[21]—existed simultaneously in the same place.[22] In Etruscan art,[23] the two types were interchangeable, and neither had any special significance.[24]

Inasmuch as the few known vases allow one to draw any sort of general conclusions, it appears that the painter was equally familiar with both techniques. The nature of the two techniques in itself determined that there should be more color on the figures of olpai numbers 1 and 2, and more incised lines on

itan Museum, 1979) no. 66, with further references; relief-pithos, Basel, Antikenmuseum, see *Kunstwerke d. Antike aus der Slg. Käppeli* (Basel, 1956) no. E 1, illustration.

17. For its history in Etruscan art and with further references, see J. G. Szilágyi, in *Kunst der Antike, Schätze aus norddeutschem Privatbesitz*, ed. W. Hornbostel (Mainz, 1977) 427–29. The motif survives not only in this strictly geometric form but also in a floral variant in which the arcs link palmettes, buds, or rosettes. This pattern appeared in Greece early in the archaic period and soon became general (fundamental also on Oriental prototypes, compare E. Kunze, *Kretische Bronzereliefs* [Stuttgart, 1931] 97–106). In Etruria it was not rare; see, for example, G. Giglioli, *Arte etrusca* (Milan, 1935) pls. 27, 44, 62; Fl. Johansen, *Reliefs en bronze d'Etrurie* (Copenhagen, 1971) pls. 41, 62–63. Near Eastern prototypes are also well known. One should not necessarily presume the geometric form to be a derivative of the floral variant. One must, in any event, distinguish between the braided arc pattern and that assuming chains of tangential semicircles in its geometric form (for example, G. Camporeale, *Buccheri a cilindretto di fabbrica orvietana* [Florence, 1971] pl. 19, a) and floral variant (*Necrocorinthia*, 155, fig. 64, F; Kunze, *Bronzereliefs*, figs. 7, 8 a-c, 9 a-b; in Etruria: I. Strøm, *Problems concerning . . . Etruscan orientalizing style* [Odense, 1971] fig. 62; J. D. Beazley and F. Magi, *Raccolta Guglielmi* I [Città del Vaticano, 1939] pl. 38, no. 44; etc.). The braided arcs pattern belongs to the Near Eastern types that appeared in central Italy around 700 B.C. (see F. W. von Hase, *Hamburger Beiträge zur Archäologie* 4 [1975] 123 ff.).

18. See *Perachora* 2, pl. 22, 422 (frg. of PC kotyle).

19. G. Camporeale, *RM* 72 (1965) 8–10.

20. The most important studies: F. Poulsen, *Der Orient u. die frühgriechische Kunst* (Leipzig-Berlin, 1912) 12, 119–24; P. Jacobsthal, *Early Celtic Art* (Oxford, 1944) 38–40; W. L. Brown, *Lion*, 28–29; P. Amandry, *AM* 77 (1962) 50–51; H. Salskov Roberts, *Acta Archaeologica* 34 (1963) 163–67; Camporeale, *RM* (see above, note 19) 1ff., and *La Tomba del Duce*, (Florence, 1967) 103, note 1.

21. Salskov Roberts, *Acta Archaeologica*, 163–66; Camporeale, *RM*, 4ff., type A and B.

22. Cf. Camporeale, *RM*, 12.

23. This was rightly pointed out against Camporeale by F. Johansen, *Reliefs en bronze*, 46. On the olpe number 5 of the Painter of Polychrome Arcs the lion's mane consists of a row of lines, on olpe number 6, a row of flames; the lions on his other vases have no shoulder-mane at all.

24. According to Salskov Roberts (*Acta Archaeologica*, 164), a flame-like mane in Greek sixth-century vase-painting "was particularly given to fabulous creatures."

Figure 9. Detail, Etrusco-Corinthian Olpe, Florence, Museo Archeologico, inv. no. 71015 (photo: Soprintendenza).

Figure 10. Etrusco-Corinthian Alabastron, Private Collection (photo: Archives of Dr. Dietrich von Bothmer).

the others. It suffices to compare, however, a lion's head, one each from olpe number 1 and olpe number 6 (figures 8 and 7) in order to be convinced that the two are by the same hand. Unfortunately, enough is not yet known to establish the chronological order of the painter's work. There is a certain likelihood that the polychrome olpai are earlier than numbers 6 and 7. Needless to say, more material must become available to discover whether or not all of his polychrome vases are earlier than his black-figure examples, to determine if he employed the two techniques concurrently. I am not aware at this time of any influence his work may have had, or that it actually continued. Nonetheless, certain of his characteristic features can be discerned on vases by other contemporary Vulcian masters.[25]

25. Compare, for example, the palmette-like styliza-

Figure 11. Detail, Etrusco-Corinthian Olpe, Florence, Museo Archeologico, inv. no. 71016 (photo: Soprintendenza).

Basically different is the historical position of the other master who employed two techniques; that is, the Pescia Romana Painter. Much of his work seems to have survived, and since he is a well-known painter, a detailed presentation is not here required. In juxtaposition to the Painter of Polychrome Arcs, the Pescia Romana Painter allows us to draw bolder conclusions, for he is one of the most interesting figures in the whole of Etrusco-Corinthian vase painting. Ten of his vases that disclose the polychrome technique are recorded.[26] Amyx's first article in which

he discussed this painter called attention to the painter's close relationship with the American Academy Painter—who is also a Vulcian master and for whom close to forty black-figure vases are known.[27] Amyx was also the first scholar to point out that the close relationship between the two painters

---

tion of the mane framing the face of the panthers on olpe number 1 with some of the panther heads of the Feoli Painter (Amyx, "Mingor Painter," pls. 36,a; 37,b; etc.).

26. For the painter and his polychrome vases, see Amyx, "Vase-Painters," 9; and Amyx, "Mingor Painter," 107; Szilágyi, *Zeitschrift Rostock*, 549; F. P. Porten Palange, *Quaderni ticinesi* (1976) 7–25; M. Martelli, in *Prima Italia, Catalogue* (Bruxelles, 1980) 118–19 and (Rome, 1981) 104–6 (references are to the later, revised Italian edition). An unpublished oinochoe of the

painter was on the American market in 1980 (Beverly Hills, the Summa Galleries Inc.; I am greatly indebted to Miss Jane Cody for photographs of the vase). The Berne olpe (Szilágyi, *Zeitschrift Rostock*, no. 38, pl. 110,1,3) was found near Civitavecchia among the ruins of an edifice: G. Studer, *Verzeichniss der auf dem Museum der Stadt Bern aufebewahrten antiken Vasen ...* (Bern, 1846) 3. I am grateful to Dr. A. Lezzi-Hafter for this information.

27. Amyx, "Mingor Painter," 97–100; J. G. Szilágyi, *Studi Etruschi* 40 (1972) 71–72 (with further references in note 16); Amyx, "Two Vases," 15–17. Below, in addition to previous attributions, a list of unpublished vases by the same hand: *Plate*, Manchester, University Museum 28863; *Alabastra*, Vulci, Museo Etrusco, ex scavi Hercle, t. 13 (two pieces); Florence, Mus. Arch. 98899, from Vetulonia; Jena, Archäologisches Institut der Universität 486 Wu (from the Weimar Museum); Stockholm, Nationalmuseet Ant. 2347.

Figure 12. Etrusco-Corinthian Alabastron, London Market (from Sotheby's Catalog, Dec. 1, 1969, no. 103).

could not be interpreted as merely that between teacher and pupil.[28] Marina Martelli maintained the same proposition but with greater emphasis.[29] She selected some of the works attributed by Amyx to the American Academy Painter and convincingly argued that they must have been black-figure vases by the Pescia Romana Painter. Further steps in this direction would prove justified. The vases discussed by Martelli cannot be really separated from other specimens earlier attributed to the American Academy Painter.[30] An analysis of the painter's complete production unavoidably leads to the conclusion that all the vases attributed to the American Academy Painter should be incorporated in the works of the Pescia Romana Painter. Unfortunately, detailed evidence to substantiate such proof requires more space than here allotted. Comparison of a polychrome and a black-figure variant of the animal figures so characteristic of this painter, each of an owl, of the head of a lion, a panther, and a goat (see figures 9–15), may serve to illustrate the identity of the master of the two series.

Since the Pescia Romana Painter is credited with nearly fifty vases, one may attempt to draw certain general conclusions. The series of black-figure vases differs in a number of features from the vases in polychrome. Hence, I also formerly believed them to be the work of two distinct painters. Of the three essential differences to which I wish to call attention, the first applies to the shapes, the second to iconography, and the third to conventions of drawing. A certain type of oinochoe,[31] as well as olpai, comprise the major number of polychrome vases—shapes missing among the painter's black-figure vases. At the same time, we do not know of

28. Amyx, "Vase-Painters," 10, but see Amyx, "Mingor Painter," 99. Compare J. G. Szilágyi, *Etruszko-korinthosi vázafestészet* (Budapest, 1975 in Hungarian) 94–95.

29. M. Martelli, *Prima Italia*, 104; see also the excellent observations by Porten Palange, *Quaderni*, 23–25, verging on the solution of the problem proposed in this paper (cf. recently M. Martelli, *Gli Etruschi in Maremma*, ed. M. Cristofani [Siena, 1981] 236).

30. Martelli, (*Prima Italia*, with reference to Amyx, "Two Vases," 18, note 19) proposed to set apart from the other works of the "American Academy Painter" numbers 1, 19, and 27 of my list. Compare, however, the sphinx of the Cambridge kylix (*CVA* 2, pl. 16,6) with that of the Vatican fragment (C. Albizzati, *Vasi Vaticani*, pl. 14, no. 141); the body of the winged sphinx on the Oxford alabastron (figure 14) and on a lost alabastron (Istituto Archeologico Germanico, Rome, Negative 36–1216) with those of a winged panther on a globular aryballos (Tarquinia, Museo Nazionale RC 1972) and a bird (figure 12) on an alabastron (Sotheby's 1 December 1969, 48, no. 103, illustration); or the owl of the Oxford alabastron (figure 14) with that on the Stockholm alabastron mentioned above, note 26; it will be clear that the three vases cannot be isolated from the other works of the "American Academy Painter."

31. For example, Szilágyi, *Zeitschrift Rostock*, pl. 112,l; *Studi in onore di F. Magi* (Perugia, 1979) 99, pl. 3. For the shape and its derivation, Szilágyi, *Zeitschrift Rostock*, 549, note 50 (local); M. Martelli, *Prospettiva* 11 (1977) 12, note 48 (east Greek).

Figure 13. Detail, Etrusco-Corinthian Olpe, Florence, Museo Archeologico, inv. no. 71016 (photo: Soprintendenza).

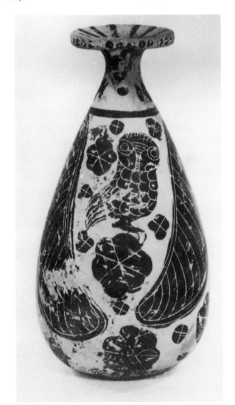

Figure 14. Etrusco-Corinthian Alabastron, Oxford, Ashmolean Museum, Queen's College Loan, no. 8 (courtesy of Museum).

any alabastron, kylix, or globular aryballos with polychrome decoration—shapes that are represented in his black-figure works and for which alabastra comprise more than half of the recorded vases. Such alabastra are all representative of the large-scale type that developed during Early Corinthian and became the dominant shape throughout Middle Corinthian.[32] A bird type that appears frequently in the friezes of his black-figure vases (see figures 10 and 15)—and one of the precursors of birds so characteristic of later Etrusco-Corinthian production—doesn't appear on his polychrome vases. Likewise, one

32. *Necrocorinthia*, 303. For the history of the shape in Etrusco-Corinthian vase-painting see J. G. Szilágyi in *Studi di antichità in onore di G. Maetzke* (Rome, 1984) 472–75.

Figure 15. Detail Etrusco-Corinthian Alabastron, Munich, Antikensammlungen, inv. no. 705 (from Sieveking-Hackl, fig. 80).

can observe on the black-figure vases that, in the drawing conventions at the front portion of his quadrupeds, double arcs or circles filled with white dots are a common feature (figures 10 and 15). This convention—inspired by Corinthian, perhaps already Middle Corinthian, models[33] that became extremely popular during the middle period of Etrusco-Corinthian vase-painting[34]—is also absent from his polychrome vases. All this clearly indicates that his polychrome works are *generally* earlier than the black-figure examples and that the vases attributed to the American Academy Painter *as a whole* represent the later period of the Pescia Romana Painter.

33. *Necrocorinthia*, 284–85, 290 and D. A. Amyx, *Corinthian Vases in the Hearst Collection* (Berkeley–Los Angeles, 1943) 220. *Necrocorinthia*, 284, n. 4 rightly notes that the models used by the Etruscan artists were Corinthian vases, referring also to the Munich alabastron of the "American Academy Painter" (figure 15). For the Greek models—chiefly MC—of the painter's black-figure vases, see Amyx, "Mingor Painter," 99–100.

34. See, for example, the vases of the Rosoni and the Bobuda Painter.

There are other signs as well,[35] but a comparison of some works (figures 9–15) will clearly reveal that one cannot rigorously discriminate between the two periods simply on the basis of technique. When vases using the two techniques are compared, it becomes equally clear that a colorfulness reminiscent of the Corinthian Transitional period is present in the polychrome vases and that it is chiefly heightened by the freshness, inventiveness, and refinement of drawing. The major number of black-figure vases, conversely, are characterized by a desire for routine, that is, the repetition of a few well-rehearsed patterns of composition—mostly of patterns that suffer mass-reproduction on the small pots of the middle and late periods of Etrusco-Corinthian vase painting. The Pescia Romana Painter was certainly not one of the

35. See, for example, the painter's polychrome plate (*CVA*, Paris, Bibliothèque Nationale 1, pl. 19, 1,4,6,8), the only shape common to his polychrome and black-figure series that became one of the favorite mass-produced shapes of Vulcian workshops during the middle period.

pioneers, nor was he one of the artists of the first generation for Etrusco-Corinthian production. On the contrary, he must have started at the end of the first period with polychrome vases in the main, and his black-figure works thereby provided a transition to the mass production of the middle period. Significantly, he established a long-surviving school of vase painting in Vulci, which became an important center of black-figure production during this period.

If some general conclusion may be reached from the consideration of these two vase-painters, it would seem that "bilingualism" in Etrusco-Corinthian figural vase-painting was typical for the moment of transition between the early and middle periods, but not in the same vein as in Athens where "bilingual" vases numbered among the first important experiments in the red-figured technique, and where "bilingualists" were then the pioneers of the new technique who confronted past and future.[36] In Etrusco-Corinthian vase-painting, polychrome and

36. See J. Boardman, *Athenian Black Figure Vases* (London, 1974) chapter 5 and p. 237; Boardman, *Athenian Red Figure Vases, the Archaic Period* (London, 1975) 15–17, 55–60, 237; B. Cohen, *Attic Bilingual Vases and their Painters* (New York-London, 1978), with full bibliography.

black-figure techniques appeared, by and large, simultaneously in the first period, and their concurrent use—after a transitional period for which bilingualism was characteristic as well—was replaced around 590 B.C. by the absolute predominance of the black-figure technique. From then on, Etrusco-Corinthian vases decorated with polychrome or merely with incised figures must be considered as isolated phenomena.

Postscript

Since the pages above were written, through the kindness of Dr. Maria Antonietta Rizzo I have had the chance to see in the Villa Giulia Museum some fragments of an oinochoe decorated in the polychrome technique, found at Vulci, excavations of the Hercle, tomb 61. The vase was obviously painted by the Feoli Painter and shows that this remarkable personality must be added to the two masters treated above as the third bilingual painter of major relevance active in the period of transition from the early to the middle phase of Etrusco-Corinthian figural vase production. The historical impact of this fact has a story of its own.

20. The Pescia Romana Painter: A Bilingual Vase Painter

MARINA MARTELLI

UNIVERSITÀ DI URBINO

In addition to the many acknowledged merits as a fine and diligent student of pottery, Darrell A. Amyx is also to be credited for having turned his attention to Etruscan imitations of Corinthian pottery and establishing fruitful advances in connoisseurship. I hope, therefore, that this tribute will engage his interest inasmuch as it proposes to address the complex and delicate interrelationships between polychrome and black-figure technique in Etrusco-Corinthian vase painting, a problem touched briefly but incisively by Amyx some two decades ago.[1]

I have had occasion to reflect on this subject in the preparation of a catalogue entry concerning one of the eponymous olpai in Florence by the Pescia Romana Painter for the exhibition *Prima Italia* organized in Brussels at the end of 1980. Thus my work on this exhibit has led me to the reconsideration of the entire corpus of this painter.

I have been impelled to return to this topic by the recent unacceptable proposal in a *Miscellany* of the Archaeological Institute of Perugia to add the olpe in the Archaeological Museum of Perugia (figures 1–4), to be discussed below, to the oeuvre of the Pescia Romana Painter. The fact that a photograph of another work that is certainly by his hand, that is, the oinochoe number 676 in the Museo dell'Opera del Duomo di Orvieto (figures 5–8), appeared for the first time in the same journal without any critical attention, also calls for the following study.

Before proceeding, it is perhaps advisable to consider the list of nine vases thus far securely attributed to the Pescia Romana Painter (omitting the olpe in Perugia):

Olpai

1. Florence, M.A., inv. 71015, J. G. Szilágyi, "Etrusko-korinthische polychrome Vasen," *Wissenschaftliche Zeitschrift der Universität Rostock, Gesellschafts und Sprachwissenschaftliche Reihe* 16 (1967) 549, 551, no. 36, with bibliography to date, pls. 110.2, 111.3;[2] M. Martelli, *Prima Italia. Arts italiques du premier millénaire avant J. C.* (Brussels, 1980; Italian edition Rome, 1981; 104–6) 118f., no. 65, with further bibliography and color photo.[3] From the necropolis of Pescia Romana (figures 13, 14, 24, 25, 30, 31).

2. Florence, M.A., inv. 71016, Szilágyi, "Etrusko-korinthische Vasen," 549, 551, no. 37, with bibliography to date, pl. 111.1–2, 4; Szilágyi, *Etruszko-Korinthosi Vázafestészet* (Budapest, 1975) 29, pl. 7, figs. 10–11.[4] From the necropolis of Pescia Romana (figures 10, 15, 16, 26–29, and 32).

3. Bern, Historisches Museum, inv. 12237; Szilágyi, "Etrusko-korinthische Va-

---

1. The translation of this article is by C. B.

2. Hereafter this work will be referred to as Szilágyi, "Etrusko-korinthische Vasen," in text and in notes.
3. Hereafter this work will be referred to as Martelli, *Prima Italia*, in text and in notes.
4. Hereafter this work will be referred to as Szilágyi, *Etruszko-Korinthosi*, in text and in notes.

Figure 1. Etrusco-Corinthian Olpe, Perugia, Museo Archeologico.

Figure 2. Second view of Olpe in Figure 1.

Figure 3. Third view of Olpe in Figure 1.

Figure 4. Fourth view of Olpe in Figure 1.

Figure 5. Etrusco-Corinthian Oinochoe (Vase no. 6), Orvieto, Museo dell'Opera del Dunomo, inv. no. 676.

Figure 6. Second view of Vase no. 6.

sen," 549 and 551, no. 38, pl. 110.1 and 3; J. Jucker, *Aus der Antikensammlung des Bernischen Historischen Museums* (Bern, 1970) 36, nos. 35 and 102, note 36, pl. 11 and cover illustration. "Angeblich aus Nola," (Szilágyi, "Etrusko-korinthische Vasen," 551, with reservations on 549, note 49).

4. Swiss market (Basel, 1961); present location unknown; Szilágyi, "Etrusko-korinthische Vasen," 549 and 551, no. 39, with bibliography to date. Provenience unknown.

5. Lugano, anonymous private collection; F. P. Porten Palange, "Olpe etrusco-corinzia in una collezione privata ticinese," *Numismatica e antichità classiche* 5 (1976) 7ff., pls. 1–5, with bibliography to date.[5] From Cerveteri.

Oinochoai

6. Orvieto, Museo dell'Opera del Duomo, inv. (Bizzari) 676 = inv. (Franci) 1105 =

inv. (Cardella) 567; Szilágyi, "Etrusko-korinthische Vasen," 549 and 551, n. 30, with bibliography to date; D. A. Amyx, "The Mingor Painter and Others: Etrusco-Corinthian Addenda," *Studi Etruschi* 35 (1967) 107;[6] D. Manconi, "Un'olpe etrusco-corinzia al Museo di Perugia," *Nuovi Quaderni dell'Istituto di Archeologia dell'Universita di Perugia* (*Studi in onore di Filippo Magi*) vol. 1 (1979) plate 3. From Orvieto[7] (figures 5–8).

6. Hereafter referred to as Amyx, "The Mingor Painter," in text and in notes.

7. Height to the top of the handle, 22.3 cm; to the mouth, 18.5 cm; diameter at the foot, 9.8 cm. The provenance from Orvieto, not mentioned previously, is recorded in the Franci inventory (by the number 1105, by which it has up to now been known in the literature). Franci describes the oinochoe among the objects "appartenenti a tre tombe, rinvenute nella costruzione del nuovo Campo del Mercato, presso Porta Romana." This corresponds in effect to the "oinochoe colla bocca a tre aperture, dipinta in rosso su fondo cenere, nella cui larga zona principale sono graffite diligentemente figure di animali (alcune delle loro membra sono segnate in bianco), e che lentamente procedono da sinistra a destra . . . ," as described by G. F. Gamurrini in *Notizie degli scavi* (1881) 104. Gamurrini further notes the oinochoe among the furnishings of the "tre antichissime tombe ad

5. Hereafter this work will be referred to as Porten Palange, "Olpe etrusco-corinzia," in text and in notes.

Figure 7. Third view of Vase no. 6.

7. Swiss market (Basel, 1956); present location unknown; D. A. Amyx, "Some Etrusco-Corinthian Vase-Painters," *Studi in onore di Luisa Banti* (Rome, 1965) 10f. (Volunteer Painter);[8] Szilágyi, "Etrusko-korinthische Vasen," 549 and 551, no. 31, with further bibliography, pl. 112.1. Provenance unknown.

8. Stockholm, Medelhavsmuseet, MM 1960:22; Porten Palange, "Olpe etrusco-corinzia," 13f. Provenance unknown; acquired in Rome (Mataloni).

Plate

9. Paris, Bibl. Nat., inv. F 1966; Szilágyi, "Etrusko-korinthische Vasen," 549 and 552, no. 61, with bibliography to date. Provenance unknown.

* * *

Figure 8. Fourth view of Vase no. 6.

The oinochoe in Orvieto, number 6, which can at last be studied close at hand and better evaluated (figures 5–8),[9] is morphologically identical with oinochoai numbers 7 and 8. I have dwelt on this Etrusco-Corinthian shape (of rather limited diffusion) on another occasion,[10] noting its adoption also within black-figure and linear-decorated Etrusco-Corinthian pottery and its establishment in the orbit of Vulci from the end of the seventh century B.C. to the first decades of the sixth century B.C.

Oinochoe number 6, moreover, shares with the example in Stockholm, number 8, certain accessory ornamental details—such as the pair of eyes on the sides of the middle

ipogeo . . . scavate nel tufo . . ." which came to light by chance in the Piazza del Mercato, *Notizie degli scavi*, 103f.; for an account of the discovery, see also B. Klakowicz, *Il Museo civico archeologico di Orvieto, La sua origine e le sue vicende* (Rome, 1972) 25 and 269f., no. 3 in particular; B. Klakowicz, *La necropoli anulare di Orvieto*, vol. 2, *Cannicella e terreni limitrofi* (Rome, 1974) 17ff., 18 in particular, no. 3, and 20, note 15.

8. Hereafter referred to as Amyx, "Etrusco-Corinthian Vase-Painters," in text and in notes.

9. I am extremely grateful to Anna E. Feruglio, Superintendent of Archaeology in Umbria, for having sent promptly the complete series of photographs of this vase and of the olpe in the Museum at Perugia for my use.

10. M. Martelli, "Per il Pittore di Feoli," *Prospettiva* 11 (1977) 10, figs. 25–26; an example from the Ciclo delle Olpai should now be added (*Kunstwerke der Antike, Münzen und Medaillen Auktion 56* [Basel, 1980] 19f., no. 42, pl. 13, attributed by Szilágyi to the Hercle Painter), likewise furnished with eyes on the sides of the central lobe of the mouth.

lobe of the mouth, the white-dot rosettes overpainted on the neck, and the cusped rays on the shoulder—details common also to number 7, with the exception of the rays, which are replaced in that case by tongues.

The frieze of number 6 (figures 5–8), as is typical for this phase of the painter's activity, is exclusively zoomorphic, consisting of horse, lion, panther, grazing fawn and boar, all arranged in a clockwise direction. The first two animals, the horse and the lion, are among the most common protagonists of the painter's figural repertory,[11] whose general accents and make-up show the final effect of orientalizing influences. Instead, the other three animals are less frequently found in his works.[12] In particular, the lion,[13] an unmistakable creation of the painter, finds its most precise parallel (among the animals that we have just listed) in the upper frieze of olpe number 4, with the identical pincer-like configuration of the mouth and even the same phytomorphic filling motif below the head.

Other typical distinguishing features of the painter are the groups of wavy lines that, in overpaint, furrow the central portion of the animals' bodies; the hooked line that indicates the shoulder; the recurrent undulating motif that marks the rumps, bellies, necks, wings, and divisions of the muzzle; the clear separation between the legs and the hooves of the horses, the deer, and the boars. Among the characteristic earmarks of the Pescia Romana Painter, the phytomorphic filling motifs register as fully the most elaborate within the oeuvre thus far brought into discussion. This motif, a "stem" divided internally by a wavy line, turns at the upper end and is enriched with trapezoidal and triangular leaves with doubly incised contours. These leaf shapes are identical to those adopted as fins on the curious wild goat-fish and on the just as unusual bird-lion-fish[14] of olpe number 5.

Because of the impossibility of including for discussion oinochoe number 8 (since it is unpublished photographically), the piece that seems most similar to the oinochoe at Orvieto in terms of the syntax of the frieze, the realization of the bodies, and the distribution of overpaint is vase number 7.

In general, however, either the five olpai, which are closely associated, down to the smallest details, or the three oinochoai and the plate are marked by considerable stylistic homogeneity.

Indeed, it is just this stylistic homogeneity that allows us to exclude without hesitation the olpe in the Museum of Perugia (figures 1–4) ascribed to the oeuvre of the Pescia Romana Painter by Manconi,[15] as indicated above. In regard to the accepted works, the olpe in Perugia shows obvious differences, whether in terms of the overall organization or in the direction of the friezes—in the Perugia olpe the friezes run counterclockwise, whereas in the previously cited works they always run clockwise—or in terms of the more elongated but less organic treatment of the figures, which are articulated by lower, smaller joints. There follow then a number of other not inconsiderable differences in the Perugia vase concerning the filling ornaments of a typology unparalleled in the work of the Pescia Romana Painter; the tails of the felines, on one hand, are, like the horns of the bull, heavily punctuated by a careless series

11. The horse, in fact, appears on numbers 1 (figure 30), 4, 5, and 9; the lion on numbers 1, 2, 4, and 5.

12. The wingless panther (more frequently depicted with wings) recurs on numbers 4 and 8; the fawn on number 5; and the boar on number 7.

13. The iconographically uncommon feline seems to me to be identifiable as a lion, precedents for which are not lacking in the orientalizing bestiary. It has been described as "Einhorn" (Szilágyi, "Etrusko-korinthische Vasen," 551, no. 30) or "felino, probabilmente un leone" (Porten Palange, "Olpe etrusco-corinzia," 12 and 20, who, however, on p. 21 designates it as a unicorn exactly in reference to the oinochoe in Orvieto).

14. See Porten Palange, "Olpe etrusco-corinzia," pls. 1,1; 3,5; and 2,4 and 5,10 respectively.

15. See D. Manconi, "Un'olpe etrusco-corinzia al Museo di Perugia," Nuovi Quaderni dell'Istituto di Archeologia dell'Università di Perugia (Studi in onore di Filippo Magi) vol. 1 (1979) 95, pls. 1–2 (the drawing reproduced on pl. 2 is, however, inverted). Through the courteous information supplied by A. E. Feruglio, we might now add the following to the scanty references so far furnished by Manconi in regard to the olpe's registration: this vase was sequestered, together with additional material, in Orvieto in October 1965, following an operation carried out by the police of Viterbo.

Figure 9. Etrusco-Corinthian Oinochoe, Florence, Museo Archeologico.

of small oblique strokes; the tail of the bull, on the other hand, is twisted.[16] Broad zones of spotting are then scattered or, rather, aligned along the neck and the length of the contour of the bodies of the animals, not to mention along the tail of a panther and even along a filling ornament. And the indication of the shoulder here becomes an irregular elliptical incision. All these elements are each so distinctly different as to reject Manconi's attempted attribution of this work to the Pescia Romana Painter and, with greater force, as to categorically deny that the vase belongs to "un momento di piena maturità del nostro maestro o della bottega che da lui prende nome."[17] The few, weak recognizable similarities, such as, for example, the overpainting of wavy lines on the bodies, do not confirm the attribution but suggest instead that the mediocre decorator of the Perugia olpe is a pupil or, rather, an imitator of much less

skill than the Pescia Romana Painter. The painter of the Perugia olpe, thus, is characterized by a hard and clumsy line that he tries to sustain with a redundancy of ornament.

The vase in Perugia, therefore, joins the Vulcian nucleus of Etrusco-Corinthian polychrome production, but it remains an anonymous work that cursorily echoes the fluent and dynamic language of the Pescia Romana Painter.[18] And, at least for the moment, it remains isolated, since not one relevant parallel is to be found in the material published to date.

* * *

It is perhaps not superfluous, at this point, to try to trace the stylistic development of the Pescia Romana Painter. The works most related to his formal expression have been identified[19] not so much with the exponents of the Polychrome group, but more certainly with the artists engaged in black-figure technique and, in particular, with the Volunteer Painter and the American Academy Painter (whose certain works have reached the remarkable number of thirty).[20] It is evident that such an evaluation, in conjunction with

16. The intertwined tail is to be found occasionally in contemporary vase painting; for example, on an oinochoe of Orvietan provenance (figure 9) and on an anonymous work of the Polychrome group: see M. Martelli, *Restauri archeologici* (Florence, 1969) 94f., no. 69, with bibliography; pls. 25,2 and 26,2.

17. Manconi, "Un'olpe etrusco-corinzia," 95.

18. My opinion is shared by J. G. Szilágyi, who has kindly sent me a confirmation by letter (3 January 1981).

19. On the painter see G. Karo, *De arte vascularia antiquissima quaestiones*, Dissertation (Bonn, 1896) 37, nos. 1–2, pl. 2,5; J. Boehlau, *Aus ionischen und italischen Nekropolen* (Leipzig, 1898) 101; Amyx "Etrusco-Corinthian Vase-Painters," 9ff.; Amyx "The Mingor Painter," 98f. and 107; Szilágyi, "Etrusko-korinthische Vasen," 549; Szilágyi, "Remarques sur les vases etrusco-corinthiens de l'exposition étrusque de Vienne," *Archeologia Classica* 20 (1968) 18 and 21 (hereinafter referred to as "Remarques"); Szilágyi, *Etruszko-Korinthosi*, 29; Szilágyi, "Entwurf der Geschichte der etrusko-korinthischen figürlichen Vasenmalerei," in A. Alföldi, *Römische Frühgeschichte, Kritik und Forschung seit 1964* (Heidelberg, 1976) 185; Porten Palange, "Olpe etrusco-corinzia"; Szilágyi, "Considerazioni sulla ceramica etrusco-corinzia di Vulci: risulti e problemi," *La civiltà arcaica di Vulci e la sua espansione. Atti del X Convegno di Studi Etruschi e Italici* (Florence, 1977) 55; D. A. Amyx, "Two Etrusco-Corinthian Vases," 16; Martelli, *Prima Italia*, 118f.

20. Most recently, Amyx, "Two Etrusco-Corinthian Vases," *Studies in Honour of Arthur Dale Trendall* (Sydney, 1979) 16, with bibliography to date in notes 13, and 17–20.

Figure 10. Detail of Etrusco-Corinthian Olpe (Vase no. 2), Florence, Museo Archeologico, inv. no. 71016.

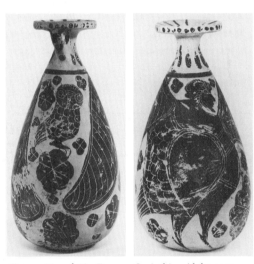

Figures 11 and 12. Etrusco-Corinthian Alabastron, Oxford, Ashmolean Museum, Queen's College Loan, no. 8.

the isolation of the Pescia Romana Painter within the Polychrome group correctly pointed out by Szilágyi[21]—not substantially affected by the olpe in Perugia—requires a detailed verification of eventual contacts between the pieces attributed to the Pescia Romana Painter and to other painters.

Amyx has already expressed justifiable

doubt[22] about Szilágyi's assignment[23] of the Cambridge kylix 1.1931, the Oxford alabastron, Queen's College Loan number 8 (figures 11 and 12), and the alabastron DAI Rome, neg. 36.1216 (figure 17), to the American Academy Painter; these are works that the Hungarian scholar had earlier recognized as "peut-être de la main d'un autre peintre du groupe."[24] I believe not only that one must agree with Amyx's rejection of Szilágyi's attribution but also that one can go further and see in these vases extremely interesting connections with various works of the Pescia Romana Painter and more than a few of his distinctive traits.

The Oxford alabastron, in particular, presents a most suggestive case as one sees in it a figurative element that, while not outside the repertory of Etrusco-Corinthian pottery and outside incised buccheri,[25] is not, however, one of the most common. This element reappears in practically identical form on at least two vases attributed to the Pescia Romana Painter: a fact that is indeed difficult to ascribe to chance coincidences or to mechanical derivation. I refer to the owl standing on the large rosette on the back of the Oxford alabastron (figure 11) and to those owls that, respectively, roost on the tail of a winged panther on olpe number 2 (figure 10) and stand on the ground in the decoration of olpe number 5.[26] By comparing the three owls in

21. Szilágyi, "Etrusko-korinthische Vasen," 549; "Remarques," 18.

22. Amyx "Two Etrusco-Corinthian Vases," 18, note 19; Martelli, *Prima Italia*, 118.

23. J. G. Szilágyi, "Le fabbriche di ceramica etrusco-corinzia a Tarquinia," *Studi Etruschi* 40 (1972) 71, n. 1, and 73, nos. 19 and 27. The first alabastron has been reproduced afterward by J. Boardman, *The Greeks Overseas, Their Early Colonies and Trade* (London, 1980³) fig. 247 on p. 207, and it has been treated by this writer (Martelli, *Prima Italia*, 118); the photograph of the second alabastron appears in A. Alföldi, *Römische Frühgeschichte, Kritik und Forschung seit 1964* (Heidelberg, 1976) pl. 9,10.

24. Szilágyi, "Remarques," 19, note 49, pl. 12, 1–2 (Oxford alabastron).

25. For as much as it concerns the first, see, for example, an oinochoe by the Feoli Painter (M. Martelli, "Per il Pittore di Feoli," *Prospettiva* 11 [1977] 4, figs. 6 and 9); for the other, see a cup from Narce (M. Bonamici, *I buccheri con figurazioni graffite* [Florence, 1974] 35, no. 37, fig. 14, with bibliography).

26. It should be recalled that this bird appears, more-

Figure 13. Detail of Etrusco-Corinthian Olpe (Vase no. 1), Florence, Museo Archeologico, inv. no. 71015.

Figure 14. Detail of Vase no. 1.

Figure 15. Detail of Vase no. 2.

Figure 16. Detail of Vase no. 2.

these polychrome and black-figure examples, one can easily establish strict correspondences of detail, in addition to the identity of the structure and general formulation, between the Oxford alabastron and the Lugano olpe in particular, even at the level of the scaly plumage. Likewise, if one examines on the Oxford alabastron the bearded siren with outspread wings that stands out as the principal subject (figure 12), it is impossible to ignore typical signs of the Pescia Romana Painter: from the linear characteristic of a double contour around the profile of the

heads, with the nape rendered as a kind of protuberance—as for example, on the sphinxes of olpai numbers 1 (figures 13 and 14), 2 (figures 15 and 16), 3, and 5—to the unmistakable cranium circumscribed by a curved line ending in a small hook. Other signs include the decidedly half-moon faces and the groups of multiple incisions, which, for example, link the wings to the bodies of the animals on the black-figure vases (figures 12 and 17) or encircle the necks of the sphinxes (figures 13–16), panthers, and lions on the polychrome vases.[27] Very similar char-

over, with open wings on oinochoe number 8 (Porten Palange, "Olpe etrusco-corinzia," 13, no. 1, and p. 21).

27. Compare, respectively, the olpai numbers 1, 2, and 4.

Figure 17. Etrusco-Corinthian Alabastron (Deutsches Archäologisches Institut, Rome, Photo neg. 36.1216).

Figure 18. Etrusco-Corinthian Kylix, Rome, Museo di Villa Giulia, inv. no. 82554.

Figure 19. Etrusco-Corinthian Kylix, Rome, Museo di Villa Giulia, inv. no. 82553.

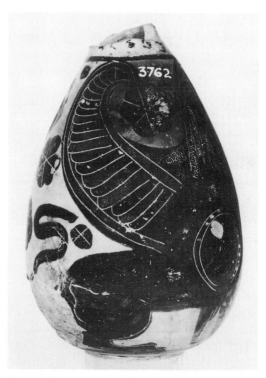

Figure 20. Etrusco-Corinthian Alabastron, Florence, Museo Archeologico, inv. no. 3762.

Figure 21. Second view of Alabastron in Figure 20.

Figure 22. Third view of Alabastron in Figure 20.

acteristics are to be found as well on the Cambridge kylix and on the DAI Rome, neg. 36.1216 alabastron (figure 17), which is even closer to the Oxford example.

If, therefore, our proposal to identify the same hand in works decorated by different techniques is not unfounded, we find ourselves confronted with a "bilingual" vase painter whose isolation within the Polychrome group comes to be fully understood as the result of recognizing him as an autonomous personality. This personality, following its own development, tends progressively (and precociously) to separate itself from its group of origin. Due to interest in the prevalent experiences and the technique most widely practiced in his center of activity, this master engages in new and more up-to-date forms, under the guidance of an increasingly intense reception of Middle Corinthian influences. The Pescia Romana Painter originates, as evident from our proposal, at the same time as a painter who is identified as the leader of the American Academy group.

On the other hand, the three vases that we have deleted from the oeuvre of the American Academy Painter along with Amyx (see above) set into motion a chain reaction, since they are linked by indubitable connections with several other vases traditionally ascribed to the American Academy Painter. If, in fact, the Cambridge kylix is strongly related formally to the pair of kylikes[28] (figures

28. For the first (inv. 82554), see G. Colonna, *Nuovi tesori dell'antica Tuscia* (Viterbo, 1970) 39, no. 26; Szilágyi, "Le fabbriche di ceramica," 72, no. 2; Szilágyi, *Etruszko-Korinthosi*, pl. 22, fig. 30; *La civiltà arcaica di Vulci e la sua espansione. Atti del X Convegno di Studi Etruschi e Italici* (Florence, 1977) pl. 19,c; Amyx, "Two Etrusco-Corinthian Vases," 18, note 23; M. Martelli, in M. Cristofani (ed.), *Gli Etruschi in Maremma, Popolamento e attività produttive* (Milan, 1981) 236, fig. 227 in color. For the second (inv. 82553), and Szilágyi, "Le fabbriche di ceramica," 72, no. 3; on this last vase one may note, by the way, a small but indicative Morellian element that supports our line of reasoning, the triangular appendage below the tail of the lion-bird (another animal, then, of hybrid composition), entirely similar to those triangles that function as fins on the wild goat-fish of the polychrome olpe number 5 (see Porten Palange,

18 and 19) from the Vulcian tomb called the *Tomba del Pittore della Sfinge Barbuta* and to the Vatican plate 16432,[29] and if the sphinxes depicted on these works stand in organic relation to those depicted on the Florence alabastron 3762[30] (figures 20, 21, and 22), then the bearded sirens of the two alabastra (figures 12 and 17) are not without firm connections with the winged despotes— likewise bearded—on the alabastron of Tomb 94 Osteria.[31] The figure on this latter alabastron, in its turn, is inseparable from the hoplite on alabastron B.M. 1928.6–14.1 (figure 23) and not just for the telling detail of the fringed perizoma on the warrior's thigh; that is to say, these alabastra are inseparable from the eponymous vase of Amyx's Warrior Painter,[32] called by Szilágyi the American Academy Painter.[33] However, the winged steinbock on the alabastron (once in the Candelori collection)[34] exhibits such a

Figure 23. Etrusco-Corinthian Alabastron, London, British Museum, inv. no. 1928.6-14.1.

"Olpe etrusco-corinzia," pls. 1,l; 3,5.

I must thank Paola Pelagatti, Superintendent of Archaeology in Southern Etruria, and M. A. Rizzo, Inspector, for the photographs and for the kind permission to reproduce the latter vase here for the first time.

29. Szilágyi, "Le fabbriche di ceramica," 72, no. 10.

30. Ibid., 73, no. 21.

31. Ibid., 72, no. 12.

32. Amyx, "The Mingor Painter," 97ff., pl. 39; Szilágyi, "Le fabbriche di ceramica," 73, no. 18. I would like to point out a small detail, that is, the hooked mark on the knees and on the heels of the warrior—perhaps to demarcate the greaves—which returns, identically, in the right claw of the owl on olpe number 2 (figure 10) and, reduced to a simple curl, on the right forelegs of the horses on olpai numbers 1 (figures 30 and 31) and 2 (figure 32).

33. Szilágyi, "Le fabbriche di ceramica," 32, note 16; see now Amyx, "Two Etrusco-Corinthian Vases," 18, note 13.

34. Szilágyi, "Le fabbriche di ceramica," 72, no. 15. This vase, together with the American Academy alabastron 543 in Rome (assumed to be eponymous vase of the American School Painter by Szilágyi, "Remarques," 18f. and note 49, pl. 11; and Szilágyi, "Le fabbriche di ceramica," 73, no. 20), and with the aforementioned plate (note 29) of the Museo Gregoriano Etrusco, has been closely linked by Amyx, "Etrusco-Corinthian Vase-Painters," 9ff., to the Pescia Romana Painter. Amyx concludes: "though I cannot yet give them firmly to the Pescia Romana Painter, are so close to this work that they must belong within the same immediate orbit, and the establishment in this vicinity of a crossing over of hands

wide range of correspondences with those by the Pescia Romana Painter that it avoids, in effect, an attribution to a different hand. Indeed, the comparison with the grazing steinbocks of olpai numbers 1 (figures 24 and 25), 2 (figure 26 and 27), and 5 is decisive with respect to the identical treatment of the eye, the ear, the horns, the beard, the subdivisions of the muzzle, and even the double little arc under the eye that the painter uses often, for

in both techniques is to be expected." Similarly, Amyx, "The Mingor Painter," 99, collecting the first list of works of the Warrior Painter, underlines "the close relationship . . . to the work of the (black-polychrome) pieces by the Pescia Romana Painter." On the other hand, Porten Palange ("Olpe etrusco-corinzia," 24f.), who has dwelt on some of the precise points of contact and details of complete correspondence in the pieces ascribed to one or the other vase-painter, concludes decisively that "il Maestro di Pescia Romana" has "decorato solo vasi con motivi incisi su fondo verniciato" (p. 23).

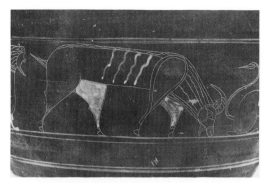

Figure 24. Detail of Vase no. 1.

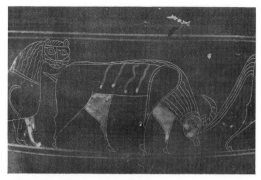

Figure 25. Detail of Vase no. 1.

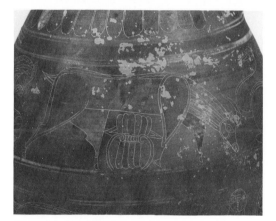

Figure 26. Detail of Vase no. 2.

Figure 27. Detail of Vase no. 2.

other animals as well.[35] In regard to the wings, one of the most fitting comparisons is with those of the lion-bird-fish on olpe number 5.[36]

Moreover, if we put, for example, the lions of the alabastra numbers 13, 20, 22, and 25 of Szilágyi's 1972 list side by side with those of olpai numbers 2 (figures 28 and 29) and 4 of our list, we might point out the analogous bisection of the mane, rendered by slanting lines in divergent directions, and the manner

of terminating the mane with a double segment. Again, we might point out the analogous arcuate mark—repeated, as a rule—that designates the lateral separation of the muzzle. We might further point out the triangular termination of the jaws and the tassel-like ending of the tails.[37]

If also in black-figure vases the shoulder of certain animals generally appears as an arc encompassing three quarters of a circle, frequently combined with rows of dots in added white, that could plausibly be explained as the result of a change of technique. It might also be explained contextually as the result of the evolution of the painter, who depends

35. This appears, for example, on the lions of numbers 4 and 6, on the winged panthers of number 5, on the winged and wingless horses of numbers 1 (figures 30 and 31), 2 (figure 32), and 5, and on the fawn of number 5.

36. The wings of this composite creature, according to Porten Palange, "Olpe etrusco-corinzia," 20, note 41, find corresponding form on the owl of oinochoe number 8.

37. For the latter, compare the plate from the Pushkin Museum (Szilágyi, "Remarques," 19, note 49, pl. 10,1; Szilágyi, "Le fabbriche di ceramica," 72, no. 9), as Porten Palange, "Olpe etrusco-corinzia," 24, has observed.

Figure 28. Detail of Vase no. 2.

Figure 29. Detail of Vase no. 2.

Figure 30. Detail of Vase no. 1.

Figure 31. Detail of Vase no. 1.

ever more on the compositional schemes and the influences of ripe Early Corinthian and Middle Corinthian. To cite a more notable example, it is sufficient to recall the profound metamorphosis in the career's evolution of a prominent figure like the Bearded Sphinx Painter.

Within the group of works cited, in short, the correspondences are certainly numerous, the connections so closely linked as to jeopardize the belief in a rigid differentiation of hands. And we are persuaded to admit, at least, a partial superimposition, rather than to consider these close correlations as the effect of a simple rapport between colleagues or disciples. This would, in fact, necessarily presuppose not so much a slavish imitation at the level of style and figural repertory—which, however, is immediately perceived in the inferior Bobuda Painter—as much as the copying and the repetition practically *ad un-*

guem of specific particularities of execution of the first painter by the second painter.[38]

A skillful draftsman then, the Pescia Romana Painter is endowed with a fluid and vigorous line; he is not a stranger to unusual or fanciful figures like the theriomorphic creatures pointed out previously on olpe number 5, the superimposed fishes on the oinochoe number 8,[39] and, if our proposal is accepted, the lion-bird and the little human figure with open arms on the kylikes Villa Giulia 82553 (figure 19) and 82554 (figure

38. I abstain from denying altogether the identity of the American Academy Painter, *for the moment*, since that would imply an integral revision of all the works ascribed to him—a task that does not fall within the scope of this essay and that is impossible to undertake at present, not solely because half the works remain photographically unpublished. But I am deeply persuaded, now, that this result is unfailing.

39. Porten Palange, "Olpe etrusco-corinzia," 13f., no. 5.

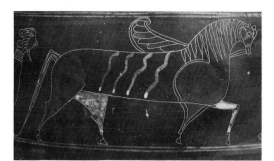

Figure 32. Detail of Vase no. 2.

18). This fanciful tendency makes the Pescia Romana Painter depart from time to time from the dominant repetitive style of the contemporary Vulcian schools of vase painting. Our painter shows an experimental attitude and an open approach. In his new operative phase, on the one hand, there are unidirectional friezes and the compositions display more articulation, with the adoption of the heraldic scheme (for example, on the Cambridge cup). He maintains, on the other hand, from his earliest formation a marked propensity for the use of incisions and added colors, not without precise suggestions of the Corinthian White Dot style.

The career thus reconstructed for the Pescia Romana Painter, however, is not an isolated event in Vulci. It is in fact the seat of activity for another bilingual vase painter, namely the Painter of the Polychrome Arcs,[40] a more slender and delicate draftsman whose style designates itself among the miniaturistic modes of Protocorinthian/Transitional derivation. Always in the orbit of Vulci the experience of bilingualism, consisting of limited adoption or an occasional approach to polychrome technique by craftsmen engaged in black-figure painting, is attested by an eminent leader such as the Bearded Sphinx Painter[41] and by sporadic examples such as the Hermitage alabastron B.9120[42] or a plate from the *Tomba della Panatenaica*.[43] The latter works correspond significantly with incised buccheri.

In the varied weave of experiences by workshops devoted to the production of vases, correlations may also be made between Etrusco-Corinthian ceramics and bucchero. If these correlations are by now clarified within the Polychrome group, particularly as concerns the Castellani Painter, and the incised buccheri from the region of Veii, another emblematic paradigm is recognizable in the Louvre amphora C 552.[44] This is found in the evident parallels in the *ductus* of the frieze and in the typology of the filling motif (disc-like rosettes with cruciform internal division) with the aforementioned plate—surely of Vulcian manufacture—from the *Tomba della Panatenaica*; this fact serves to severely invalidate the attribution of the Paris amphora to Cerveteri.[45]

In the study of vase painting, which, for many generations, has involved archaic Etruscan handicraft, the moment has perhaps arrived to evaluate the diverse means and expressive languages explored by some vase-painters in multiform and articulate experiences under the concomitant stimulus provided both by local traditions and by external influences. This model is to be preferred, in my estimation, to the previously formal approach that granted too much to the compartmented distinction between techniques and to a fragmented parcelling out of hands.

September 1981

40. See Szilágyi, "Considerazioni sulla ceramica etrusco-corinzia di Vulci," 55.

41. F. Zevi, "Nuovi vasi del Pittore della Sfinge Barbuta," *Studi Etruschi* 37 (1969) 44; see in particular the upper friezes of the olpai on page 55, numbers 2, 5, and 35, pls. 16,c-d and pl. 17,d.

42. Szilágyi, "Etrusko-korinthische Vasen," 550 and 552, no. 57, pl. 114,1; Szilágyi, "Remarques," 17, pl. 14,1.

43. Szilágyi, "Etrusko-korinthische Vasen," 550 and 552, no. 62; Szilágyi, "Remarques," 17f.; G. Riccioni and M. T. Falconi Amorelli, *La Tomba della Panatenaica di Vulci* (Rome, 1968) 43, no. 26, with figure.

44. M. Bonamici, *I buccheri con figurazioni graffite* (Florence, 1974) 51f., no. 67, with bibliography to date, pl. 30, a-b.

45. Ibid., 135.

21. Six Corinthian Red-figure Vases

IAN MCPHEE AND A. D. TRENDALL

LA TROBE UNIVERSITY, MELBOURNE, AUSTRALIA

At some point within the period 440–420 B.C., Corinth began to produce its own red-figure pottery in imitation of, and in competition with, the red-figure vases imported from Athens. A great many examples of this local fabric, found in the American excavations at Corinth since 1896, have recently been published,[1] but this material is for the most part fragmentary and does not give as complete a picture as one would like of this important local red-figure fabric. It therefore needs to be supplemented by the publication of whole vases. With this in mind we take the opportunity to present six vases that have found their way to museums outside Greece: two pelikai in Winchester and Reading; a bell-krater in Vienna; an oinochoe in New York; two skyphoi in Toronto and London.

Pelikai

The collection of classical antiquities at Winchester College includes a small Corin-thian red-figure pelike (inv. no. 2), some 18.3 cm high (figures 1 and 2). The pictures on both sides are bordered above by a strip of egg-and-dot pattern and below by a reserved band. The scene on the obverse is set in the palaestra: a young athlete stands in frontal view, head to right, at a stele, grasping a strigil in his left hand. To the right of the stele, a second youth leans forward to left against a staff, a himation wrapped about his lower body and his legs. Both figures wear white wreaths. On the reverse of the vase is another draped youth, standing to right beside a stele, his right arm extended.

Both the shape and the general scheme of decoration are based on Attic pelikai of small dimensions produced in the latter half of the fifth century, such as Munich 2352 and 2357.[2] A close parallel for the composition of the obverse may be found in the tondo of an Attic cup, Ferrara T.1168, to be dated circa 410–400 B.C., approximately contemporary with the Corinthian pelike.[3] The main difference is that the athlete wears a himation.

The obverse of another Corinthian red-figure pelike in Athens, N.M. 17472, also has a palaestra scene: a stele, a jumper to right, and a trainer who stands frontally, head to left. A fragment of a third pelike, in

---

1. Sharon Herbert, *Corinth* VII, 4, *The Red-figure Pottery* (Princeton, 1977); Ian McPhee, "Local Red-figure from Corinth, 1973–1980," *Hesperia* 52 (1983) 137–53. Of particular importance is the publication of the fragments from Perachora, with general remarks by P. E. Corbett: T. J. Dunbabin, ed., *Perachora* 2, esp. pp. 286–89 and pl. 116. For permission to publish vases in their charge and for ready assistance, we are grateful to Mr. Arthur Morgan (Winchester), Miss Jane F. Gardiner (Reading), Dr. Dietrich von Bothmer (New York), Mr. Brian F. Cook and Dr. Dyfri Williams (London), and Dr. John Hayes (Toronto). We are also much indebted to Sir Walter Oakeshott and Mr. J. M. Hammond in respect to the vase in Winchester.

2. *CVA* Munich 2, pl. 71, 3–4 and pl. 72, 2, 7–8; *ARV²* 1136, 9 (Hasselmann Painter), and 1104, 15 (Orpheus Painter).

3. S. Aurigemma, *La necropoli di Spina in Valle Trebba*, vol. 2 (Rome, 1965) pl. 124b, *ARV²* 1399, 2, Painter of Bonn 1645.

Figure 1. Obverse, Corinthian Red-figure Pelike, England, Winchester College, inv. no. 2.

Figure 2. Reverse of Pelike in Figure 1.

Corinth (C–70–42a),[4] has two athletes, one with javelin, the other with strigil, standing on either side of a stele. On the reverse of the Athens vase is a draped youth holding a stick; only a small fragment (C–70–42b)[5] remains from the reverse of the Corinth vase, but here, too, there was a male figure standing to right, arm extended. The Athens vase and the Corinth fragments are by one hand, the Pelikai Painter, as Sharon Herbert has called the artist,[6] and the Winchester pelike may be attributed to the same painter. This is especially clear from the drawing of the eye, facial profile, and torso of the athlete. The Pelikai Painter seems to have been active during the last quarter of the fifth century. To judge from the more fluid linework, the Win-

chester vase is probably later than those in Athens and Corinth and may belong in the last decade.

The Ure Museum of Greek Archaeology in the University of Reading has a Corinthian red-figure pelike, RM 87.35.25, that is on permanent loan from the Reading Museum and Art Gallery[7] and appears to have belonged to the Bland Collection (figures 3 and 4). Nothing of its earlier history is known. It is in good condition, though the glaze has flaked in places and there has been some retouching. The pelike is 24.4 cm high. The vase is a little taller than the Winchester pelike, but the shape is in general similar, except that the handles do not rise as close to the lip. The pelike seems to have been one of the more important Corinthian shapes, particularly the pelike of small size (less than 25

4. *Corinth* VII, 4, 29, and pl. 1, 2a. The pelike Athens N.M. 17472 is mentioned by Herbert, *Corinth* VII, 4, 12 and 29, but has not, to our knowledge, been published.

5. *Corinth* VII, 4, 29, and pl. 1, 2b.

6. *Corinth* VII, 4, 5–6.

7. The Reading pelike is mentioned in *Corinth* VII, 4, on p. 28. We owe observations on the present condition of the vase to Miss Jane F. Gardiner.

Figure 3. Obverse, Corinthian Red-figure Pelike, England, Reading University Museum, inv. no. RM 87-35-25.

Figure 4. Reverse of Pelike in Figure 3.

cm in height), and a not uncommon grave-offering.[8].

The pictures on the Reading pelike are bordered above and below by pattern-bands: on the obverse by a sort of bead-and-reel, on the reverse by bands of chevron. The bead-and-reel pattern is, to our knowledge, unparalleled in Corinthian red-figure. A variation, however, is used on the neck of an Attic red-figure column-krater of the late fifth century from Montesarchio.[9] A chevron-pattern is to be found again on the reverse of the Corinthian pelike in Athens, N.M. 1473.

The Reading pelike has two figures on either side.[10] On the obverse a bearded satyr

leans forward to right, one foot raised on a rock, talking with a maenad, who is seated to right on a bunched himation, looking back at the satyr. The maenad wears a peplos and holds a mirror in her left hand. Her bracelets and her necklace are indicated in added white, as is the satyr's fillet. Between the two figures is a sprig of ivy. On the back of the vase are two draped youths standing on either side of a stele. The arrangement of the reverse is close to that of certain Attic red-figure pelikai of the first quarter of the fourth century, such as Sydney 44 or Upsala, Gustavianum 2106.[11] The bearded satyr is also derived from Attic vase-painting of this time.[12] In Corinthian red-figure the combi-

8. See the remarks of Sharon Herbert, *Corinth* VII, 4, 28. On the funerary use of pelikai see also S. Karouzou, *BCH* 95 (1971) 138–45.

9. M. Napoli, *La tomba del tuffatore* (Bari, 1970) 196, figs. 115, 116. The pattern is just as unusual in Attic red-figure, but it recurs more frequently in South Italy, in both Apulian and Paestan.

10. Miss Gardiner informs us that preliminary sketch

lines are visible on the woman's body and on the satyr's upper right arm.

11. The Sydney and Upsala pelikai are by one hand; by the same hand is Bucharest, MIRSR 16826, from Istros, *Histria* IV, pl. 48.

12. See the right-hand satyr on the obverse of a pelike in Rhodes: *Deltion* 18/B2 (1963) pl. 373 c-d; *BCH* 89 (1965) 877, figs. 3–4.

Figure 5. Obverse, Corinthian Red-figure Bell-Krater, Vienna, Kunsthistorisches Museum, inv. no. IV 3735 (Masner 344).

nation of seated maenad and standing satyr will be found again on a pelike in New York, MMA 57.43, which Herbert attributes to her Hermes Painter.[13] At present the Reading pelike stands stylistically alone, though general resemblances may be noted between the treatment of the youths on side B and those on the reverse of such a vase as Corinth C–37–237.[14] The pelike is probably to be placed in the first quarter of the fourth century.

Figure 6. Reverse of Bell-Krater in Figure 5.

Bell-krater

Vienna IV 3735 (Masner 344) is a small bell-krater, about 20 cm high (figures 5 and 6). According to Masner it came from the Blum-Blankenegg collection that was given to the Oesterreichisches Museum in 1886.[15] The provenience, "Thebes," recorded by Masner, must derive from the inventory written by the original owner.[16] However, the vase is not Boeotian but Corinthian, as the clay indicates. Boeotia might seem at first sight an unlikely findspot, but at least two other Corinthian red-figure vases, the bell-

kraters in Athens, N.M. 1384 and 1391 (C.C. 1927), were unearthed in Boeotia, and other Corinthian vases, not red-figure, were exported there in the fifth and fourth centuries.[17]

The Vienna krater has been recomposed from fragments. In places the glaze has flaked or has been abraded.

The lip is decorated with a single row of laurel leaves running to left. Below each handle is a palmette flanked by upright leaves. The groundline is formed by a reserved band that encircles the vase. The obverse has two figures, a maenad and a satyr. The maenad, who wears a belted peplos, stands to right, holding a piece of fruit or an egg, it may be, in her left hand, and calmly watches the bearded satyr as he dances toward her, a fruit or egg in one hand, a drinking-horn in the other. The "fruit," and the wreaths worn by both figures are in added color.

13. *Corinth* VII, 4, 7, 31, and pl. 32.
14. *Corinth* VII, 4, 37, no. 30, and pl. 7.
15. Karl Masner, *Die Sammlung antiker Vasen und Terracotten im K. K. Oesterreichischen Museum* (1892) 54, no. 344.
16. Ibid., p. vi.

17. For example, some Sam Wide vases: A. D. Ure, *JHS* 69 (1949) 18. For the red-figure bell-krater, Athens N.M. 1391, see A. D. Trendall, *Phlyax Vases* (London, 1967) 25f. Dr. Elizabeth Pemberton also informs us that there are fifth and fourth century Corinthian vases in the Tanagra (Schimatari) storeroom.

Figure 7. Corinthian Red-figure Oinochoe, New York, Metropolitan Museum of Art, acc. no. 64.107.

The reverse has only one figure, a youth in himation standing to right, a stick in his out-stretched hand. In front of him is a pillar supporting an egglike object painted in added color. Added color has also been used for the youth's fillet.

Oinochoe

The Metropolitan Museum of Art has two Corinthian red-figure vases: a pelike, 57.43, which has been published elsewhere, and an oinochoe, Beazley's type 2, 64.107 (figure 7).[18] The oinochoe is 16.45 cm high. On the

neck is a short strip of Z-maeander. The body is decorated with a youth standing in three-quarter view, head in profile to right. He wears a himation off the left shoulder and holds a strigil in his left hand. Beside him is a stele. An irregular reserved band serves as groundline. The scheme of decoration is again derived from Attic red-figure, in this case from oinochoai dating to the end of the fifth and first quarter of the fourth centuries, such as the oinochoai of the Painter of Ferrara T.782 and a series related to the F.B. Group.[19] These vases stand out from the normal run of Attic oinochoai of the time by restricting the scene to a single figure and by placing a short pattern-band on the neck, not on the shoulder. An unattributed Attic oinochoe in Ferrara, from Valle Trebba, T.784, provides a parallel for the design of stele and athlete with strigil.[20] The left-hand figure in the tondo of a cup in Ferrara, from Valle Trebba T.1168, is very close in attitude and in garb to the youth on the New York oinochoe.[21] On the basis of shape and style, the New York vase is to be dated in the early fourth century.

Skyphoi

The skyphos (figures 8, 9, and 10) of Attic type Toronto 919.5.5 (C.421) has long been known and was published in 1930, but as South Italian.[22] The vase is, however, defi-

---

18. The pelike is published: *BMMA* 21 (1962–1963) 9, fig. 10; *Corinth* VII, 4, pl. 32. The oinochoe was the gift of Harold F. Anderson and was identified as Corinthian by Dietrich von Bothmer.

19. For the Painter of Ferrara T.782 cf. *ARV²* 1356–57; the two oinochoai from T.782 (inv. 2490 and 2492) are illustrated by L. Massei, *Gli askoi a figure rosse nei corredi funerari delle necropoli di Spina* (Milan, 1978) pl. 13, 2; inv. 2492 is also illustrated in N. Alfieri, *Spina: Museo Archeologico* (Bologna, 1979) fig. 261. For the series related to the F. B. Group, see *ARV²* 1493 and 1696. *ARV²* 1493, 1, is inv. 9800, Massei, *Gli askoi*, pl. 79, 2; *ARV²* 1493, 2, is inv. 9799, Massei, *Gli askoi*, pl. 70, 2.

20. Ferrara T. 784, Aurigemma, *La necropoli di Spina*, pl. 35.

21. Ferrara T.1168, Aurigemma, *La necropoli di Spina*, pl. 124b, *ARV²* 1399, 2.

22. D. M. Robinson, C. Harcum and J. Iliffe, *A Cat-*

Figure 8. Obverse, Corinthian Red-figure Skyphos, Toronto, Royal Ontario Museum of Archaeology inv. no. 919.5.5 (C.421).

Figure 10. Handle Zone of Skyphos in Figure 8.

Figure 9. Reverse of Skyphos in Figure 8.

nitely Corinthian. The pale clay is covered with a red wash; the glaze is dull and greenish to brownish-black in color. The vase has been mended from fragments and a large section is missing from the reverse including almost all the head, the neck, and part of the torso of the draped youth. The skyphos came from the collection of W. A. Sturge, of Icklingham Hall, Suffolk, but of its earlier history nothing is known.

The obverse is decorated with two figures, a maenad and a bearded satyr. The maenad stands in profile to right holding out in her right hand a round object (red wash over added white). With her left hand she pulls aside her peplos at the knee. Her hair is

bound with a cord painted in red with three white dots at either end. The second figure, the satyr, is shown in three-quarter view, head in profile to left. He holds in his right hand a basket that is thought of as full of food (reserved area with five white objects). The satyr wears a wreath painted in red.

Both the maenad and the satyr are named. Behind the head of the woman, from left to right, are the letters Τ I A, and behind the satyr's head, a single letter, probably O. In their publication, Robinson and Harcum give ΠΟΝΤΙΑ for the maenad's name, and Κάδωρος for that of the satyr. ΠΟΝΤΙΑ occurs in Pausanias (2.34.11) as an epithet of Aphrodite at Hermione but is not found, as R. S. Stroud kindly informs us, in the prosopography of Corinth. Κάδωρος is not intelligible, and Robinson and Harcum suggested that the name was perhaps a variant of Κάδωλος. Since only one letter of the inscription is now legible, any interpretation of the name can only be highly speculative.[23]

These are the only inscriptions at present known in Corinthian red-figure pottery. They might be thought to be modern (nine-

alogue of the Greek Vases in the Royal Ontario Museum of Archaeology, Toronto (Toronto, 1930) 224, no. 454, and pl. 83. Only the obverse is illustrated. The height is 16.6 cm.

23. For assistance with the inscriptions we are most grateful to J. W. Hayes (Toronto) and R. S. Stroud (Berkeley).

Figure 11. Obverse, Corinthian Red-figure Skyphos, London, British Museum, inv. no. 1955.4-18.3.

Figure 12. Reverse of Skyphos in Figure 11.

teenth century), but insofar as one can tell, they seem to be genuine: the added red of the letters, for instance, is just that used for other details on the vase.

On the reverse of the Toronto skyphos is a single figure, a draped youth who stands in profile to left holding the top of a stick in his right hand. Given the drawing of the himation, the youth's left arm was probably placed akimbo. A sash (red wash over added white) hangs in the field.

Under each handle is a single palmette with spiraling tendrils that end in buds. Such buds are not common in the handle-florals of Corinthian red-figure vases, but something similar will be found on a hydria in Athens (N.M. 12260).[24]

The drawing of the women on the Athens hydria is close to that of the maenad and satyr on the Toronto skyphos. One may also compare the figures on the two oinochoai, Athens N.M. 1544 and 1543, which are certainly, as Herbert has already seen,[25] by the same hand as the Athens hydria. The Toronto skyphos appears to be by the same painter, who must have been active within the last twenty years of the fifth century, as is suggested not only by the drawing but also by the shape.[26]

The skyphos London B.M. 1955.4–18.3 (figures 11 and 12) is small, only 11 cm high.[27] It has been recomposed from numerous fragments, and a small piece is missing from the lip on the reverse. The glaze was applied thinly, and the surface has been much rubbed. The main side is decorated with two figures: a youth, with a cloak draped in the manner of a shawl over his arms, stands in three-quarter view to right, looking at a woman who is seated to left, in peplos and himation, holding up a cista with her right hand. The heads of both figures reach the lip of the vase so that the woman appears to be larger than the youth. On the back of the London skyphos are another two figures, satyrs this time: the first, youthful, with his head and body shown in three-quarter view, executes the dance of a reveler; the second, whose face has unfortunately been obliterated, strides to the right looking back at his friend, a thyrsus grasped in his left hand and an unidentified object (two corners remain) in his right. Finally, under each handle is a palmette flanked by vertical tendrils.

---

24. *Corinth* VII, 4, pl. 19, and pl. 20, 121.
25. *Corinth* VII, 4, pl. 21, 125 and pl. 22, 126.
26. The skyphos in Corinth C–37–439, *Corinth* VII, 4, 66–67, no. 151 and pl. 25, is similar in shape but

perhaps a little later. Compare also the skyphos formerly in the Agalopoulou Collection in Athens, *Catalogue d'une collection d'antiquités grecques* (Athens, 1927) 5, no. 55 (ill.): "a) Cavalier au galop en chlamyde et pétasse. b) Devant un pilier, un jeune homme en himation tenant un strigile."
27. Dr. Dyfri Williams informs us that the skyphos formed part of lot 61 in Sotheby's *Sale Catalogue*, 14 February 1955.

A youth standing before a woman who holds a cista recalls scenes in which Polyneikes presents the necklace of Harmonia to Eriphyle, a story set in the Peloponnese and certainly known in Corinth. In Attic representations, at least, the box is normally held by Polyneikes and the necklace is visible. Since scenes of myth are so few in Corinthian red-figure, the subject here is probably drawn from everyday life.

The striding figure on the reverse of the London skyphos is a favorite in Corinthian red-figure. Dionysos takes this attitude on Athens N.M. 1405, as does a satyr on New York MMA 57.43 and a youth on Corinth C–37–439.[28] Less common is the three-quarter head of the left-hand satyr, but, concerning this, compare Perachora 2792 and Corinth CP 534 + 2710.[29]

The skyphos of Attic type is a popular shape in Corinthian red-figure: the earliest examples begin in the last quarter of the fifth century; the latest belong to the second quarter and the middle of the fourth, to the last phase of the fabric. The London skyphos has the slight double-curve to the profile, which, by analogy with Attic examples of the shape, suggests a date in the first quarter of the fourth century B.C.

28. *Corinth* VII, 4, pl. 27, pl. 32 and pl. 25 respectively.

29. *Perachora* 2, pl. 116 and *Corinth* VII, 4, pl. 14, 73.

22. Import of Protocorinthian and Transitional Pottery into Attica

DENISE CALLIPOLITIS-FEYTMANS
ATHENS

During the span of a century, from about 725 to 625 B.C., Attica did not import Corinthian vases of the same high quality as those purchased by yet independent Aegina. In fact, no other ancient center of mainland Greece or in Magna Graecia managed to acquire such a quantity of large figure-decorated Protocorinthian vases, painted in the "big style" by the best of artists. At all sites other than Aegina, Protocorinthian vases, even the finest, are chiefly of small dimensions and carry linear decoration or, at times with figure motifs, are of a miniaturist style.

During the eighth and seventh centuries B.C., the importance of *Aegina* in the history of Protocorinthian pottery can be explained by its commercial and maritime strength—that is, by its economic wealth—by its vicinity to the Corinthian port of Kenchreai on the Saronic Gulf, and by the poor quality of its own clay, which would serve only crude wares for domestic use.[1] Likewise, one should perhaps not forget the human factor that some wealthy families in the port of Aegina might have been enlightened amateurs who had direct contact with the best workshops of Corinth—an assumption based on the evidence that exceptionally fine Protocorinthian has not been found on the island with the exception of the site once called "the col-

umn," that is, the ancient city north of the modern harbor on the west coast of the island facing the Argolid. It is here in the area of the sanctuaries, particularly that of the successive temples of Apollo, that large Protocorinthian vases,[2] together with Attic, Argive, and oriental imports, have been discovered. Unfortunately, these vases are presently in very fragmentary condition as a result of the circumstances of their discovery, which dates from early times, owing to the easy accessibility of the site that has always attracted archaeologists and clandestine excavators.[3] There is no evidence that fine

2. Most of them are in the Aegina Museum. See W. Kraiker, *Aigina. Die Vasen der 10. bis 7. Jahrhunderts v. Chr.* (Berlin, 1951). Reviewed by T. Dunbabin in *Gnomon* 25 (1953) 243–48. There are other fragments, once taken to Berlin, and some more fragments, still unpublished, bought in the Athens market in 1916 and taken to the Berlin Museum in 1936 (R. Eilmann and K. Gebauer, *CVA* Berlin 1, 5), mentioned by T. Dunbabin and M. Robertson (*BSA* 48 [1953] 172–74 and 177). According to these scholars, these fragments should belong to some vases published by W. Kraiker (*BSA* 48 [1953] 179, no. 2a). Kraiker did not publish all the vases and the fragments with linear decoration that were found in the same area: see L. Pallat, *AM* 22 (1897) 277, fig. 9; 278, fig. 11 and 294, fig. 19.

3. In 1837 the Ephor of Antiquities, Pittakis, transferred the old finds from Aegina to a house near the Erechtheion in Athens where they were seen by Konze and Michaelis in 1860. They were later taken to the Athens National Museum (G. Loeschke, *AM* 22 [1897] 259) and finally transferred to the present Museum of Aegina in 1926. Organized excavations have been conducted by Stais, *ArchEph* (1895) 235 (cf. Pallat, *AM* 22 [1897] 265), A. Furtwängler in 1904–1907, and P. Wolters and G. Welter (*AA* [1937] 25). Since 1966, H. Walter and his collaborators have resumed systematic exca-

1. Pollux, 7.197 (ed. Teubner): Τὴν δ' Αἴγιναν χυτρόπωλιν 'ἐκάλουν (they called Aegina a pot-seller).

Figure 1. Late Geometric Kotyle fragment, Aegina, Temple of Aphaia.

Figure 3. Fragmentary Protocorinthian Aryballos, Aegina, Temple of Aphaia.

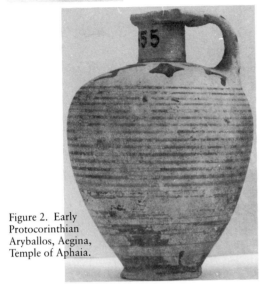

Figure 2. Early Protocorinthian Aryballos, Aegina, Temple of Aphaia.

thian vases[5] and many Protocorinthian and transitional vases with linear decoration of a fairly ordinary type. Apart from the aryballoi and the kotylai,[6] there are some fairly large vases with linear decoration—oinochoai with conical bodies and tall necks.[7] The few small vases with figure decoration are in silhouette or, more rarely, painted in a miniaturist style.[8] These mainly date from

Protocorinthian vases had served as funerary offerings in the contemporary graves in the city. The graves seem to have been modestly furnished primarily with small drinking vases of mediocre quality.[4]

Other sanctuaries that were situated on Aegina far from the port area seemingly were not equally favored, and the dedications to them are rather ordinary. Thus, the predecessors of the temple of Aphaia, at the east of the island, received Late Geometric Corin-

vations of the entire site down to the prehistoric level (publication pending). There are numerous finds from the eighth and seventh centuries B.C. (for example, *Archaiologikon Deltion* 25 [1970] B 1, pp. 136–37; hereafter cited as *Deltion* in notes), some of which will doubtlessly permit more complete restoration of Protocorinthian vases presently in the museum.

4. *ArchEph* (1910) 177; *AA* (1928) 612; (1938) 511. For the seventh century B.C., *AA* (1938) 517, see also *Deltion* 25 (1970), B 1, chr., 132; place called Livadi, grave 4: tall Early Protocorinthian pyxis, cf. Friis Johansen, *Les vases sicyoniens* (Paris, 1923) pl. 11. Height, 290 mm, lid not preserved (not mentioned in the article but seen in the museum magazines).

5. A. Furtwängler, E. Fiechter, and H. Thiersch, *Aegina, Das Heiligtum der Aphaia* (Berlin, 1906). Neck with trefoil mouth from a Late Geometric II round-bodied oinochoe, p.449, no. 172, pl. 126. Kotyle fragment (69/55 mm) decorated with a heron whose long wings are flanked by heavy lines: Late Geometric II period (figure 1).

6. Early Protocorinthian round-bodied aryballos, Furtwängler, *Aegina, Das Heiligtum*, pl. 126, no. 5. Ovoid aryballoi: pl. 128, no. 14 and no. 6 (drawings) (figure 2) (H. 73 and 80 mm). Cf. Kraiker, *Aigina. Die Vasen*, pl. 23, no. 294.

7. Furtwängler, *Aegina, Das Heiligtum*, pls. 126, 128. Complete Early Protocorinthian examples, pl. 126, nos. 2 to 4; in Kraiker, *Aigina. Die Vasen*, pl. 36, nos. 481 to 483.

8. Furtwängler, *Aegina, Das Heiligtum*, pl. 128,10, p. 449, no. 160 (drawing) (figure 3): surface weathered, neck missing. Preserved height, 62 mm. Naked youth walking to the right, head turned back, framed by four dot-rosettes, between two triple line concentric circles; on the other side, dog running left, framed by dot-rosettes. Cf. *Perachora* 2, pl. 2, 26. On the shoulder row of hooks; rays above the foot bordered by a triple line; Late Protocorinthian I. Furtwängler, *Aegina, Das Heiligtum*, pl. 128,16, p. 454, no. 232, rider; Late Protocorinthian I. Aryballos (pl. 128,17) and kotylai (pl. 126,11) with running dogs in silhouette; transitional period.

the Late Protocorinthian II and transitional periods.

This summary serves only to illustrate the difference between the history of Protocorinthian imports in Aegina and of Protocorinthian imports in Attica.

* * *

Unlike those of Aegina, sanctuaries in *Attica* have received very few dedications of Protocorinthian vases. On the Akropolis at Athens only a few aryballoi and quite late alabastra of mediocre quality have been found.[9] Nevertheless, it is possible that some temples and votive monuments of the city were originally richer in Protocorinthian vases.[10]

Because of the location, the sanctuaries on the southeast coast of Attica were more favored, as, for example, the sanctuary at Cape Sounion, where a "bothros" contained some small Protocorinthian vases of good quality, together with a figured ovoid aryballos that seems to belong to the Late Protocorinthian I period.[11]

Eleusis is an exception to the rule, since its sanctuary received quantities of Corinthian vases from the Early Protocorinthian period on (*Necrocorinthia* 185). This Attic harbor is nearest to the isthmus of Corinth and its sanctuary enjoyed religious preeminence. Furthermore, Eleusis at the time was more influenced by Megara than Athens.[12] How-

ever, we again have the same small vases found in the rest of the Greek world; that is, we have kotylai and aryballoi with linear decoration[13] or, less often, with figure motifs.[14] There are also offerings of alabastra[15] and of vases also found in graves: pyxides with concave sides[16] and a small oinochoe with a conical base and a tall neck.[17] The most unusual find is an object in clay—a pomegranate—that is certainly related to the cult of Kore.[18] If Protocorinthian dedications are relatively numerous for an Attic sanctuary, apart from the Early Protocorinthian aryballoi with linear motifs, they generally comprise small vases of mediocre quality.

Before dealing with the problem of the graves, we should examine the places that are intermediate between the sanctuaries and the cemeteries. These are the Mycenaean tombs, which had become sites of hero-cults since the Geometric period.[19] In Attica the most important such tomb is the tholos tomb at Menidi, where the offerings had accumu-

---

9. B. Graef and E. Langlotz, *Die antiken Vasen der Akropolis zu Athen*, vol. 1 (Berlin, 1909) pl. 15. They call Protocorinthian some Early Corinthian vases, for example, no. 428 (R. J. Hopper, *BSA* 44 [1949] 189) and no. 405 (*Necrocorinthia* 283, no. 370).

10. According to Rodney S. Young (*Hesperia, Suppl.* 2, 139, 142–45), the fill in the well of Kolonos Agoraios (first half of the seventh century B.C.) is seemingly uniform and consists of offerings from a shrine; 10 per cent of the vases are Corinthian with linear decoration (chiefly kotylai, some aryballoi, and a concave-sided pyxis).

11. In the National Museum. *ArchEph* (1917) 197 fig. 9, 4. Cf. *Perachora* 2, 18, no. 42, where Dunbabin associates it with Furtwängler, *Aegina, Das Heiligtum*, pl. 128, 15.

12. Megara, near Eleusis, had at the time a greater commercial importance than Athens. Large Early Pro-

tocorinthian vases of good quality, like the stirrup-handle krater with figure decoration (*Athens Annals of Archaeology* 2 [1969] 343, fig. 2; *Deltion* 25 [1970], B1, pl. 79), have been found in graves there.

13. *ArchEph* (1889) 177; Johansen, *Vases sicyoniens*, pl. 4,4 and 4,6, and p. 17; Johansen, *Vases sicyoniens*, pl. 4,8 and p. 17 is the most carefully executed piece (Dunbabin, *Perachora* 2, 13).

14. *ArchEph* (1889) 177; of the "Silhouette Neck Group" (Dunbabin and Robertson, *BSA* 48 [1953] 173).

15. Eleusis 782, in the Late Protocorinthian style; *Necrocorinthia*, no. 30, pl. 9,7.

16. K. Kourouniotis, *Eleusis, A Guide to the Excavations and the Museum*, translated by Oscar Broneer, 1936, p. 110, fig. 55. Johansen (*Vases sicyoniens*, p. 93, no. 21) has rightly associated it with the Phaleron pyxis (*AJA* 46 [1942] 37, fig. 21), which seems to be by the same artist but has a different composition. Here, hunter attacking a deer; hunter attacking a lion; lion and boar facing each other.

17. Johansen, *Vases sicyoniens*, 21.

18. *ArchEph* (1898) pl. 2,5. Cf. Hahland, *Festschrift für Frederick Zücker* (Berlin, 1954) 187. Dunbabin, *Perachora* 2, 129. According to Axel Seeberg this is not a pomegranate but the fruit of a poppy (*Acta ad archaeologiam et artium historiam pertinentia. Institutum romanum Norvegiae* 4 [1969] 7).

19. C. Blegen, *ArchEph* (1937) vol. 1, 389–90. G. Mylonas, *Mycenae and the Mycenaean Age* (Princeton, 1966) 181–86.

lated in the "dromos." Among the many Attic vases that often have a ritual character,[20] there are some fragments of small Late Protocorinthian vases, as well as the tall neck of an oinochoe with a conical body[21] not unlike the many examples from the temple of Aphaia on Aegina. This type of vase, except in reduced size, is rarely found in Attic graves. The Mycenaean tomb of Velatouri at Thorikos, which also received a hero-cult,[22] contained the fragments of Late Protocorinthian kotylai and aryballoi of second-rate quality, as its earliest dedications.

As for the funerary offerings, we shall not consider the Protocorinthian vases that are isolated finds or those for which the provenance is uncertain. We shall limit ourselves to the examination of a few cemeteries, large and small.

In sharp contrast to Aegina, most Protocorinthian vases in Attica are found among the funerary offerings, but, as elsewhere, these are mainly small vases. It seems that the cemeteries richest in early examples are those located on the southeast coast of Attica; that is, in the coastal plains that were ruled at the time by a land aristocracy.[23] In the east, the cemetery of *Anavysos* contained many Attic Geometric vases and some small Late Geometric Corinthian examples that are earlier than the period with which we are here concerned. These are black kotylai with white paint decoration near the lip[24] and a kotyle[25] that heads a series of examples decorated with two long-winged confronting herons separated by wavy lines.[26]

The graves of the *Phaleron* cemetery[27] contained small Corinthian vases dating from the Early Protocorinthian period to the sixth century B.C. Those contemporary with Early and Middle Protocorinthian had aryballoi and kotylai with linear decoration,[28] but the aryballoi are missing from the more recent graves. The cemetery is distinguished from other Attic cemeteries by its wealth in pyxides dating from the Middle Protocorinthian period on. Most of the early pyxides belong to the type with straight sides, whereas the later pyxides, which date to the Late Protocorinthian and transitional periods, have concave sides. They have a linear decoration, except for number three of grave thirty-two, NM 14960 (figures 4, 5, and 6), dated in the Late Protocorinthian period,[29] which is one of the most interesting vases of the cemetery. F. Johansen has already noted that it is probably by the same artist who produced the pyxis of the Eleusis sanctuary.[30] Felice Gino lo Porto has compared it to a pyxis from Taranto (52720) and to an example from grave 428 at Syracuse.[31] The Tar-

20. D. Callipolitis-Feytmans, *Les "loutéria" attiques* (Athens, 1965).

21. G. Nicole, *Catalogue des vases peints du Musée National d'Athènes* (Supplement, Paris [1911]) no. 838 (2035). P. Walters, "Vasen aus Menidi," *JdI* 14 (1899) 124. There is also an alabastron and a kotyle fragment (*loc. cit.*, 110, no. 26 and 124, no. 63).

22. Of a different form than at Menidi, the vases here offered are buried in the grave itself, which has a rectangular form with two apses. J. Servais, *Thorikos*, vol. 1 (1963) 30. The "dromos" of the Mycenaean tomb at Aliki Glyphada also contained votive offerings from the Geometric period on, but probably not Corinthian vases (*PAE* 1955 [1960] 96–99).

23. C. W. Eliot, *Coastal Demes of Attika. A Study of the Policy of Kleisthenes* (Toronto, 1962).

24. *PAE* (1911) 120, fig. 15 and 16. Cf. *Perachora* 2, nos. 595, 596, 586. J. K. Anderson in *BSA* 53–54 (1958–1959) 141, nos. 45–46.

25. Athens National Museum 14476, *PAE* (1911) 110. Johansen, *Vases sicyoniens*, pl. 10,1 and p. 24. J. Coldstream, *Greek Geometric Pottery* (London, 1968) pl. 19,k and p. 100. R. M. Cook, *Greek Painted Pottery* (London, 1966) pl. 8,B. Cf. also above, note 5 and figure 1.

26. For the appearance of the aryballoi after the kotylai, see Vallet-Villard in *BCH* 76 (1952) 341.

27. S. Pelekidis, *Deltion* 2 (1916) 13. The publication of the early graves, resumed and studied chronologically by Rodney S. Young, *AJA* 46 (1942) 23: it is to this publication that we refer here. For comparison with the cemetery of Cumae, see Vallet-Villard, *BCH* 76 (1952) 342.

28. See above, note 27: In Middle Protocorinthian graves, some aryballoi have figured motifs in silhouette; birds on no. 10, grave 19, fig. 4; running dogs on no. 4 A, grave 37, fig. 14; man between boars on no. 4 B of the same grave, fig. 14. From the end of the Middle Protocorinthian period: black-figure aryballos, no. 2, grave 18, fig. 17.

29. Johansen, *Vases sicyoniens*, pl. 24,1; *AJA* 46 (1942) 37, fig. 21,3.

30. Johansen, *Vases sicyoniens*, pp. 93–94. See note 16.

31. *Annuario della scuola archeologica di Atene* (1959–1960) 39–40 and p. 37, fig. 26, e.

Figure 5. Top of Pyxis in Figure 4.

Figure 4. Late Protocorinthian Pyxis from Necropolis of Phaleron, Athens, National Museum, inv. no. 14960.

anto pyxis and those from Phaleron and Eleusis are certainly by the same hand[32]— interesting evidence for the extent of Corinthian export of that period. Importantly, at Phaleron was found one of the earliest examples of a "powder-pyxis" (grave 71 of the Late Protocorinthian period).[33]

The Phaleron cemetery was one of the first to provide a firm basis for dating Protoattic vases in relation to Corinthian pottery. Unfortunately, the Attic examples are small and inexpensive vases that have not helped to solve the most important problems of Attic production.[34] These problems may be more easily resolved by the finds from *Trachones*, in the fertile plain east of Phaleron, at the foot of Mt. Hymettos. Here is located the property of J. M. Geroulanos, who has carefully excavated the occasional finds of his farmland, for which he has published the eighth-century graves.[35] The few small Cor-

Figure 6. Side view of Pyxis in Figure 4.

inthian vases and the more frequent Attic offerings were found in cremation graves in which the ashes were placed in large Athenian vases or, less often, in pithoi. The Corinthian vases consist of kotylai and aryballoi with linear decoration but of good manufacture. These allow us to date the fine Geometric and Protoattic vases from the burials. The earliest graves belong to the Late Geometric II period (grave A 23, "Grabsitten," pls. 11, 16, and 30) and contained kotylai similar to those found at Anavysos (see notes 24 and 25). From the period of interest to us, there was discovered a sumptuous lidded pithoskrater, which imitates a Cycladic model, grave A 30 (pls. 13, 18, and 37), with two Early Protocorinthian aryballoi of an intermediate form between the globular and ovoid type. Graves A 8 ("Grabsitten," pls.

32. The pyxis British Museum 65.7–20.7 (Johansen, *Vases sicyoniens*, pl. 24,2), which also seems to come from Phaleron and which dates from the Late Protocorinthian II period, might be a later work by the same artist.

33. *Necrocorinthia* 293, note 8.

34. They have only helped in dating second-rate vases like the miniature conical oinochoe from the Akropolis no. 583, Graef, *Die antiken Vasen*, p. 63 (for the type, cf. Beazley, *ABV*, p. 444,E) after the vase no. 4 of grave 36, fig. 26, which belongs to the transitional period.

35. J. M. Geroulanos, "Grabsitten des ausgehenden

geometrischen Stils im Bereich des Gutes Trachones bei Athen," *AM* 88 (1973) 1–54. Hereafter referred to in the text as "Grabsitten."

12, 20, and 32) and A 12 ("Grabsitten," pls. 19 and 32) contained aryballoi dating from the period between Early and Middle Protocorinthian. For the Middle Protocorinthian period there were two burials: one with two kotylai decorated with rays above the foot ("Grabsitten," pl. 23), and the other—a handsome Attic amphora ("Grabsitten," pl. 24)—with a slightly later kotyle and a concave-sided pyxis like that of Phaleron.[36]

The cemeteries of *Eleusis* received as many small Corinthian vases as the sanctuary itself, and this is natural. Here again, the earliest graves possessed the best Protocorinthian vases. These pithoi contained kotylai with linear decoration[37] or with a black surface displaying an hour-glass decoration on the lip like those known from Anavysos.[38] Another drinking vase is more unusual—a cup with a vertical handle and with linear decoration.[39] From the Early Protocorinthian period there are aryballoi that are later than those found in the sanctuary. Some have figure decoration without incision over the whole surface[40] or just on the shoulder.[41] Finally, some small vases that are rare in Attic graves have been found at Eleusis: the kalathos[42] and a small squat oinochoe with a broad neck.[43] But the cemetery west of Eleusis, which was used from the Mycenaean times to the fifth century B.C., contained very few Protocorinthian vases.[44] Compared to

Figure 7 (left). Miniature Protocorinthian Oinochoe, Vari. Figure 8. Miniature Protocorinthian Kotyle, Vari.

Attic vases, their number is insignificant.

The tymbos of *Vari*,[45] about eight hundred meters from the cemetery of Anagyrous, is distinguished from the other known cemeteries of the southeast coast of Attica by the fact that no Corinthian vase earlier than the transitional period has been found there.[46] Numerous Corinthian vases, often broken and fragmentary, have been found outside the graves, scattered over the whole excavated area and in all levels. These are chiefly aryballoi with a scale pattern. A single small vase is more rare in the graves; namely, a miniature oinochoe (51 mm) with conical body and tall neck (figure 7).[47] The most remarkable find, however, was a large vase, a dinos (figures 9 and 10), with figured decoration, which, unfortunately, was in highly fragmentary condition. The decoration consists of a continuous zone showing the fight of Herakles and the Hydra—the scene sepa-

36. *AJA* 46 (1942) 37, fig. 22.

37. Eleusis 666, *ArchEph* (1898) pl. 2,11. Johansen, *Vases sicyoniens*, pl. 9,5. K. Kourouniotis, *Eleusiniaka*, vol. 1 (1932) 164, fig. 124.

38. Eleusis 1020, *ArchEph* (1898) pl. 2,3 and p. 119. Johansen, *Vases sicyoniens*, pl. 9,2. Coldstream, *Geometric Pottery*, pl. 21,d. Cf. Anavsos.

39. Eleusis 675, *ArchEph* (1898) 91. Johansen, *Vases sicyoniens*, pl. 10,4 and p. 34.

40. Eleusis 786, *ArchEph* (1889) 177. Dunbabin and Robertson, *BSA* 48 (1953) 173.

41. *ArchEph* (1889) 177. *ArchEph* (1912) 37. Johansen, *Vases sicyoniens*, pl. 4,7. Eleusis 33, *ArchEph* (1898) 59.

42. Eleusis 851. Johansen, *Vases sicyoniens*, p. 67. Cf. *Perachora* 2, 91, n.2, and 93, fig. 6.

43. *ArchEph* (1898) 92, fig. 21. Middle Protocorinthian.

44. G. E. Mylonas, *To Dytikon Nekrotapheion tes Eleusinos* (1975). The Protocorinthian vases serve as

furniture to burials in a pithos. These are the aryballos of pithos 17 (pl. 243, no. 173) and the concave-sided pyxis of pithos Z 12 (pl. 308, no. 394) of the Middle Protocorinthian period.

45. *Deltion* 18 (1963) A, 115–34, pl. 40–62; *Deltion* 20 (1965) B1, 112–17, pl. 75–85 (V. Kallipolitis).

46. This occurs apart from a single Late Protocorinthian aryballos, of which the surface is eroded. Linear decoration with a zone of dot-rosettes on the shoulder and on the belly bordered by zones with check-pattern; cf. *Delos*, 10, pl. 21, nos. 140, 143, 145.

47. Probably used as a lekythos (Dunbabin, *Perachora* 2, 26, n. 1). On the belly, zone with running dogs in silhouette and dot-rosettes between two zones with triangles and over a red line. Check-pattern on the handle. The other small vases are aryballoi decorated with horizontal lines, some kotylai with linear motifs, a miniature kotyle (height, 4 cm) with running dogs in silhouette (figure 8), and some fragments of concave-sided pyxides.

Figure 9. Corinthian Dinos fragment, Vari.

rated from komasts dancing around a standed dinos by two processions of riders.[48] This vase would have been worthy of import to the city of Aegina, and it is the only large Corinthian vase to have been found thus far in a cemetery on the southeast coast of Attica.[49]

We know that the public and private cemeteries of Athens were situated along the roads running from the gates of the city. The only cemetery that has been systematically studied over a long period of time and over quite a wide area is that of the *Kerameikos*, outside the Dipylon gate. It has been excavated by the German Archaeological Institute of Athens, and the scholarly publications[50] show the relative importance of the Protocorinthian finds. Small vases, similar to those of the coastal cemeteries, are few. The earliest kotylai might date from the beginning of the Early Protocorinthian period.[51] For Middle Protocorinthian the examples are

offerings in cremation graves: three examples have linear motifs[52] and only one has a figured decoration.[53] Of the aryballoi, none seems to be Early Protocorinthian. They are mainly Middle Protocorinthian and one is figured. Finally, one complete aryballos and some fragments also belong to the Late Protocorinthian or to the transitional period,[54] to which the alabastron number 965 (*Kerameikos*, vol. 6, 1, pl. 61) belongs. Some large vases have also been found, and this distinguishes the Kerameikos cemetery from almost all cemeteries of the southeast coast. The earliest is number 661,[55] a standed bowl that belongs to the Attic repertoire from the Late Geometric II period on, but that was particularly in vogue during the Early Protoattic period. This is therefore a Corinthian imitation of an Attic prototype. Number 661 still has the wide lip and the thick foot of the Attic Late Geometric II style. It is, however, Early Protocorinthian, and its decoration has been associated with the Cumae group. The other large Corinthian vases of the Kerameikos belong to the standard repertoire of Pro-

---

48. Callipolitis-Feytmans, "Dinos Corinthien de Vari," *ArchEph* (1970) 86–113, pls. 30–34.

49. The northeast coast of Attica, facing Euboea, seems poor in Protocorinthian finds. We may mention the cemetery of Velatouri near Thorikos where some small Middle Protocorinthian vases of mediocre quality have been found: see J. Servais, *Thorikos*, vol. 1, 52 ff.

50. *Kerameikos. Ergebnisse der Ausgrabungen*, Berlin. Hereinafter cited in the text and notes as *Kerameikos*.

51. *Kerameikos*, vol. 5, 1, grave 98, pl. 132, found with two Early Protoattic cups with high foot (pl. 126) and *Kerameikos*, vol. 5, 1, grave 99, pl. 132 and p. 271, published as Attic. On these, Dunbabin, *Perachora 2*, 51. The fragments of kotyle 1376, found in the filling of b/XIII (*Kerameikos*, vol. 6, 1, pl. 67) might be of the

same period, as also the fragments of two kotylai, *Kerameikos*, vol. 6, 1, pl. 68, offering trench K/XIX.

52. 1273, offering trench a/IV, *Kerameikos*, vol. 6, 1, pl. 59; 97, offering trench E/XII, *Kerameikos*, vol. 6, 1, pl. 61, p. 26; 966, *Kerameikos*, vol. 6, 1, pl. 61.

53. 1355, grave 8/VIII, *Kerameikos*, vol. 6, 1, pl. 60 and p. 114. *Perachora* 2, 51, n.1.

54. *BCH* 98 (1974) 596, child's grave. Middle Protocorinthian with linear decoration: *Kerameikos*, vol. 6, 1, pl. 56, grave 62/LXII. Fragment with running dogs in silhouette on the shoulder, offering a/IV, pl. 67, and p. 15. Area K/XIV, *Kerameikos*, vol. 6, 1, pl. 67. Aryballos with a zone with running dogs in silhouette on the shoulder and belly, inv. 4215, *Kerameikos*, vol. 12, pl. 19, 1 and p. 78. Same subject, *Kerameikos*, vol. 6, 1, pl. 68, fr. Aryballos with figured scene: fighters; inv. 78, offering β/IV, *Kerameikos*, vol. 6, 1, pl. 67, by the Aetos Painter, *BSA* 48 (1953) 176, no. 8. The only aryballos that might date from the Late Protocorinthian period is no. 4282 (unpublished), a pointed aryballos decorated with lines. The only piece perhaps from the transitional period is the fragment with scales, *Kerameikos*, vol. 6, 1, pl. 68.

55. *Kerameikos*, vol. 5, 1, pl. 127, grave 67; *Kerameikos*, vol. 6, 1, pl. 56, grave 1/I. Dated and associated with the Cumae group by K. Kübler and T. Dunbabin (*Perachora* 2, 128).

Figure 10. Corinthian Dinos fragment, Vari.

tocorinthian shapes.[56] The oinochoe with narrow foot and trefoil mouth, number 1267, has also been compared with the Cumae group to which it stands close, but it is Middle Protocorinthian.[57] The few olpai belong to the transitional period.[58] Finally, there are three kotylai-pyxides of the Middle Protocorinthian period.[59] These fine large

vases are mainly decorated with linear or vegetable motifs. Just a few have animal zones: the lid of the kotyle-pyxis number 1278 and the superimposed zones of the olpai. None of these Protocorinthian vases, however, can compete with the best from Aegina.

The other cemeteries that are situated along the ancient roads are often found by chance during road work or other construction. In these cases the Greek Archaeological Service undertakes rescue excavations that cannot extend over the whole cemetery but are limited only to nonbuilt areas. We should note here that Protoattic graves are rare and that they do not often contain Protocorinthian vases. The small cemetery of *Kallithea*[60] on the road leading to Phaleron contained a few such vases. Unfortunately, they were first discovered by the workmen, before

56. However, the trefoil-mouthed, round-bodied oinochoe, inv. 83, *Kerameikos*, vol. 6, 1, pl. 56, which should be Middle Protocorinthian since it was found in grave 62/LXII with aryballos 87, has a shape that seems unique to me. It might derive from a Middle Geometric oinochoe with ovoid body, tall neck, and trefoil mouth, like Corinth T 2455 (Coldstream, *Geometric Pottery*, pl. 18) and Corinth CP 1892 (*Corinth* VII, 1, 19f. and pl. 11, no. 70).

57. *Kerameikos*, vol. 6, 1, pl. 57–58 of offering trench a/IV. For its relation with the Cumae group, see Dunbabin and Robertson in *BSA* 48 (1953) 174. But its shape is more developed than that of the Early Protocorinthian Cumae oinochoai (Payne, *Protokorinthische Vasenmalerei* [Berlin, 1933] pl. 7, 1–3), because the conical neck with straight sides and the rounder body look more like those of the oinochoe in Toulouse by the Toulouse Painter (*loc. cit.*, pl. 12), a work of the beginning of the Middle Protocorinthian period (*BSA* 48 [1953] 175).

58. No. 1358 from grave 21/XXII, *Kerameikos*, vol. 6, 1, pl. 64; no. 68 from offering trench μ/XXI, *Kerameikos*, vol. 6, 1, pl. 63; *BSA* 44 (1949) 241, no. 1, and no. 1357, offering trench λ/XV; *Kerameikos*, vol. 6, 1, pl. 68; *BSA* 44 (1949) 241, no. 2.

59. Nos. 1268 and 1269 found in the same offering trench a/IV, *Kerameikos*, vol. 6, 1, pl. 59, as the oino-

choe 1267 (see n. 57) and no. 1278, *Kerameikos*, vol. 6, 1, pl. 60 from the offering trench β/IX, which contained also the aryballos 78 (see above, note 54); cf. *Perachora* 2, 100, n.1.

60. Callipolitis-Feytmans, "Tombes géométriques de Callithéa en Attique," *BCH* 87 (1963) 404–30. Next to these were fifth-century graves with Attic black-figure lekythoi. In April 1963 (*Deltion* 19 [1964] B1, pls. 62–63 and 65–67), again in Theseus Street of Kallithea, graves with Late Geometric II vases were found that might belong to the same cemetery.

Figure 11. Protocorinthian Aryballos (inv. no. 1086). From Kallithea.

Figure 12. Protocorinthian Amphora (inv. no. 1083). From Kallithea.

the Archaeological Service had been notified. Hence, it is not certain whether they come from the same grave. The three Early Protocorinthian aryballoi (for example, figure 11) might have been together.[61] There were also two large Protocorinthian vases, one of which, a tall pyxis, is a type known mainly from the cemetery of Thera and also from a grave of Aegina (see note 4). It is a fine vase with thin walls, and it belongs to the Early Protocorinthian period, but it is in too fragmentary a condition to be illustrated satisfactorily.[62] The other vase is the amphora 1083 (figure 12), which is more difficult to date;[63] the neck-handled amphora is rare

during the Protocorinthian period. This vase, like the standed bowl number 661 from the Kerameikos (see note 55), is inspired by an Attic Late Geometric prototype. In fact, the shape of the amphora from Kallithea is the same as that of some Attic Late Geometric Ib products of the Dipylon workshop.[64] This shape is still produced in conservative Late Geometric IIa workshops;[65] modified later, it was used in some Early Protoattic workshops.[66] But the amphora from Kallithea keeps the Attic Late Geometric proportions, like the standed bowl number 661 of the Kerameikos. The two vases have another similarity: they are decorated in the manner of the Cumae group but are much less close to

61. The aryballos no. 1086 (figure 11) (BCH 87 [1963] 419, figs. 10 and 11) is close to nos. 1–4 of group A of Dunbabin and Robertson (BSA 48 [1953] 173) for the composition and the choice of linear motifs. Cf. also K. Kübler, Kerameikos, vol. 6, 2, p. 139, n. 187.

62. Cf. Johansen, Vases sicyoniens, pl. 11. For the example from Aegina, see above, note 4. The pyxis from Kallithea (BCH 87 [1963] no. 1094, p. 425) was broken into 65 pieces, only eight of which joined. Probable height, 120 mm, diam. at mouth, 80 mm. Thin walls, glaze turned red, large metope with six superimposed rows of zigzags framed by vertical lines. Belly with horizontal lines interrupted by a zone with zigzags.

63. BCH 87 (1963) 422–23, figs. 12 and 13; 421–25.

64. Coldstream, Geometric Pottery, pl. 8,d, Munich 8748, but this has a shorter neck and shorter handles.

65. Ibid., pl. 15, a, Kerameikos 816. Cf. also K. Kübler, Kerameikos, vol. 6, 2, 152.

66. Cf. New York 21.88.18, BSA 35 (1934–1935) pl. 50. Cf. also the amphora in the same style, Deltion 23 (1968) B 1, chr., pl. 45 and p. 82.

it than the oinochoe number 1267 of the Kerameikos (see note 57) because of their mediocre technique and their clumsy and overelaborate decoration. It is possible that they were made in a single workshop that used Attic shapes in order to attract Athenian customers.

The most important of the occasional finds of Protocorinthian vases was that of the demos of *Tauros* in 1969, in the southeast suburbs of Athens, along the ancient road that probably ran from the Melitides gate. The excavation and the finds have been carefully published by the Ephor D. Skilardi.[67] Among other graves, the cemetery contained cremation grave 20, which contained burnt furniture: small Protoattic vases, a Protocorinthian concave-sided pyxis, and, finally, a piece of exceptional value—an oinochoe with small foot and trefoil mouth, decorated with a figure zone in the "big style," showing three centaurs carrying tree-branches and attacking two lions (pls. 42–45). D. Skilardi rightly dates the vase to the Middle Protocorinthian II period and associates it with the Syracuse oinochoe (p. 145), a work of the Aegina Bellerophon Painter (*Necrocorinthia*, pl. 7), while admitting that the style is somewhat different.

The find of the dinos at Vari and that of the oinochoe of Tauros prove that the inhabitants of Attica occasionally bought beautiful and large Protocorinthian vases decorated with figure scenes painted in the "big style."

They did not dedicate them in sanctuaries, as in Aegina, but offered them in graves,[68] which is regrettable, since the inhabitants of Attica during that period burned the offerings to the dead.

* * *

It is not difficult to understand why Protocorinthian imports were less important in Attica than on the island of Aegina. Athenian pottery had, to a certain extent, retained the acme reached during the Geometric period. If it had lost its reputation in the Greek world, it nevertheless continued to produce vases for local consumption. As in all other places, it is the small Protocorinthian vases that are imported, particularly kotylai and aryballoi, the technical virtuosity and careful execution of which are difficult to equal. As the best Geometric and Protoattic workshops mainly manufactured middle-sized and large vases, it is the modest workshops that imitated these Corinthian types but that executed them with a certain clumsiness. From the Late Geometric II period, they produced kotylai that later followed the evolution of Protocorinthian works.[69] However, since the aryballoi were more difficult to manufacture, the globular aryballoi introduced in the Early Protoattic period did not change shape during the seventh century B.C.[70] Because of their technical superiority in this field, Corinthian workshops continued to export their vases to Attica.

---

67. *ArchEph* (1975) 66–149, pls. 30–45. Hereinafter cited in the text by page and/or plate number.

68. The Protocorinthian imports for everyday use seem unimportant. Cf. Eva Brann, *The Athenian Agora*, vol. 8, *Late Geometric and Protoattic Pottery* (1962) 104–5, nos. 636 to 648, pl. 41. Mainly kotylai from the Early Protocorinthian period on, ibid., p. 50 and pl. 9, nos. 155 to 158.

69. Coldstream, *Geometric Pottery*, 87 and 110, n. 1. Early Protocorinthian period, Brann, *Agora*, vol. 8, nos. 153, 159, and 162, pl. 9 and pp. 50–51. *Kerameikos*, vol. 6, 2, pp. 184–86, pls. 70, 75, and 99.

70. J. M. Cook, *BSA* 35 (1934–1935) 212 and 214. Brann, *Agora*, vol. 8, p. 38. At Trachones, *AM* 88 (1973) pl. 32. Rather late example, Athens National Museum no. 18031.

23. A Note on a Grotesque from Corinth

WILLIAM R. BIERS

DEPARTMENT OF ART HISTORY AND ARCHAEOLOGY,
UNIVERSITY OF MISSOURI, COLUMBIA

Among the ceramic finds from the early excavations at Corinth is part of a grotesque plastic face (figure 1). The fragment, broken on all sides, preserves a portion of the face, which includes the lower half of an eye with its lower lid, an exaggerated large, hooked nose with nostril terminating in a roughly stylized volute, and a heavy, curving mouth with a thick and slightly protruding lower lip. The lower portion of the face is decorated with rows of roughly semicircular indentations that doubtlessly intend to represent the stubble of an incipient beard. The fabric is a dark, red-brown, fired gray at the core; the surface is covered with a mottled red-brown to blackish metallic glaze.[1] Although but a single fragment, the subject portrayed, the fabric, and the technique clearly indicate that the figure is a grotesque of the Roman period. The type is well known in the popular art of the time in terracotta as well as in other media.[2]

The coarse, exaggerated features, especially the hooked nose and thick lips, suggest that the head must represent a particular type. The many examples that exist of grotesque male figures sharing these characteristics are generally considered as representing actors in the Roman mime.[3] One of the most important characters in these broad, popular entertainments was depicted as bald, deformed, ugly, and stupid—that is, the "mimus calvus," or bald mime. An alternate designation for this character—"Stupidus"—as used by some scholars, is based on the exaggerated features and on what little is known of the character's role in the mime itself.[4] Whether our grotesque is in fact a "Stupidus," or is simply an undifferentiated grotesque, is difficult to determine, for surely not all grotesques represent actors in the mime and unfortunately the figure's head, bald or otherwise, is missing.

The fragment from Corinth was originally

---

1. Corinth inv. no. C–33–1479 (MF 1798) found 26 May 1933. Ph. 0.074m Fabric, interior circa 5 YR 5/4 to 5/3; fracture between 5 YR 5/6 and 2.5 YR 5/6 to gray. I must thank Dr. Nancy Bookides of the Corinth Excavations for providing photos and the Munsell readings and Dr. Kathleen Slane for sharing her observations on this object. This brief article is not intended as an exhaustive study either of the type of vases to which this fragment belongs nor of the fragment itself. It is simply an opportunity for me to make some contribution to honor D. A. Amyx, whose scholarship and friendship have been important to me over the years.

2. For examples of grotesques in metal and glass, see P. La Baume, *Römisches Kunstgewerbe zwischen Christi*

Geburt und 400 (Braunschweig, 1964) 223, fig. 204; 227, fig. 207.

3. For the mime and its actors, see H. Reich, *Der Mimus* (Berlin, 1903); G. Michaut, *Histoire de la comédie romaine, sur les tréteaux latins* (Paris, 1912) 321–24; J. Cébe, *La caricature et la parodie cans le monde romain antique, des origines à Juvénal, Bibliothèque des écoles françaises d'Athenes et de Rome*, vol. 206 (Paris, 1966).

4. So Cébe, ibid., 40, 56. The simpler, undifferentiated term *mime* is often used for these bald, large-nosed caricatures, M. Bieber, *The History of the Greek and Roman Theater*, 2d ed. (Princeton, 1971) 248–49.

Figure 1. Face fragment, Corinth, Museum, inv. no. C-33-1479 (MF 1798). Courtesy of Corinth Excavations.

Figure 2. Lagynos, Cairo, National Museum, inv. no. 86635. From *MonPiot* 51 (1960), pl. IV; permission of the Academie des Inscriptions et Belles-Lettres.

Figure 3. Head from a Lagynos, Alexandria, Archaeological Museum. From *BABesch* 55 (1980), 111, fig. 6c; permission of Stichting Bulletin Antieke Beschaving.

published as a part of a terracotta mask.[5] However, its size and shape indicate that it is in fact part of a plastic vase. Its fabric points to the group of relief wares that seem to have been manufactured in Asia Minor, probably at Knidos or in its vicinity.[6]

Cups in the form of heads are known in this ware, but the closest parallels to our fragment are from lagynoi. Such lagynoi, of sharply carinated profile, were produced in two piece molds and bear relief decoration

in itself derived from the molds. The decoration, figural or vegetal, adorned the shoulder of the vase, for which the neck, molded separately and later joined to the body, is in the form of a human head. Often, the vessel's mouth protrudes from the top of the plastic head, thereby giving the vase a stressed vertical axis to counteract the spreading form of its body. These head lagynoi were made in Asia Minor from the late first century. A series in African Red Ware, which must have begun in the third century, was most likely derived from imported examples of the older

5. G. R. Davidson, *Corinth* XII, *The Minor Objects* (Princeton, 1952) 60, no. 441.

6. For a general statement, see J. W. Hayes, *Late Roman Pottery* (London, 1972) 411–12. the specific attribution of this group to Knidos can be found in D. M. Bailey, "Cnidian Relief Ware Vases and Fragments in the British Museum Part 1: Lagynoi and Head Cups," *Rei Cretariae Romanae Fautorum Acta* 14–15 (1972–1973) 11–25. See also J. W. Salomonson, "Kleinasiatische Tonschalen mit Reliefverzierung," *BABesch* 55 (1980) 65–135; D. M. Bailey, "Cnidian Relief Ware Vases in the British Museum Part 2, Oinophoroi and Jugs," *Rei Cretariae Romanae Fautorum Acta* 19–20 (1979) 257–72.

series. Unfortunately, very few head lagynoi have been published or even illustrated.[7] The well known and almost complete example in Cairo is illustrated here (figure 2).[8]

The grotesque head on the Cairo lagynos appears to be very similar to the Corinth example in general shape, in the treatment of the eye, and in the method of indicating the unshaven cheeks. One distinctive feature of the Corinth fragment—the termination of the nostril in a tight curve (figure 1)—is also found on another lagynos head now in Alexandria and published in a photo by Salomonson (figure 3).[9] Here the grotesque appears to be bald and so might be designated a "Stupidus." The huge nose and coarse, heavy lips are shared by both examples, but the example from Corinth is better modeled.

Unfortunately, no other fragments of the vase of which our grotesque forms a part have been found in Corinth. Consequently, it is difficult to state at this time whether this Roman visitor was in fact a "Stupidus" or whether he only exhibited some of the characteristics of a "Stupidus."

7. A recent publication by Salomonson discusses a number of examples and also provides a full bibliography, "Der Trunkenbold und die Trunkene Alte," *BABesch* 55 (1980) 65–135. More recently, a number of examples of both lagynoi and head cups in African Red Ware have been published by Salomonson; *Römische Kleinkunst Sammlung Karl Löffler* (Wissenschaftliche Kataloge des Romisch-Germanischen Museums Köln, vol. 3, undated—1982?), 159–76.

8. Cairo, inv. no. 86635. L. Ghali-Kahil, "Un lagynos au Musée du Caire," *MonPiot* 51 (1960) 73–91.

9. J. W. Salomonson, *Römische Kleinkunst*, n. 7, 111, fig. 6c. First published by E. Breccia, *Terrecotte figurate greche e greco-egizie del Museo di Alessandria*, vol. 1 (Bergamo, 1930) pl. 34, 6.

Index